TWO MEN NAMED JESUS

TWO MEN NAMED JESUS

S. Eugene Cohlmia

Two Men Named Jesus

Copyright © 2013 by S. Eugene Cohlmia

ISBN 978-0-617513-83

All rights reserved

No part of this book may be reproduced, stored in a retrieval system or tranmitted in any way by any means, electronic, mechanical, photocopy, recording or otherwise without the prior permission of the author except by U.S.A. copyright laws.

Scripture quotations marked are taken from the Orthodox Study Bible (O.S.B.) Copyright C 2008 by St. Athanasuis Academy of Orthodox Theology.

This novel is a work of fiction. However, several names, descriptions, entities and incidents included in the story are based on the lives of real people.

The opinions expressed by the author are solely his own.

Published by Cohlmia Issa Publishing
1433 N. Stratford Lane. Wichita, KS   U.S.A.

Book & Cover design concepts by Cohlmia Issa Publishing
Cover art by Richard Stroud
Interior design and print by PawPrints POD

Published In the United States Of America

ACKNOWLEDGEMENTS

As always I must acknowledge My Holy Master God - Jesus Christ, all The Saints and of course my overworked Guardian Angel. At times when there are no others around I spend time talking with my Angel and constantly ask for help from them. Yes I say them for it takes many Angels to keep me on the right path!

In my first published book, The Chains of St. Peter, I failed to acknowledge what I attempt to rectify at this time! I was remiss not to have mentioned those three people who have lent themselves in true fashion to the development of this human being and to my writings though they be want I am sure.

First I must mention my dear Mother who always encouraged me to read, absorb and enjoy the written word along with teaching me a way of life pleasing to God and those around us. Although it was during the Great Depression of the 1930s and 40s when money was short she did all in her power to beg or borrow written materials from her friends where after digesting and enjoying the read it was given to me. Always with thoughts for others and a true charitable character I will never forget her willingness to volunteer for the most impossible endeavors which she carried out with grace and love.

Then my dear friend, Mentor, Teacher and remarkable human being Rachael Clapper. She encouraged, with a force that told me I could reach any potential I could dream, constantly yet casually dropping hints and encouraging me. As I look back my dear Mother and this Teacher left me knowing I could do whatever I dreamed so that I grew to believe I had "IT" within me. Under Ms Clappers instruction I signed for two years of Latin and with her talent she made each day more fun than the previous. Later she insisted I try out for a high school drama of which I won the lead and just that quickly I was transformed from an introvert to a happy extrovert. Once again this amazing instructor encouraged me to put my thoughts on paper!

Of course I leave to the last the most important person in my life. A Lady to whom I give all the credit in the world who put the finishing touches upon my life and my Character. My wife is the most important person in my life and together Our Master allowed us four of the most precious men ever gracing this World and who are an extension of her benevolence for Helen M. Cohlmia's thoughts have never been of herself but her immediate and extended family as well as her fellow man. She takes the back seat in all her actions when the fore is truly hers; my love to her always.

TWO BABES BORN – DIVERSE BACKGROUNDS

The midwife Amira dipped a five gallon bucket into the flowing stream of water and with her five foot five stature and meager one hundred and twenty pounds used all the strength she could muster to lug the container to the cauldron ten feet away. The big man took the bucket pouring the water into the cauldron then stoked the fire and added several large logs cut from a large cedar unfortunately downed by a bolt of lightning. The fingers of fire that had been licking the belly of the cauldron retreated into the abyss and as each piece of fresh wood was thrown in the hot searing fingers extended and elongated hugging each log attempting to pull it closer to its boiling bosom. The slight wind made the fire retreat under the cauldron for just a moment as though it would expire then suddenly in the cool September air the cinders caught and the large hot fingers of the flame massaged the cauldrons huge belly. Very soon there would be loads of hot water necessary for sterilization.

Amira stood waiting away from the fire watching the children playing tag. One could feel the warm air of summer mixed with the approaching soft winds of the north forcing their way into the area to cool the air. Noticing the water making a roiling sound she dropped her pail into the cauldron holding a rope tied to the handle assuring her of no burn, she lifted the pail out of the cauldron and moved slowly toward the house, Chagi seeing the elder midwife struggling reached onto the handle and towering over Amira lifted the heavy load out of the smaller persons grasp, her five foot ten one hundred seventy pounds effortlessly carried the bucket over the threshold into the darkened room.

Chagi thinking back a half hour ago when she and Adva, the other midwife knocked at the door of Amira pleading, "Shiphra has begun her labor and as always Y'hanaton is becoming nervous, could you please come now." They explained that the wife's water had broken several hours before which signaled a possible long and tedious childbirth, "But," replied Shiphra, "the previous births were short and uncomplicated so settle the husband down he should know better, ha, ha." Throwing her head back she laughed pleasantly.

Now stepping into the house she breathed heavily, "So God willing we will be here to take care of her whatever problems He may challenge us with." Clapping her hands together she shooed the children out the door, "Now Y'hanaton," it is your job to stoke the fire and keep the children out of our way or they may not be blessed with a new child in this house."

Amira's reputation was well known in Nazareth and throughout the District of Galilee. She turned to check on Shiphra lying in a pool of perspiration on the pallet prepared for this birthing. Because of her slight stature Amira had invented this birthing pallet designed several years before to make it easier on the midwives as well as the mothers. The bed was almost twelve inches taller than a normal bed. It was much easier to perform ones duties when ones back did not pain especially when one knew it would take some time.

Chagi poured olive oil into Amiras palm. She rubbed her hands together as if washing them then ran them over the mother's midsection rubbing softly and feeling the child moving inside the womb. Experience told her this child would be a strapping baby boy for she could feel his movements turning to make his way into the world.

Shiphra stifled a scream as she bit hard on the damp cloth Amira had given her. Adva stepped forward with a small pan of cool water and a cloth which she dipped into the water and wiped the head of Shiphra. Two additional pails of hot water, one carried by Deborah and one by the husband, was brought in and set near the cooking area. Jonathan did not hesitate he spun and almost ran out the door; he did not want to displease the midwife for he knew she would have words for him he did not want to hear. Prior to the beginning of the birth Amira told him, "Dig a large pit, build a fire and put the cauldron over it, fill it with water from the stream," he grumbled under his breath and continued his mumbling for Amira was intent with her instructions. He also knew her reputation from previous birthing of his other children and wanted nothing beyond this day to do with her. She heard him swear that he would have no other offspring because of her. She just laughed and clapped her hands at the older children, "Come Dears help father for he is only two hundred eighty pounds and six foot six but may need help for this is truly an exertion of which he is not accustomed, ha, ha, ha," that happy laugh of hers contagious making Shiphra's neighbors and friends laugh as they stood waiting at the entryway.

If he could hear what she was saying quietly, "Lazy man doesn't deserve such a wife never had a permanent job never attends Synagogue, I doubt if he knows what the Torah is."

But this was not the understanding of Shiphra for she knew positively her husband was a great provider. Sure he had been in jail from time to time but it was always a mistake, for, as he told her, there was a rake and a drunkard living somewhere near who resembled him and it seemed the authorities were always mistaking him for that terrible man but he was always home within a week or less. She loved her husband and adored her three children.

Deborah the eldest was her pride and joy although not home much for as was the custom in lesser fortunate families she, like other friends hired out to the wealthy and was making a very good living. Her mother pretended to not know that Deborah put several denari a week into the clay jar above the fireplace and it was taken for granite by mother, or she would lie and tell all, the money was from Jonathan.

Shiphra was a very good mother but allowed her children to roam wherever they would. Deborah was now almost thirteen with her sister Naomi at six and Nouri at four. Deborah had seen her father several times in the bowels of the City, when with another servant of the family they worked for, went into the oil store to fill their jugs. They went into the lower parts of the city for the prices were much less than in the market near the gates of Nazereth. That is where she saw her Father for the first time gambling and drinking along with known thieves and the unsavory. This was an area of the town where even the local police shied from for they were not wanted and the only time they entered the area was out of necessity possibly to search for a wanted criminal or just to make the usual walk through unannounced and always with a large cadre in order to protect themselves and possibly get lucky and solve one of their long time pending cases. Deborah knew this is where her father hung out and this was his lifestyle. She would never say anything to debase her father in front of her mother for she had great respect for her mother. She did not appreciate the life she knew he lead but as long as Shiphra was happy Deborah would give a sigh of relief but say nothing. She would keep her eye on them and be there in case anything untoward happened.

Two Men Named Jesus

Deborah did love her father but hated his lifestyle. All her girl friends told her he was a very good looking man with his thick black hair and beard and his blue eyes always looking out of that dark leathery skin. His constant smile fooled almost everybody which made it easier to con anybody out of his or her belongings. He played a board game with dice and his friends seldom bested him but they always presented others to play against him which gave them a chance to bet on him for there were always those gamblers hoping to turn their meager monies into large winnings.

****

Now! the infant could not wait, for when he began the trip through the canal of life he wasted no time. Abruptly Amira shouted, "Bring the rags and the hot water this youngster is hastily entering the world," and she pulled the child into the air and slapped him on the back opening a set of lungs worthy of an announcement that the world was now to see a boy child who would grow into a man of enormous proportions, following the path of his father and those kinsmen who were of very large stock. His mother laughing and reaching out to receive her prize took him and folded him with great effort into her bosom offering him the milk of life. The child's head almost spun searching for his first meal and making his mother wince, shudder than laugh proudly. Jonathan and Deborah dragging the other two children burst into the room at the sound of the fourth child to make entrance into this family. The two smaller children hung back until their mother bade them touch their new brother. Yet bashful they stepped forward and put their hands on his little hand as Nouri laughed out loud for his sibling grasped onto his thumb with surprising strength. Not backing away Nouri giggled with great pleasure shouting, "Look Oomy (my mother) he is squeezing my hand wow he's tough." And his voice screeched with excitement. They all noticed and it pleased them to see this. Deborah leaned down to kiss her mother and brother and whispered that she would be home for a couple of days to help. Shaphira smiled, pursed her lips saying, "Thank you my child you are a true blessing to me."

****

So this was the entrance into the world of a man whose life would somehow become interlaced with the most famous person in the world, that of Jesus Christ also of Nazareth in the district of Galilee who entered the world near the same time, the child who would become known among other titles as King of Kings, Lord of Lords, Savior of The World!

****

At the same hour, far from Nazareth to the south in Judea, a child was born behind an Inn in the stables at the edge of Bethlehem. A very bright star hung in the night sky over the manger of that Inn as Angels heralded His birth and from many, many mille around peasants, commoners and Kings came to pay respect and honor to this child born of a humble Jewish couple. He would be called Jesus, a common name, for a worldly unusual personality born of a Virgin promised by God of this unearthly miracle. This child' father Joseph, as instructed by an Angel of God, had searched every Inn in Bethlehem for a room but there was no room to be found. Approaching the last inn with apprehension Joseph walked in knowing by the look on that face there were no rooms. The owner verified Josephs' thoughts and smiling told him, "You are welcome to take whatever room you may need in the manger, use the straw for your beds, I am sorry that is all I have to offer you. Yes the most important life ever would be launched from this lowly manger.

The star beckoned many to this location as the Angels of Our Lord heralded the birth of Gods only Son. Those wise men directed here brought riches only Kings could afford and all noticed they rode horses, only the affluent owned such pleasures. Others not as earthly fortunate as the Wise men came on camels and yet others such as shepherds being directed by Angels came to see this long awaited birth predicted from the earliest days foretold so many hundreds of years prior prophesied by God and told from one generation to another.

These two lives would cross one day and unknown to the big giant, another Jesus, his life would follow a totally different style than The Savior for Christ's Disciples would teach all men who listened a new commandment and teach the world a new approach to life that of love and forgiveness and the gift of saving life. Unlike Barabbas' life destined to be just the opposite for he would take lives and live a life of lies, deceit, and murder. He would meet many of those men chosen by the Savior and possibly become friends with many others whose lives he would cross. Then not far from now the world would acquiesce to one of them and deny the other. Proving that the world, when offered options that would eventually change ones way of life, would unthinkingly select the easier paths toward wealth and security rather than one relying on acts of good works.

****

As he grew Barabbas was a handful for both his mother and father. This was a child who one could get through to by reasoning although that was not his father's way. His mother on the other hand presented a placid more loving and understanding being never assuming bad of anybody. She would ask Barabbas to do something for her which as generally was never accomplished although his intentions were a one so she did it herself or asked one of the others to help her. His personality was almost identical to his father for neither of them were good handymen for their hands just did not fit tools of manual labor. As Barabbas would say and his father always agreed, "That kind of work is for servants." How he knew what a servant was none knew. Deborah was the only person he would do anything for and when her mother remembered, and if it were important Shiphra asked Deborah to ask the *Giant* for a favor.

That nickname came into play when a group of young children were making fun of Ayoub, a young man with a clubfoot. This young man was not a large kid for a ten year old but we all know how impossible children can be. His dark eyes flashed and his flesh, which was normally sallow, turned a bright red. Ayoub stood five foot four as tall as most of the others but had large hands and he and the other children were about to find out how large they were. As one young brave came toward him with a noisy growl Ayoub brought the full force of his right hand around meeting the young man's left temple and down he went Ayoub's ebony hair flying in the wind. Two other youngsters jumped into the fray and that was a sign for the other four to do the same. They overpowered Ayoub and threw him to the ground at the same time Majheed and Barabbas came around the corner. Barabbas loved a good fight but he did not condone this for it was unfair. One of the youngsters shouted, "Here comes that Giant let's get out of here." The crowd dwindled hastily in many varied directions. The nickname stuck like glue.

Barabbas never denied his big sister anything, for he considered himself her protector and besides she always saw to it that he had plenty of his favorite foods to eat especially if he came home late and missed dinner. He had not missed many dinner's for the mothers of his two friends Majheed and Ayoub always saw to it that he shared food with them if he were there during that time of day.

Deborah made it a point to come home each evening in time to help her mother prepare the evening meal and she was the teacher of the family having schooled her other two siblings so when her youngest brother was of age she began bringing him along. She taught them all she knew and even brought in ideas from the Priests of the Temples although she knew little for none of her family made a habit of going to Temple so it went, sadly to say, by the wayside.

Barabbas was what one might call a mischievous little imp. He and his two companions were forever in trouble with the community. By the time they were twelve they were a force to be reckoned with. Yes, they would steal anything they could get away with.

The three of them turned twelve and now they thought they were men. There was no reasoning to it but they decided to see what the market would be like without their parents. As they strolled along the aisles of foods such as fruit, vegetables, cloth, thread, clothing, clay pots from the up country, utensils of all kinds and so much more, Barabbas winked at his two buddies jerked his chin down toward the scrumptious looking pears and peaches then looked away as he bent his body over the fruit and with one movement transferred some of the luscious fruit from their bed of shredded paper to the pocket in his tunic. Ayoub gasped at the shameless act of Giant; surprisingly it gave the other two a boost of adrenaline and their confidence flowed freely. Before they knew it they were pocketing all kinds of things. They all three stopped at the same time looking at each other and laughing out loud. Their confidence was shattered as they turned toward the market exit for they were looking into the face of two Legionnaires with their Praetorian Lieutenant starring at them with disgust.

That had to be the meanest looking face any of them had ever seen and the Romans were quite imposing. They had never been this close to their Roman conquerors and two of them were frightened but Barabbas' face only showed concern and his mind was racing. He knew he could beat them in a fair fight but he had nothing that resembled a weapon and here stood three very large representatives of the Governor. The six foot six Lieutenant was glaring directly at him and said, "Alright big guy I know what you are thinking and your exits are blocked." He raised his sword pointing it toward them and the legionnaires aimed their weapons at the other two. Barabbas quickly thought, "This is the time to back off and make them think I am giving up then as soon as we go through the gate we will make our escape." He was hoping they would take them through the west gate, known as the Damascus gate, for it was the nearest and largest of all the gates in or out of Nazareth and there was always a flow of people entering and leaving by this gate. Barabbas had one advantage and that was he knew his own power. At twelve Barabbas weighed one hundred sixty pounds standing at six foot. He did not learn the trick of easing himself into these types of situations from anyone he simply developed it knowing it worked whenever needed.

The Lieutenant pointed them toward the Damascus gate when one of the shop owners asked if they were going to cuff them the officer laughed and said, "No, no they are youngsters and I am just going to scare them." When Barabbas heard that remark he decided to do whatever was asked of him feigning submission which would give the Roman guards a false sense of self assurance thus relaxing their guard. The officer led them to the right around the corner of the City wall and stopped in the shade of a large tree. "Face me!" He shouted at them and they spun toward him as if they were part of his army knowing they were about to face some real tough choices. "Give me your names he shouted," seeing the frightened looks of the two smaller youngsters, sheepishly Majheed said, "My name is Joreo, his is Mondana and the big guy is Pampa." Ayoub and Barabbas almost burst out laughing both of them coughing to keep from giving the lie away. The officer ordered a lady passing with an empty basket, "Woman set your basket on the ground,"

Two Men Named Jesus

and turning to the three young men, "empty your pockets into the basket." When they finished their little task there were needles, food, jewelry and a child's toy they had dumped into the basket along with fruits and vegetables. He then asked, "Do you not have money with you?" They looked at each other wondering why the guard asked such a stupid question. Barabbas said quietly, "We have no money why do you think we took the fruit, we are hungry!" "If you are hungry you should go to home for food, but since you have none and cannot pay for what you have stolen then I am forced to take you into the dungeon to await your trial." Majheed and Ayoub looked at each other terrified as to what might happen to them. Yes they were shaken, but not the Giant. He would wait and see what the next few minutes brought and if it presented itself he would force a change. The Legionnaire said, "You must work off your fine," he glared at them to make a point, "you have no history of stealing so, be at the Judgment house near the jail first thing in the morning you will clean the forum area and whatever else he might think of which will pay off your charges."

As Ayoub and Majheed approached the Judgment house the sun was warming in the east and they spied the Officer from the previous day. Majheed and Ayoub still with sleep in their eyes yet looking as though they had not slept at all proceeded slowly and sheepishly toward the big officer. He knew they were behind him but thought he would let them suffer an additional moment or two. Reaching his arms in the air stretching pretending he was exercising turned slowly then smiled and said, "Well my young thieves are you here to rectify your past deeds?" They just stood there not knowing what he asked. Then looking around he asked, "Where is the big guy who was with you yesterday?" The shrugging of their shoulders told him they did not know where Barabbas was, "I know now who that giant of a young man is for I have had several run in's with his father whom he resembles; my men and I have arrested him several times and he has spent many nights in my dungeon." He laughed loudly, "Oh yes I remember that giant of a man whom I have chased many times for he outran all of us more times than I want to count, where that man got his release money I will never know." Then, "O k you two get busy picking up all the trash around the Judgment room and the Magistrates office and those two buildings." He pointed to two large government buildings nearby the Tetrarchs office. Once again he asked, "Where is your buddy, when I find him I will double his work load." Not saying anything but keeping their eyes to the ground they began the clean up. "When you see him tell him for his own good he best get in touch with me to clear his name and he owes the Governor a day's work. He started to walk away then said, "If he does not show up when I see him again I will imprison him." He pointed to two legionnaires saying, "If you become thirsty let the guards know they will give you water. When you are finished cleaning to our satisfaction you will be allowed to leave.

Barabbas watched all this from atop a home near Judgment hall by conning an apartment owner to allow him on the roof. He saw the apartment owner sweeping the front of the building and walked up to him with no compunction praising the building, its color, its height and the setting. As an exceptional con artist Giant was extremely glib and this time was no exception in fact he may have been one of the best ever. When he was finished with all his baloney he asked," "How tall is this building did you have it built especially for you and your family?" By that time the owner was under a blanket of egoism and he offered to allow the young man to come to the top of the building where his garden was, "Come, come with me and I will show you my garden atop my house you will see it is a beautiful courtyard, come have a refreshing drink of homemade lemoun hamith" (lemonade). So it was that Barabbas watched as his two best friends worked off their obligations. He laughed for he had outsmarted, oh so he thought, the police for the first time and it gave him an ego boost that would send him into another phase of his life, a crossroads allowing him to change his direction.

This then was this young man's decision-making time that would direct his footsteps into a life of good or evil, it was never a decision that required any thought, although it probably should have. This false feeling of accomplishment was so strong it blanketed the id and polished the egocentricity of his brain, which would now guide him into a life of crime. Again a burst of laughter leapt from his throat as his back arched in the air then fell back on the large pallet under the huge umbrella enjoying the cool winds.

He lay there his mind in the clouds thinking back to his earlier childhood, the picture coming to his mind showed himself with those two friends remembering when they first met and what they had named their own secret club, just the three of them. Nobody was allowed to follow them deep into the oasis, past the caravans and all the travelers. They had fallen upon what came to be their secret hideout where they swore to be friends for the rest of their lives and vowed never to tell anybody about this place or anything that took place there. They gave each other secret nicknames, another something that would be just theirs. It took almost an hour to decide what nicknames suited each of them. Ayoub would be Ab, Majheed new name, Maj and Barabbas was tagged Bas that's when Majheed pulled a knife out of his belt and said, "We will make a small slit in our fingers just enough to bring blood then we must hold our fingers together so the blood will mix together making us brothers." Barabbas cringed at the thought but when the other two showed no compunction he was embarrassed not to be a part of this lasting friendship. They did so and pointing the bloody fingers toward each other touched them together so, as they said, made their blood mix together and now *would* forever be blood brothers.

The following day laughing and remembering their ordeal they walked toward the south gate of Nazareth and Barabbas continued questioning his two best friends about their big day cleaning up the area around the Government buildings. "Did they feed you anything, did they bring you water, did they furnish rags to wipe your sweat from your brow?" Each time he asked a question of them he laughed out loud uttering, "Good, oh yeah and finally you didn't tell them where I lived did you. I knew they would never mess with me they know I would be hard to handle and they couldn't take me I'm too damn tough for 'em." Majeed and Ayoub stopped, glaring at him, Majheed arms akimbo brows furrowed, his eyes like lasers saying, "Ya subby (young one), and looking up at his towering friend, "what do you think; after all we are supposed to be your best friends." Barabbas' big arms reached around them both pulling them to his body saying, "Ah come on guys you know I am just joking, O K?"

Majheed and Ayoub trying to pull away from the strong grasp of Giant, not realizing his strength for their heads were locked in his grasp and they were looking at four of the largest legionnaires they had ever seen. Barabbas had no idea what the two youngsters were trying to say for he was laughing so loud he heard absolutely nothing. He loosed them and took one step backwards still smiling then seeing the fright in their eyes looking passed him he spun too late. The legionnaires had been schooled in the art of capture and they would now subdue this big young giant. The four legionnaires were the strongest in the troop and had been trained in this type of seizure. While one of them flipped a slip knot onto Barabbas' right wrist and pulled him off balance making him raise his right leg that limb was lassoed as was his left wrist then it was a simple thing to cinch the final limb and now he was trussed completely, so they thought; everybody` but Barabbas. Each of the policemen were holding their end of the ropes as taught as possible making sure they gave this big guy no quarter. "Hold tight don't give an inch, this guy is huge, wow!" Giant looked like a human X standing there waiting the next move and he had already decided the next move would be his. He breathed a huge sigh of relief as his entire body relaxed. He dropped his arms to his sides and sighed deeply once again as if to tell them he had given up his face mirroring defeat which convinced the guards he had ceded for his chin dropped to his chest as he exhaled which took all of fifteen seconds and they assumed his entire body would succumb to the ground as he almost sat down where he was. He stood like that for some time bent over his arms touching the ground his knees bent and the officers were convinced he had surrendered for the tautness had gone out of the fetters. The largest of the four guards inched his neck out toward the Giant and began slowly walking toward him. Seeing this, the other three did the same. That move was exactly what Barabbas had anticipated so suddenly and unexpectedly Giant made several swift movements in one fell swoop as his arms arched upward and he inhaled so loudly one would think all loose objects near would be sucked up into his air passage. Then suddenly he jerked hard on both ropes tied to his wrists and the two legionnaires on the working ends of said ropes were careening toward each other and although they tried they could not stop and came crashing into one another at such a speed there was the resounding clash of bone on bone and surely something had to give.

Giant utilized the surprise factor to its utmost for just as the two legionnaires met head on he dropped to the ground rolled onto his back and jerked his legs hard and the other two policemen were on the ground. Now it was a matter of a very few seconds all four of the ropes were off him and his feet flying up the hill toward the cover of the forest at the edge of the City. Barabbas was fifty yards ahead of them as they sprang to their feet in hot pursuit. This was Giants own ground's for he spent many hours here guided by his father pilfering from the many caravans that found this oasis a temporary respite from their travels through the plains of Esdraelon or as most called them Megiddo. A few seconds later the four lawmen made it to the top of the small hill, stood there surveying the area from north to south, east to west but could see nothing of the escaped giant. The sergeant of the crew shouted one word, "South." And pointed in that direction a tall black haired man could be seen making his way speedily through the crowd of picnickers made up of caravan travelers who were trying to keep a semblance of home. They could see him a quarter of a mile ahead jumping through, around and over those having an evening meal. As he made his speedy way through the throng he grabbed a piece of fruit here a leg of chicken there and so on his way south into the throes of the Plains ahead of him for it was a possibility he would try to throw them off and it looked as if he may be headed for the small town of Salim or Aenon then into the valley below Mt. Ebal and across the Jordan river which at that point was fed by Sea of Galilee which flowed through the small communities and fertile valley where these peoples made their livings raising the fruits and vegetables of the region.

Coraee, near Alexandrium, Phasaeks, Jericho, Tarsus and Cyprus all those living here always thankful for the Sea of Galilee which made its way through those towns then into the extremely large lake Asphaltitus or Dead Sea as it came to be called.

Surprisingly he turned north up the hill toward the elevated plateau. This they thought would not be a normal escape route but yet why not even though it was up hill all the way he seemed not to slow as the plateau crawled speedily down to meet his plodding feet. The Giant did not stop although he did pause as he glanced back his eyes scanning the horizon below from east to west to make sure the Romans were not closing on him. Here he was five hundred feet above Nazareth one of his favorite places in his hometown for he loved the panoramic view. To the north he could see the Plateaus of Naphtali and Zebulun and especially the Mountains of Lebanon with snow covered Hermon towering above. He stopped and looked west to the blue waters of the Mediterranean and the coast of Tyre where his mother's aunt Najeeba lived. He had been quite young when he had come up here with his father and grandfather and heard them talking of Mt. Caramel and he remembered the story of the struggles of Elijah against someone called Baal. Turning southwest he would follow the crest then when reaching that end he would slowly move toward Ginae a small town just outside the plain.

Knowing he was still in the Tetrarchy of Herod Antipas, this he recalled for he had been told by his sister that Herod controlled the area west of the Sea of Galilee south to Judea then west to Perea. Barabbas had overheard his father speaking to some friends telling them of a convenient hideaway near the Dead Sea southwest of Judea that abutted the sea. Although it was a wilderness it made for an ideal location for none of the Centurions would allow their men to enter the area with less than half a brigade for not only was it a wilderness but there were so many depressions and caves unless one were familiar with the area it was a nightmare of canyons and rock formations and especially at night could be a remarkably forbidding arena of dark sights and sounds that would rock ones spirituality reaching into ones id and ego shaking some of the bravest of men.

****

Majheed and Ayoub missed their friend for he was a mover and shaker that always made things happen showing them a funny side of life so evening after evening they sat reminiscing. "He will be back soon I know for he can't stay away very long, he will miss us as much as we miss him." Said Ayoub and they had a good laugh. This was one of Barabbas' good traits which made him a forever optimist and part of his great personality that pulled people in to him for his conviction ever seemed to be just the right thing at the right time.

****

Three months after the escape of Barabbas during a beautiful evening the two friends were sitting outside the east gate, or more commonly known as Stephens gate, of Nazareth enjoying a cup of the famous Turkish coffee along with cheese and fruits. The discussion turned, as it usually did, to the buddy whom they had not seen for several months. "I sure hope he gets in touch with us one of these days and I hope nobody has caught him yet." Majheed answered, "I am sure soon he will send us a message and then we can hopefully go to him that is unless he is in the pokey." That loosened them up somewhat and they began telling jokes, laughing and relaxing. As Mahjeed reached for a juicy looking plum a young man approached and asked if they knew anybody by the name of Ayoub or Majeed. Ayoub almost jumped out of his skin answering the question but stopped short for Mahjeed kicked him and shook his head no. Majheeed, with his left hand on Ayoub's arm, asked the man what his name was and as if he did not understand the name he asked him to repeat his question. "My name is Sladeen and I have come from Taurus a few days hence and met a huge giant with a marvelous personality, we sat and drank arrak together. He told me he was from Nazareth and soon he would be going home then asked me where I was headed, when I informed him I was coming here he asked me to look up a couple of friends of his and gave me the names of Mahjeed and Ayoub and he insisted I speak to them and only them. He is such an imposing being while smiling he threatened me with my life if I dared to tell anybody other than them. Perhaps you know of the two men I speak, if you do I would appreciate your assistance." Mahjeed stood and put his arm around the shoulder of Sladeen saying, "I know of these two good young men and if you will give us a moment to finish our coffee, would you like a cup, we will take you to them." Sladeen shook his head but answered in the negative as to the coffee.

They walked through the gate with Sladeen at their side and started up the grassy slope toward the oasis where Barabbas was last seen. They walked into the clearing where all the wagons and travelers were and continued on through and past the crowds then at the edge of the dense tree line turned to look at the mass of humanity most of them getting ready for their evening meals. Mahjeed put one arm around Sladeen's shoulder with the other around Ayoub and they stood there for a few seconds then Mahjeed turned looking at them and pushed them toward the forest than leading them into the deep greenery. He told Sladeen to follow closely then stopped as he took a large rag out of his tunic and tied it around Sladeen's eyes assuring him that was necessary and not to be worried. After several minutes of turning and twisting through the underbrush and dense growth, taking a surreptitious route, they stopped facing a wall of trees and vines. Ayoub put his hand deep into the growth and separated the vines, which opened into a small cathedral type area looking like a large room. Here was their secret hiding place.

Mahjeed removed the blindfold from Sladeen's eyes and told him to sit. There were large rocks used for seating and a board placed over the top of two of the rocks to make a table. One could see pallets of straw, which had been placed around the perimeter of the room evidently used for sleeping. Sladeen said, "Wow what a great place it's really neat." "O K Sladeen we are the two who you are looking for, you can now give us the message." "No not yet for you see there is one more thing he said if you were his buddies you would tell me his nickname and then I will know who

Two Men Named Jesus

you are." Mahjeed gave Sladeen the name Bas. Sladeen told them he was happy to know them and said the message is that he will be coming to see them at the next full moon and to meet him at the usual place. They were happy to get the message and gave the messenger two denari with their thanks then put the blindfold back over his eyes and escorted him out of the forest releasing him on the west side. When they released him they said if he ever tried to find that hideaway they would be forced to find him and do harm to him. He assured them he would be heading back to his home in Syria. They had no idea where that was but they knew they had never heard of it so it must be many miles from them and it was several hundred miles north and west.

Walking back to their homes Mahjeed asked Ayoub when the next new moon would be and Ayoub shrugged his shoulders saying he thought it was something like ten or more days away. Mahjeed screwed his face up as if what does that mean then asked how they would find out and Ayoub told him his neighbor was an old man whom he called Uncle Naseem and said he knew everything. "I will find out and tell you tomorrow." He shouted as he scampered across the street to his small abode rushing as if the advance of the night would crash in upon them. Mahjeed waved as he reached for the front door of his Grandmother's home.

****

THE WILDERNESS - HOME?

"Mahjeed, Uncle Naseem said it would be only three days to the new moon he has charts and maps and all kinds of things that tell him many things about our world. I will take you to him one of these days and he will tell you things you will find unbelievable. Uncle has told me so many things I have forgotten but his stories are real and many, you'll see some day. When Giant returns I will take you both to him and we will all listen to his stories. In fact he is a very good friend of the Priests in the Temple and you know some of them are seers and some of the smartest men in the world. I'll bet you didn't know they can read and write." Majheed stood there with his mouth open for this was the first time Ayoub had talked like this and all he could say was, "Unjuud, (for truth?) I can't wait to hear him?" Then, "Okay now along with being great with numbers you are also one of those history guys too huh?"

On a cool evening later that week the two friends

were sitting out in front of their houses looking up at a full moon. "I never really noticed the moon before now, Ayoub it is something to behold. How come we can be in this world and not notice such pretty things as the moon, stars, giants and all things around us. I think this has given me a different outlook on life." Ayoub nodded his head in agreement then in deep thought, "Maybe we should go to the place tonight and wait 'cause he may be there now; he did say the full moon didn't he?" Majheed agreed and they were off to their secret place.

To watch them move through the dense overgrowth of this place one knew they had been there many times for even in the total darkness they found their way easily. It always took a good eight minutes to arrive at the hiding place for it was deep into the forest. Majheed reached his arm deep into the overgrowth then jumped back for someone inside grabbed his arm. He muffled a shout and held it deep in his throat. As is normal when one has been in the darkness for a short time the eyes discern and what Ayoub saw in his buddies face was abject fear and without thinking he grabbed Majeed's arm to help him pull him back out of the thick vine growth. Then they heard a deep growl of an animal they had never heard before and then the thing was upon them. Immediately they knew it was their old friend Giant for the guttural laugh coming out of him was unmistakably their own Barabbas. In between his laughter he asked, "Hey guys good to see ya, didn't scare ya did I. Where ya been I've been waiting for several hours, I thought maybe my messenger didn't find you." At first frightened then ecstatic and euphoria came upon them making them giggle like small children for happy they were to have him back and they laughed as a few tears drained down their faces then they lashed out playfully hitting Barabbas all over his body as he drew back trying to get away from them; finally they all three crumpled to the ground laughing so hard their sides and cheeks ached and if any could see them they would know these were three very, very happy human beings.

****

Ayoub and Majheed awoke to a most pleasant odor, which would soon be their breakfast. They separated the extremely heavy vines acting as a doorway between two massive dogwoods where Barabbas was just lifting off a home made skewer of the most delightful looking charcoaled meat with a remarkable aroma. They could hardly contain themselves as they held out their hands awaiting the first taste of this delectable meat. They were eating heartily saying nothing and licking their fingers over and over. This was the best meal they had eaten for some time, Ayoub, in between bites, "Where

in the world did you learn to cook like this Giant and what kind of meat is this?" "I began cooking weeks back when I ran from those Roman guards; do you really like my cooking?" Majheed still with a mouth full of meat, "Umm best I eber ate, what is it?" It's a little white and gray fury animal I think it is called arnab (rabbit) and I love it roasted as I see you do also. I gained a friend who has a hideout in the Wilderness of Judea and he taught me to catch and cook several types of animals. Just wait until you taste snake," they both almost jumped out of their skins, "you won't believe the taste for it is better than chicken in fact much sweeter." All they could say is "Wow!" Then, "Are we going with you to the new hideout?" "Yea, sure now you two get some sleep and I will wake you when I'm ready to leave and we will take what is left over from this fine meal with us."

****

It was yet dark when Barabbas awakened his two cronies to begin their sixty odd mile trek to their new hideaway very near the dead-sea inside En-gedi or wilderness of Judea. As they made way through the thick forest Ayoub and Majheed paused for they were sure somebody was following them. "Giant," Ayoub whispered loudly, "somebody is following us." Yes," came the answer, "it is my new friend Schmuel (Samuel) and he is the one who has taught me the art of cooking the animals we catch. Than as the new friend approached, "Schmuel meet my two best friends in the world Ayoub and Majeed." Giant explained, "As you guys know I was running from those Legionnaires and Schmuel was running from others who would do him harm." Schmuel added, "I had arrived first at a cave and as I entered it this big guy threw me aside and piled into the cave." "Oh no Schmuel I was there first and you came after me," Barabbas answered loudly. "Wrong again bird brain," Schmuel said.

Laughing uproariously Giant said, "Before I knew what was taking place this guy, a brave youngster, drew a saber and threatened to use it if I gave him any trouble." Another enjoyable laugh by all then they settled down inspecting the cave. "Wow it's large enough for twenty or thirty people," Ayoub shouted from deep in the cavern. "Come see how far back it goes." But seeing a wall from which Ayoub's voice was coming Mahjeed shouted, "Where are you Ayoub?" Came Ayoubs voice, "See the wall that looks like the end of the cave, go to the left and it opens into another passageway that is impossible to see until you turn the corner, it meanders back into the canyon wall then splits into three other passageways." Barabbas told them, " I haven't had time to inspect the rest of the cave but go back and check to see that no animal has made a home their." "Now I have another thing to tell you about our new buddy Schmuel, "I believe he is the fastest man I have ever seen throwing a knife 'cause I saw him throw his knife splitting a bamboo cane thirty feet away." That brought broad smiles from the two friends and they said they would like to see Schmuel use his talents. He assured them he would show them his talents later. They thought it unusual that Schmuel did not spend the night in the hut and he said he would rather be in the open than inside a cave or den. He explained it was the only thing that made him nervous was to be in a confined area very long. Barabbas said, "Come now we can visit as we walk so step it up I think we can make at least twenty-five miles by daybreak." He warned his two buddies they needed to get in shape for their lives were about to take an upward turn and they would need to increase their stamina, at that he laughed out loud, saying, "You will learn to outrun the Romans."

****

They did not follow a trail but made their own moving southwest toward the Jordan River following that south then around the two towns of Coraee and Alexandrum remaining very near the river edge just inside the tree lines where accessible so as to avoid human contact. Unexpectedly they arrived at the confluence of the Jordan and the Jabbok River which told them they had made excellent time putting them over half way to their destination. As it was dawning they decided to look for a place to camp hoping to find a dense area near. They saw they were within a hundred yards of a caravan just awakening and making ready to continue their journey. Barabbas told them, "Find hiding places in the tree line but get as near as possible while it is not yet dawning for most of those in the caravan are yet sleepy act as if you are with the caravan and take what you can reach from the wagons." On second thought he added, "Try to steal some foodstuffs that will keep us from going into a town for we should avoid contact with people." He warned them, "Try to stay low and don't do anything that will draw suspicions to you, take no more than a few minutes and we will meet near that stream nearby where we will sleep." He then assigned them all watch times and told them they would continue on their way at first light.

Schmuel had taken the last watch so now as the sun pushed against the eastern sky to reach its agenda he awakened them offering fruit and goats cheese as they rose tying their napkins around them. Taking a large bite out of the cheese and trying to ask Schmuel a question along with tying his shawl around his waist Majheed asked, "Where did you get this cheese it is some of the best I have ever eaten." Schmuel laughed and pointed toward the departing caravan and holding up a large bag saying, "They were a very rich caravan and look at this." He pulled a tall solid copper oil container with a very small mouth out of his bag laughing. Ayoub said very casually, "When you laugh you sound like my sister." And he laughed thinking it funny. Schmuel walked away quietly shrugging his shoulders then shouted back at them, "Didn't any of you take anything from those wagons last night, you sure missed a lot of goodies. I'll get rich on the things I took, he haw, he haw!" Ayoub and Majheed looked at Barabbas sheepishly and watched him pull out an ahrrkellah (water pipe) from his bag.

There was a seascape painted on its side in gold, green and yellow and the same colors snaked around the smoking pipes with a mouthpiece of genuine ivory. He put it back into his bag saying, "You guys are going to have to start carrying your weight so start learning some more tricks of the trade."

Now up ahead was truly a wasteland for there was little grass, few trees and lots of cacti, so many forms of the water bearers from flat ones on the ground to many resembling tall men on a horse or one that resembled a birthday cake with candles on top and so many indescribably beautiful and yet some dangerous plants. There were a few trees scattered throughout the area and one could see this area received very little moisture. They wove in and out between the cacti and anthills and soon Barabbas turned to them saying, "Well my friends we are almost there and I will venture to say as bright and intelligent as you think you are I will give five dinary to the one who finds the cave in fact I will guide you within twenty-five feet of it and you must find it on your own." He laughed as he moved ahead of them again.

Approaching the area where the cave would be one could not see the entrance for there were several small mounds that resembled large anthills standing from four to seven foot tall. So many could be seen across ones vista many were grouped together in threes, fours and even more. Schmuel stopped in front of a group of three anthills saying, "How could you possibly have a cave here in this desolate country everything here is atop the ground." Barabbas laughed while his two buds just smiled looking at the unbelieving stranger. Now they were on their own turf and they felt much better for being with Giant gave them both a new confidence they had not felt for quite some time. Yes they were far from home but anyplace was home as long as their rafika (friend) was with them.

He lead them to the right about fifty yards around a group of hills then to the left another fifty or sixty yards then turned an immediate left walking behind a large grouping of anthills that were formed in a circle. In the center of this circle were two hills butted up against each other. Barabbas stood there in front of the two hills and turning to Schmuel, "Do you suppose you can find our cave Schmuel?" The young man stood there looking all around first in one direction then in another. The other two were very confident they could find the cave. Barabbas sat down on a small mound situated within the confines of this inner area. If one looked around at the surroundings it would seem they were inside a miniature city and outside the city they were guarded by a multitude of cacti.

They searched for the cave for a good fifteen minutes. They wove in, out and around the humongous mounds of solid earth; Aboud began slowly looking over some of the mounds by running his hands over them.

Later one by one they all approached Barabbas and sat on the ground or on other small mounds around him and in turn shook their heads as if to say, we give up! They sat there for almost a full minute then finally all three of the seekers began speaking somewhat loudly. They could not be understood but Giant knew what they were saying. Slowly he turned walked left toward one of the anthills stopped in front of it for a second then turned away and walked to another and stopped. He turned looking at the three of them knowing they were expecting him to show them a cave. He heaved a huge sigh then turned back toward them walking past them toward the two huge mounds butting up to each other. The base of the mounds was twenty to twenty five feet in circumference. Because they were of the same color it looked as though they had grown together and only about six inches apart. Like a backdrop a magician uses one could not really tell there was other than the very small space one could see. As huge Giant walked toward the center of the two and continued through the opening. Now as he made his way toward the interior he suddenly stepped to the right and disappeared. They could not believe what they were seeing and sat there for several seconds until they heard Giant's voice calling to them to come on back into the cave; they could hear that deep guttural laugh of his enjoying this new game.

    One by one they followed each other, into what they did not know. As they turned right they saw a small opening into the side of the chasm and it looked as though it were almost directly in front of them. They walked toward it and saw that Giant was walking into a cave. As he did he ducked his head so as not to scrape it on the opening. "From back there," he turned facing the direction they had just come, "it looked as though the cave was too small for any of us, but look as we get nearer the mouth it seems to get larger." From Majeed, "Looking from back there I expected Giant to get down on his hands and knees and crawl into the cave. Then when I saw him walk upright into it I realized it was an illusion." Schmuel was awed as were the other two as they continued to walk in and out of the cave looking up toward the area they had come, for they could see but not make out the opening from which they had just come it looked as though the anthill had eaten them alive. They shouted and laughed and shook Giants hand and hugged him. Majheed said, "Giant you are a genius." Schmuel faced Giant with a puzzled look on his face saying, "How in the world did you find this place did someone lead you to it or," his voice trailed off.

"Before I answer that question, and I will soon, don't you guys want to look over your new home? There are so many rooms you won't believe it." Standing in the mouth of the cave they all turned to look inside.

The large area they were looking at was a good forty feet deep and at least that wide maybe larger. Toward the back of the cave on each side were passageways into other parts or rooms of the cave. They explored for thirty minutes, as there were three passageways that led into many other caves. This could hold a large family of several generations and probably did at one time for there was table like slabs of stone set upon four legs of the same stone and around it several of the same, yet shorter, resembling seating. In the back areas were ledges cut into the walls of the cave that looked to be where one could crawl into and sleep. There were several of these in four of the rooms.

When they tired of inspecting their new lodgings they all sat or laid around in various postures not saying too much for they were by now worn out from the two days trek. After resting for a while Barabbas said; "Ok guys now we are going to go get something to eat." They all looked around the cave wondering what he meant. "Here in this en-gedi" and he pointed outside, "there is to be found loads of fresh foods. I will take you outside and show you what I mean but first check this out," and he put his forefinger on what resembled a half inch circle in the huge door like boulder," each of you put your eye to this hole; you will notice you can see one hundred and eighty degree outside so before you leave the cave take a look and make sure there is nobody to see you enter or exit, now follow me and do not talk!"

They followed him outside and watched as he walked around looking at the cacti. He stopped at a funny looking cactus plant with fruit hanging from some of the branches. Gesturing to them to pick the fruit off saying, "Be careful for those barbs are sharp and can cut your hands so grab them with your fingers in between the stickers." The three of them picked several cactus pears and put them in their bags. He then took a long cord out of his belt and made a small 12" circle with it on the ground pulling some olives out of his bag dropping them inside the circle. Holding on to the large portion of the cord he began walking toward a large hill letting the cord drop to the ground and kicking dirt onto the cord to hide it. The others saw what he was doing and they took over hiding the cord. He walked behind a very large hill and motioned for Aboud to come with him. He handed his pal the cord and whispered in his ear. "Now watch for an animal with long ears and a muff for a tail; then wait till the animal begins eating, when you think the animal is concentrating on the food and only if he is inside the circle than jerk the cord, make sure you jerk hard and you will snare him." He handed the cord to Aboud and left him hiding behind the anthill. He did the same in two other locations, repeating the identical instructions he had given Aboud. He made sure the distance between them were far enough away that one's actions would not bother the other.

They ate well that evening in their new home for they had snared two rabbits and a snake. Mahjeed & Aboud looked at one another with trepidation although Giants words did not resound well in either of their minds. They each picked up a small piece of the sautéed lizard and with closed eyes threw it into their mouths and began chewing. Slowly their eyes opened as a smile broke over their faces. "Wow that is really good," Aboud said, "I know Bar you switched the snake with chicken!" Barabbas laughed and answered, "No my little buddy that *is snake* see I told you!"

Finished with the meal he took them outside near a flowing fresh clean pool and showed them the beautiful growth of kale growing under water showing them which greenery to pick that was edible. So they had enough to enjoy a repast of meat and vegetables then he showed them how to peel the cactus pears that ended a fine meal and each relaxed in his own space where he would sleep. Aboud said, "Ah that is great fruit so juicy that's the first time I have eaten such fruit." Mahjeed said, "Ok Bas now tell us how you found this great hideaway.

****

JERICHO

He began his story. "I traveled south staying near the Jordan River and soon came upon a group of young men eating their evening meal. Upon seeing me some of them became afraid while others invited me to eat with them. They were a band of men who roamed the area from the districts of Samaria on the north to Idumea south then east to Nabatea and north to Perea. Their leader and I became friendly and he took me under his wing, his name is Isaac and he taught me many things such as going to the market area in any town and talking with those clerks who sell all manner of things. The first thing he showed me was a bag sewn inside his large tunic the bottom came to his knees and open at the shoulder line. He asked to see my knife and scabbard which I gave him; now holding it in his right hand he raised it above his head than brought his hand down behind his back then brought his hand or fist to his chest. When he opened his hand it was empty. He asked me if my eyes were fast enough to see what happened to the knife. He explained to me how he "palmed" the knife hiding it in his hand and dropping it into the bag under his tunic without me even noticing what he had done. I thought he was wiping his hands on his skirt. He then explained to me that the bag would hold many things. He took me to the market area where he pointed out one of the stores and told me to go visit with the clerk and keep him busy, pretending to shop.

While I asked questions of the clerk faking interest in purchasing something Isaac lifted many worthwhile items and placed them in his bag. Although the clerk would turn to look at him from time to time Issac was never caught for he kept one eye on the clerk while stuffing valuables into his bag.

Continuing, Barabbas told them Isaac took him to an Oasis where many caravans were parked for the evening. "We waited for night until the guards fell asleep then we would sneak up to the wagons and quietly rifle through them to find valuables; we almost got caught once when a girl awoke and sounded an alarm; but we got away. By rifling through the wagons we could steal many things." Ayoub looking up at Barabbas with a very puzzled face asked, "But what would you do with all those fine things you stole?" "Well you see, in the bowels of the City, there is an area where the Roman guards hesitate to enter for it is infested with those of us who make our living on the edge of the law; many lawless men who will buy anything of value from us. The Roman guards are afraid to descend into that area for there are more of us then there are of them. These men are never short of money and there are times when we can make a better deal with gold or silver items. You guys will be surprised at the amount of shekels we make each week. One day I will show you a place where I can bury anything and none will ever find it."

Mahjeed stood with his arms akimbo his eyes cavernous sending unseen darts toward his friend. Now frowning, but before he could say anything Barabbas realized he had put them off too long laughed saying, "Ha Ha, oh I'm sorry you are wondering how I found this great hideout; well here goes. One night being alone I watched while a large caravan of at least eight wagons pulled into the outer limits of the Oasis. The sun was setting as they pulled into a semi-circle and made a big thing of pulling one of the wagons into line between the third and fourth. I found that wagon masters always put the wagon carrying the most valuables toward the front of the train so all can keep watch on it. I waited for at least an hour until they were asleep and crawled on my hands and knees very slowly toward that main wagon. At one hundred yards I crawled very slowly and it took some time to reach that wagon for I had to keep my eyes on both ends of the train to make sure nobody was watching me. This was a very sharp wagon master for they never lit any lanterns. I slowly pulled myself up to the wagon where I could raise the cover just enough to look inside I saw some of the richest pieces of gold and silver gadgets I have ever seen. As I could only see six or eight inches inside the wagon I put my hand inside to see what I could pull out without any trouble. I reached in and felt a large pitcher with a handle on it. As I pulled it out something stung my wrist so hard I yanked my hand out and before I knew what was happening, one man from each end of the wagon jumped down. I turned and ran as fast as these legs would carry me and as you know I can run fast but that night I was really scared for the first time in my life. I continued to look back and never slowed and knew I was putting many mille between us. I was surprised that they did not give up for we had now run at least two miles. When I realized they were slowing I breathed deeper and sped up and soon put enough space between us until I could not make them out in the night sky. I ran until I thought I had exhausted them for I was exhausted myself and breathing hard.

I finally ran deeper inside the en-gi (wilderness) running around and in between those large anthills. I paused once to listen and heard them outside the en-gi. As I turned and ran I hit those two anthills that look like they are one with a path between them. I thought I would stop but my speed and body carried me through that opening that is now our entrance. I fell and tumbled and as I picked myself up I saw what I thought was a small opening in the wall of the chasm that I could crawl through but when I came to the opening as if magic it became a huge mouth which I ran into as far as I could go. I was afraid they would find me but they scoured the area as well as they could yet they never found the opening that would direct them to the cave. I stayed there all night and fell asleep.

When I awoke I slowly crawled out of the cave and back up to the anthills. I stood behind them and listened for at least five or more minutes; then decided to go on out. Remember I stumbled into the place and thought I could find it easily. I sat down then decided I was terribly hungry for I had not eaten since morning and now it was late night. As I sat there very still the moon came out and I saw several arrnab (rabbits) as they would hop a short distance then look around, hop a little further and look around again. I knew now what my next meal was going to be but I had no idea how to catch one. Reaching in my tunic I came out with that roll of string I always keep and set up a snare as I did for you guys to catch those arrnab, here's the catch and I'm sure you will get a big kick out of this I couldn't find my way back into the cave. I swore I could find it easily but it took me a good two hours for I searched and searched and searched. Finally in total frustration I sat down on the ground not far from where I had set my snare (which I should have remembered) and as I looked up toward the full moon then back down, there in front of me was the double anthill. I breathed a sigh of relief went back into the cave cooked my meal and fell asleep again." They laughed and applauded his

Two Men Named Jesus

presentation and he bowed as though he were an actor of some repute. "Now we will rest and tomorrow I will take you on a visit to an area where there are great riches and we will increase our wealth considerably." They wanted to know where he would take them and pestered him to tell them but he held steady while snickering like a child with a great surprise.

****

The noise in the cave woke them. Subtle noises yet time and again the noise was metal on metal that awakened them. "Well sleepy heads you two finally woke huh? Where is Schmuel?" "I thought he was next to me," from Aboud, "at least he was when I fell asleep last night." Majheed nodded his head rubbing sleep out of his eyes then they all began looking around for the fourth member of the gang. Giant went to the left into the interior of the cave and as he went shouted Schmuel' name over and over. Suddenly the lost one was not lost anymore for there he was standing in front of Giant stretching as one does when arising of a morning. Barabbas shouted forward to the other two, "I have found the lost one." He turned and said, "What happened to you did you decide to take a separate bedroom for yourself Oh Kingly one, do you not like our company, I see you have found the small pond back yonder for it seems you have bathed and all the earth has been removed from your body." He paused and walked around Schmuel slowly inspecting him as one would inspect an animal to purchase. "If you insist on your own sleeping quarters I shall take a slight bit more of your earnings than I do from your cohorts." By then the other two were standing near and listening to the conversation. They strode over to Schmuel, Majheed came close and sniffed him then patted his hair. Schmuel slapped his hand hard and told him to keep his hands to himself and, "Never touch me again or I will smack the khatta (shit) out of you." The young man was truly irate for his face turned beet red and he stood there eye to eye with Majheed then pushed him away.

The other three dropped back looking at the brave Schmuel as none of them knew what to say. Barabbas stepped between them and told them if they wanted to remain in this gang they must all accept each other's faults and try to understand each other. "This is going to be the beginning of something that will make us all rich beyond our wildest dreams." Then he became very serious and unsmiling and the sternest look they had ever seen came over his face. He said nothing for a few seconds then told them, "From this date know I am leader and we will not allow fighting among ourselves for that will tend to ruin us. We will vote on those selected to join us, if and when there are disagreements we will hear arguments as a team and will take part in any final decision. I am sure this will meet with problems for some of you, so think it over. I will hear any helpful suggestions or grievance but if left up to me I will get rid of any found guilty of our rules." Some of them were shocked and they remained very quiet and each of them softly stole away to a space of their own for now they wanted to be in a place where there was no Barabbas for just a little while, long enough for them to become accustomed to the new Giant they had come to revere and love. They were stricken but not for long for they all realized Barabbas must take charge if he were to be the leader and, "After all he is a most just person."

Barabbas was proud of himself for he had never done this before but it gave him a new look at life and realized that he *was* in charge and he would accept the part of boss. He was not surprised of his own worth for his ego was exceedingly large and now grew another realm to extend that ego for the good of all

****

SAUL OF TARSAUS

Barabbas waited for an hour long enough he thought for them to have digested his intentions as well as his words then as if there had never been a quarrel he roused them from their thoughts, brought them together and told them they must pack what they wanted in their carry bags for they would be gone for quite some time. They were happy for he was smiling and his effervescence carried over to them. This was exactly what he wanted for he expected them to put aside their differences, small they may be, and become one team.

He had learned this and much more in a few months from the man who became his second mentor, Isaac. A very important thing Isaac taught him was the art of masquerade or altering ones appearance so drastically that even ones closest kinsmen would not recognize one. He thought possibly this would be a good time to put on a false moustache, beard, wig or other contraption that he had in his carry bag just to give them an idea of what was to come. Thinking on it he decided this was not the time or place so he deferred it. He raised his voice just a tone to tell them he would wait for them outside the cave then they would start on the next phase of their lives.

When they had gathered outside and ready to move he told them they were about forty stadia from their destination. Their sound systems were wide open for they wanted to know where they would be going but they dare not ask for the earlier outburst was enough for them for several years. So they waited to see if he was going to say anything. Lake Asphaltitus (Dead Sea) was at their backs as they moved west out of the Wilderness. At the foot of the small Giant range they turned north toward Judea and Sumaria. Jameel and Majeed, always the all knowing one) whispered, "Aha we are going to Jerusalem for there is much gold and silver and ancient relics to be taken." "You are a great guesser Majeed", Aboud told him, "but you are only a guesser for you never know what you are talking about, you just talk, ha, ha, ha." He laughed heartily which brought Giants head looking back toward them and encouraging them to pick up the pace he told them for I would like to make the twenty stadia mark by nightfall.

****

Isaac had schooled him telling him his cave and the Wilderness (En-gedi) was just east of the small city of Hebron thus Jericho would be approximately forty stadia from that point. He would not tell them where they were headed until they arrived. They probably did not know that Jericho was as large a city as Jerusalem and a very important City for that is where Moses is buried. He was thinking as he strode considerably ahead of the others for when Giant walked, thinking he always speeded his gate. "I know Isaac told me a lot of important things about Jericho but I can't remember what he said something about a large Cathedral building (whatever that is) and many other things." Nightfall was slowly closing in on them for soft lights of large lanterns shined in the distance ahead guiding him toward the small town of Qumram which would be approximately twenty stadia from Jericho. He turned to wait for them. They stopped and asked if this is where they would sleep tonight and he told them to follow him. Qumram was on the north edge of Lake Asphaltitus and they were very near the lake. He led them to a heavily treed area overlooking the lake and threw his napkin down onto the grass saying, "O K guys snack on some of that dried meat we brought and some of the cactus pears; get some sleep for the rising of the sun will awaken you. I am sure you will sleep well for the breeze coming across the lake will keep you cool."

The following morning they watched the sunrise as they began their trek to Jericho as they nibbled on the goat cheese and a large box of figs they had confiscated from a sleeping traveler that morning. "It is a great breakfast," commented one of the group, no shame these guys, for that was their plight in life to live off of others when possible. This was Isaac's motto, allow others to put forth their efforts then capture those efforts.

Giant was lagging behind trying to unravel several knots in the long cord he carried with him. As he pulled at first one line than another he looked up from time to time assuring he did not fall into a hole or trip on a boulder. He heard Aboud say something about somebody looked like they had not had a bath for quite some time. Whoever he was talking about the other two seemed to think something was funny for they were laughing. It seemed the harder he tried to unravel the cord the worse it got and he was becoming frustrated engrossed in the raveling problem. He heard Majeed's voice shouting, "Hey what the heck is going on, watch out guys those dirty men are attacking us, here comes a monster with a huge club!"

Giant looked up to see four of the grimiest looking humans he had ever laid eyes upon. The biggest, over six foot tall, his ruddy face pushing through the layer of filth that seemed to suffice for his skin a gigantic nose protruded below a pair of brooding eyes. It looked as though the beard had been washed with mud for it was caked heavily. He was rotund to the size of a baby elephant and as he ran ever closer rounds of blubber bounced under his tunic, if one could call it running his size fifteens slapped the ground resembling an otters tail, two rows of decaying teeth shined through that huge mouth and the grin of an ignorant uncouth person, term loosely used.

The other three were duplicates of that huge unwashed being though they varied in height, weight and definite repulsiveness running as hard as they could to impede the three travelers for by this time Giant was nearly fifty feet behind his group. Hearing the commotion he looked up to see four of the most motley humans he had ever seen rapidly bearing down upon them clutching huge clubs. He shouted instructions to his men, using the Greek language of his mother, "Wait for them to raise their clubs to strike when they near you then dive to the ground rolling hard toward them knocking them over like bowling pins, grab their clubs and protect yourselves." Giant sprang, running full speed toward the huge grinning elephant of a man and did not slow at all but continued on what seemed to be a crash course with the dirty, stinking man. Watching, one could see the assurance in the eyes of the rotund large footed person. Neither of them gave ground and all watching knew this was going to be the collision unlike any had ever seen. They were less than a yard away from each when giant threw his cord hard at the feet of the attacker. It was like the felling of a huge oak tree. Trying to break his fall the tree reached out and suddenly everything seemed to be in slow motion for the large wooden club he had raised in the air went flying across the sky. There was no overgrowth for this trail had been beaten down year after year by the movement of many travelers there was absolutely nothing to break the fall of this mammoth so as the huge human hit the ground the reverberation and tremor across the ground was as that of a mountain having blown its top.

Giant looked to his cohorts to see how they had fared and there on the ground were his three pals but all that could be seen of their attackers was the heels of three speeding humans for they too had had all they wanted of this crew. They turned back just in time to see that the fallen oak who had loosed himself and was on his way running with a very noticeable limp, and mumbling loudly something about not being fair and it wasn't his day. They did hear him shout back, "My name is Truboosh and I don't know who you are but I'll darn sure remember your ugly face and I'll see ya' agin." They were laughing so hard they could not pull themselves up off the ground.

****

Jericho was proud to be one of the largest and richest cities in the entire area. This Ancient City was known as Moon City situated in the Jordan Valley. This would not be the last time Barabbas would be in this city. They climbed the last of the high hills, which looked down upon the beautiful city just as the sun beckoned the moon to take its place in the night sky as it lowered itself into the western hemisphere. They slowly descended into the valley as fires of many lanterns from homes nearby extended their fingers reaching out into the night. Majheed remarked with nostalgia, "What a beautiful sight from this vantage point it gives me a sense of real security and makes me wish this was my home."

As they dropped to the floor of the valley Barabbas brought them together briefing them on their behavior and explaining what he expected of them. "You are to act as if you had visited here many times." He gave them specific instructions as to what their first jobs would be. He turned and pointed toward the nearby forest of trees saying, "Their, I am sure, inside this forest we will find a place to live." They followed as he led them into the densest part of the woods. They heard the gurgling of water and knew they were near a small brook. Barabbas turned away from the water into the deep undergrowth. He had only to go a few yards where a growth of large vines clustered together overgrowing an area reaching upwards and almost engulfing a huge oak tree. Moving along the line of vines growing up, down and out between the trees he placed his hand over the vines and slowly dragging his hand over the overgrowth until he found a small opening. He stopped and with both hands separated the vines. Starting at his chest level he divided the vines to make an opening that would be used as a door. They looked inside to find a natural clearing where they could rest and relax, then if and when needed hide from the authorities. He told them, "Get some rest, tomorrow we will begin an exploration of the City which might take several days and so I do not forget, I will tell you now, do not steal anything nor attempt anything that might bring the authorities down on us and talk little, absorb everybody and everything and be polite."

Thinking back Barabbas thought of all the things Isaac had taught him in just a few months and how many of the teachings he was utilizing. The following morning they began their exploration of the city.

"Wow I've never seen so many people in one place in all my life!" Aboud remarked, Majheed and Schmuel nodding agreement. They gaped at everything in their view and remarked as to the gigantic walls of the city that seemed to reach as far as one could see. They came closer to the south gate and stopped again for they were astounded at the number of stores each with their own canopy, under each counters and tables full of fruits, vegetables, pots & pans, such a variety of Jewelry, pins, broaches, gift stores of so many items never seen by them before now, small tables encrusted and inlaid with some of the most beautiful landscapes and seascapes and lacquered to the highest sheen possible. There were even chairs, couches of all kinds and all of this went on for several blocks. This was an education for these young men never having seen anything like this.

"Barabbas, Barabbas nephew, is that you, what pray are you doing here are your parents here with you if so we need help." Surprised that someone knew him he turned and quickly motioned for the others to get lost then turned back to the voice shouting to him from across the area. A small five foot five gray-black haired man a weathered complexion and a soft natural smile beaming toward Barabbas and a woman to match his stature as well as ilk also an inviting smile walked toward him. The lady was quite old and one could tell she was at least sixty-five and reaching around Barabbas as far as her stature would allow and gave him a hug then stepped back looking at him. An old man about the same age stuck out his hand to Giant, shook his limp hand then hugged him and stepped back his eyes and his entire face smiling, Barabbas standing his face a complete puzzle for he did not recall this dear man's face who said, "My what a strapping man you have grown into for when last we saw you as a small boy has been years. Look wife how he still resembles Y'hanaton!"

"What a surprise to see you here in Jericho, how is my Brother Y'hanaton and your dear mother Shiphra, tell me about your brothers and sisters." The woman who must be this man's wife said, "Joshua quit rambling and allow him to answer." He interrupted his aunt Sussanne, "Aha now I know who you are, wow I am so very happy to see you Auntie; by the way what were you saying, you need help, what is wrong possibly I *can* help you?" At that she began weeping and sobbing while trying to explain something yet no matter how he tried he could not understand for the sobs held words and the words gushed from her mouth uncontrollably so never recognizable. He and uncle led her out of the crowd toward the wall of the city and sat down on the seats hugging the wall. She stopped sobbing, looked to her husband to explain. Barabbas' uncle began, "We have very little saved and all our massarri (money) comes from what your aunt cooks to sell and what I make in my shop, which is not much for I do not work as fast as I once did yet we were doing well until three months ago a very mean tax collector, his name Saul, came to us and raised the amount of taxes we are to pay. We cannot possibly pay him although we have given him all the massarri we could, keeping very little for what we need."

She began sobbing again and Barabbas put his arm around her and pulled her to him, "I will do what I can my dear aunt, when is this Saul to come back to collect the rest of the taxes?" His uncle said, "He will be here in two days for he told us if we did not have fifty dinar by that date he would take our house. He would allow us to keep my small shed which houses my woodworking shop." Barabbas told his kin to wait there and he would be back soon. He turned back toward the market place finding his buddies. He signaled them to follow and they moved away from the booths and tables. "Find your way to the hideout and I will join you in a couple of days." He handed Ayoub a few coins saying, "Buy what your needs may be and I remind you again do nothing that could put us in jeopardy. As you notice those are my kin and I must be with them for a few days to straighten out some of their problems." As he walked away he turned and shook his finger at them; they knew exactly what that meant.

****

The tax collector was a man of average stature, five foot nine inches tall approximately one hundred and sixty five pounds with a down turn to his lips, his brows automatically frowning. His hair and eyes were dark brown his beard was long but what one noticed first was his searing eyes that seemed to bore through ones entire body. It was hard for most people to look at him while he was talking for he would furrow his brows and annunciate some of his words that felt like they were knives waiting to cut into one.

He introduced himself, "I", sharply annunciated perhaps to frighten, "am Saul of Taurus I am "**Chief Taxcollector"** (proudly & loudly announcing) appointed by Herod to collect back taxes of Jericho." He told them, "I am proud of my reputation for collecting more taxes than any other tax collector before me," a gruff guttural noise let itself out of his lungs and from that sound one may have expected to see fire attend the sound. He shifted his weight and stood extremely erect and glared at them which did not trouble Barabbas although the taxman did his best to demean them all before meeting this young whippersnapper. He stood at the entrance of the home waiting for this huge man to move away that he might enter for never had he been intimidated by any person and this was not going to be the person to do so. Uncle Joshua spoke softly, "Nephew please step back out of the entrance to allow Saul to enter." Giant slowly stepped back to the side of his uncle's chair and dropped his hand on Uncle Joshua's shoulder. Aunt Sussanne motioned to a chair, "Won't you sit Saul?" Glaring at them, "I will stand, do you think this is the only house I will make my presence known today, I have much more important people to see and cannot waste my time with you lowlifes, now where is the fifty dinar that will win you another three months to remain in this hovel you call a home?" One could see rage building up inside the huge one for his demeanor rapidly changed from his normal pleasantness as he seemed to grow another head taller. Aboud, if looking at his buddy, would say watch out for here come's the steam from his ears.

Barabbas slowly stepped toward Saul but his uncle put his arm out in front of the young man's leg and stopped him. "Wait my son and let us see if we can strike a bargain with this tax collector."

Saul stood with his eyes glaring and his brows furrowed a mean twist to his mouth saying, "I told you to have the massarri today or I would take your house, now if you do not have it I shall leave and will return with the Roman guard who will take you into jail, then I will take your house and sell it."

Barabbas gently took his uncle's hand away from his body and walked toward the tax collector. He stood as a statue directly in front of the man his own eyes glaring viciously. He said nothing for a moment then he reached down, a hand under each of Saul's arm pits and raised him to his own eye level. Now speaking softly to the tax collector so his two relatives could not hear, and grinning; "You little twit I will twist your head off and throw it into the hog pens where they will make mush of it. Now when I release you watch your mouth and become their mentor and do what you will to help them or so help me you will not see another day is that clear to you?" Neither his aunt nor uncle could hear what their nephew was saying although it must be pleasant for their nephew had a huge grin on his face as he whispered to Saul. Two minutes later Barabbas, still smiling, slowly returned the tax collector to the floor and released him. Saul stood red faced but smiling while Barabbas brushed imaginary lint off of the man's shoulder as one would for a friend.

Saul stood as tall as he ever could then turned to the two elders in order to address them. Before he began he smiled broadly bowed somewhat and said, "It seems your nephew is very persuasive and speaking to him I understand that he seems to know some of the Government officials in this city. We have come to an agreement that I will wait six months and allow you good people to build your finances. I promised the young man he will be in charge of your health and welfare and you are not to worry for I have given him my word that I will not speak to you again for six months, oh yes and if you do not have fifty we will settle for ten dinar, which by the way I will pay myself for your benefit."

Saul stood smiling, looking up at the big man with a question in his eye. Barabbas looked down at Saul with a frown, nodded his head saying, "Do not forget who Barabbas is and, as I suggested, be sure and look in on Uncle and Auntie occasionally and I will reward you, tax collector, when I return." Saul's head seemed to be on a spring as he nodded his understanding and his smile froze upon his face. Before Saul's exit Barabbas said, "Oh yes tax collector, none can tell you when I might return perhaps tomorrow, next week, or next month but I will return to check on my dear relatives and I am sure you will make every effort to aid them if they need it. Saul was happy to get out of this man's sight but his voice would not come so he gave them all a very wide grin nodding his head as he backed out the door then as soon as he was free of that opening he turned and swiftly fled throwing back a gold piece from his purse.

****

BARABBAS' SCHOOL FOR THIEF'S

He stood before them teaching the tricks of the trade. Now Barabbas had his own experience's as well as the topical's he learned from Isaac. As he talked he wondered if he would ever see Isaac again. "It is never a good thing to operate alone it is always better when there are at least two of you; the first to keep the clerk busy with questions while the others casually pick up the most expensive items. You must watch the clerks and as they look your way keep your head down yet maintain a clear view of him at all times and expect instantaneous glances from them."

Barabbas had on a black cloak the hem of which almost reached his ankles and once again the inquisitive Majheed was about to pose a question. Noticing the inquisitve one, Barabbas held up his hand. Barabbas' right hand was clasping the left opening of the cloak; his left hand clasping the right opening and as he talked he walked back and forth. Barbbas turned walking up to

Majheed who was standing at the back of the clearing, standing in front of Majeed and smiling his hands still clasping the opening of his garment, when suddenly, another pair of hands reached out from the cloak grasping Majeed's head. Majheed and the other two were shocked for they had never seen anything like this in their lives. "Wha', well uh, oh my, he stuttered." Schmuel asked him if he had four arms and Barabbas laughed knowing he had their attention then opened the coat revealing two fake arms somehow extending out from under Barabbas' arm pits complete with sleeves.

Then he showed them the inside of the coat and sewn inside at variable levels hung fishhooks of many sizes. They gasped, gawked then laughed and began shouting questions at him. He raised the palms of his hands toward them.

He explained how the coat was to be used. "Any who looks your way can see your hands and assumes there is no need to watch you of course what they do not know the hands they can see are fake, not your hands. Move close to the items you want to take, look around once again making sure you are not watched then slowly sieze it. Work with caution and watch me as I show you the correct movements." He said they would not begin until he thought they were ready and that their schooling started now.

He taught them the rules he had learned from his mentor, Isaac as he strowed along. "The first thing, check for soldiers or police watch them closely without meeting their eyes make note of their routes. Do a walk through of the area, know the exits and walk through them so you will know what is on the other side. No matter how it looks you must have your cloak on notice how swift I grab and go." With the cloak opened so they could watch his movements and the fake hands holding the cloak his real hands resembled a snake striking its prey as they reached out oh so very fast, then pressing them onto a hook under the cloak. He continued, "When there is just two of you never take over two items then move on to another shop. Depending on the number of clerks in a given area number one will engage them in conversation while number two, will begin his gathering. After each item taken glance at your partner before you take another." Their schooling lasted into the early morning before they were allowed to take a rest. They didn't eat and they were very sleepy and the three of them dropped off where they sat.

****

The following morning Barabbas left to begin his planning of the three large market places, one located at the south gate, he assumed this was the largest until he came upon the east gate. He could not believe what he saw for the sun was ascending into the eastern horizon and this area was a beehive of activity.

This gate faced a hill that reached about forty feet at

its crest so he climbed to its top for a great advantage point. Never had he seen so many vendors or wagons in all his life and the array of merchandise was incredible. Where were all these farmers coming from? Jericho must have one of the largest populations in the world. He bought some fresh peaches and goats cheese for he was hungry and this would give him a chance to sit near the action and study this market. He watched the movement of the ten largest stores in the souk and some of those spaces were designed so there was only one entrance and one exit. He must remember to tell them, those would be the stores to stay away from. He sat and watched the movements for forty-five minutes when at the far end of the market he caught site of a formation of soldiers marching two by two.

They were lead by a Centurion and when they came adjacent to the market two men dropped out of the formation, which left six. They walked to the center aisle of the souk, which extended to the west end. Good, Barabbas thought, as he began to count slowly; he would time their walk from one end to the other. The two soldiers strolled slowly along the aisles of the souk. Many of the market owners were Phoenicians who may have traveled from Yemen bringing spices such as Frankincense, Muir and such delicacies as fuzzdutt (Pistachios).

Barabbas and team were stopped by one of the shop owners saying, "Gentlemen taste my wares you will find these to be the juiciest fruits ever." Handing each of them a pear or peach," Schmuel taking a bite said, "Truly this is fruit for the Gods." By the time they had reached the west end of the market, at Giant's best count, it had taken them approximately twenty eight minutes. They sat down near the souk and watched the action. Barabbas would wait a little longer until the two soldiers began their return to the east end. Evidently they would walk back and forth or around the souk while maintaing their vigilance of their area.

The Centurion came around the corner and the soldiers stood and slapped their fists to their chests saluting him. He nodded and continued walking. Barabbas watched as the Centurion strolled into the center of the market nodding at first one farmer than another. Barabbas smiled as he rose and walked the crest of the hill heading back to the hideout.

****

Ayoub & Mahjeed were awake and waiting outside the clearing as Barabbas came out to greet them. "We are excited to begin this great adventure Giant and we have talked about it all morning." Ayoub spoke for them. Before they left for the city he instructed them fully on his investigation the day before. He swore them to secrecy and told them if they were caught they should say nothing, warning them, "Never give the others away, always say you are alone and be careful for the traps the Tribunes or Centurions might set for you, listen carefully and do not answer even if you are beaten." He made them put their fists over their hearts then their other hands extended one on top of the other. They were to work the souk less than an hour, take those things of great value then immediately go back to the hideaway and stay there until Barabbas's return. Majheed was sent to the west end of the souk, Ayoub at the east with Schmuel in the center. He reminded them that the wealthy owned horses so his next move was to steal one horse. The day before he made note of three different gentlemen each with his own entourage of servants and all three rode horses. The third rode an Arabian while two servants trailied his carriage. He hoped to find this last man and follow him to his home. He watched Schmuel who picked up a gold plate, looked it over then dropped his hands into his cloak and hung it on a hook. Barabbas smiled approving the speed with which Schmuel operated. He breathed a sigh of, "Fast!" Strolling the outside of the souk, looking for nothing in particular until he saw the tall Canaanite with blue eyes and fair complexion the usual facial features with beautifully trimmed hair and beard and he wore his Fez as only the wealthy can. His servant, an Arabian, leading his Master had to be at least sixteen hands tall as the horse pranced and danced as though putting on a show then nodding his head powerfully and snorting until his owner turned and waved at him. The horse gave a nod of approval and settled down.

****

Ayoub had already stolen three gold cooking ladles and a large brooch. He was casing the next booth slowly looking everything over as he walked the aisle. He spied a ten inch silver tray with very unusual inlay and could not take his eyes off of it. Ayoub let desire and greed enter into his mind although his id attempted to whisper, telling him not to. He scanned the area well spotting the clerks locations then reached down to pick up the tray. The weight of the tray took him by surprise and it slipped out of his hand but he grabbed it before it hit the floor. His sudden movement caught the eye of one of the clerks just entering the booth from behind the wall. He had forgotten to look for the exits. Panic overtook him and he grabbed the tray without putting it in his bag and began to run for the exit. The female clerk shouted, "Askarri, (soldiers) askarri!" The soldiers were some fifty feet away but they heard the voice of alarm and headed toward it. They saw the clerk shouting and pointing toward the rear exit. Ayoub could not run well for his foot did not allow it. As he came out into the bright sun a small child running ran into him and he fell and smashed into the ground, the silver tray falling from his hand and landing in the dust. At this point the soldiers arrived and grabbed him raising him to his feet allowing him to brush off some of the dust asking, "Do you know the penalty for stealing, we will take you to the Magistrate for jailing?" Majheed having left his area was headed back to the hideout when he saw Ayoub running out the exit at the west end of the souk. He lurched forward thinking he could aide his brother Patriot but stopped suddenly when he saw the askarri take Ayoub into custody. He thought to follow them when his better judgment took hold of him and he directed his footsteps toward home.

The soldiers shackled Ayoubs hands behind his back then took the walking path back toward the gate to go into the city. As usual the noise level was extremely high for there was activity everyplace and they did not hear the heavy footsteps approaching them from the rear. Those who could see and hear the big giant descending upon them from behind had to dart to the left and right in an attempt to avoid being run down. As each foot hit the ground a guttural sound came from his throat. The huge man was bearing down upon the crowd and none knew exactly his destination. Barabbas was counting on the clamor of the crowd to muffle whatever din he would make as he ran full speed toward the two guards and Ayoub. The people knew to fall back and away from soldiers making an arrest for many times the soldiers would slash out toward anybody in their way.

Those watching were whispering and pointing at a huge mass of a man who seemed to be falling from the sky; the mass was the Giant Barabbas and with both arms extended outward his hands made into fists the two askarri never knew what hit them. They fell hard into the ground where they remained not making a move and in one fell swoop the big man picked up Ayoub and was gone before anybody really knew what happened. They watched as this giant now carrying the young man headed for the outskirts of the city to the west.

Barabbas did not want to lead any who might follow into his hideaway so instead of going directly east he ran in the opposite direction. Two other soldiers approached the two on the ground kneeling to inspect them but they were still unconscious. One of the soldiers was questioning some of those in the crowd but gleaned no information for as one said, "It happened so fast all we saw was a giant of a man come flying out of the sky knocking down the soldiers, picking up the young man and ran over the hill to the west." The soldier glanced up the hill but saw nothing unusual shrugged his shoulders then leaned down to help his partner to awaken the other two soldiers.

****

Barabbas sat in his catbird seat in the clearing talking to his gang. He told them these things can happen when one does not investigate fully. He turned to Ayoub, "Noticing the size of the tray you should have picked it up before you decided to take it then you would have known its weight and you had reached your limit you should have quit, I hope this was a lesson to you, all of you, *remember what I said about greed?"*

Giant and his gang gathered enough merchandise in a week that it took up a large area in their den. The stack was some three feet tall and stretched twelve feet along the west wall. As yet not having a way to haul such a load they bought a canvas which they placed over the stolen goods and upon which they threw dirt, sticks, stones, small limbs, cedar droppings and pine cones making it look as though it was simply a mound of earth near the rear of the den. He then took them to Jericho and to the lower depths of the city to inquire as to the best place to sell his ill-gotten treasure. He knew he would not trade it here in Jericho for that was one of the first things a thief learns he told them, "Never sell or leave your gains in the same city they were taken."

****

The next day he led them out of the forest area entering the west gate of Jericho and hugged the wall of the city until they came upon a large doorway built into a convex wall much over twelve feet tall. Very little traffic was seen entering or coming out of that doorway for if one looked into it the first thing to be seen was the huge face of an extremely large unkempt human. He was ugly an and filthy being sitting on a grog barrel dangling what one would assume were his feet, although such encrusted pieces of flesh may be shoes. He was wearing clothes also encrusted with the soil of earth, matching the rest of his inhumanity. If one glanced at this unhealthy ogre like being inside that wall one would think one might be looking into a nightmare.

Giant waved his hand at the ogre whereupon the offensive one grinned back, his black cavity loaded mouth gaping back. Majeed, Ayoub and Schmuel almost lost their breakfast. "It's as if the devil is smiling back at us, ugh, what an ugly looking beast, is he really human?" asked Majeed, the others laughing.

They walked past shop after shop of café's, whiskey sellers and other stores vending products of known and unknown merchandise reeking of a combination of odors that hung in the air as fingers of repugnancy unable to tell the good smells from the sickening. The vendors as well as their customers were a varied but motley bit of humanity generally an unwashed drunken lot with tunics hiding weapons of various sizes fitting their own needs. They also saw a few well dressed foreigners dressed unlike those of this land.

Barabbas and his gang soon stopped at a large bazaar containing all types of silver, gold, wood and glass utensils used in the home. Engraved reliefs on short, small tables of which most of them had never seen as well as carvings of gold, silver and wood faces. A shout came from behind a wall at the rear of the shop, "Barabbas my friend, Ahlain, Ahlain,(welcome, welcome) it has been too long, how are you and who are the new ones with you?" The two clasped hands over wrists in a greeting and Barabbas said, "Ya Ibn Dahour, (Aramaic) (Oh you

Son of Dahour) or (Jewish) (Bar Dahour) you old reprobate who have you been stealing from this day?" That brought a loud guffaw from the man who almost matched Giant in height and breadth greeting him with a large mouth, which filled an even larger ruddy face over which a huge pock marked beak of a nose forcing its way out of that face and commanded those who beheld it as a mistakable landmark. The dark reddish brown hair spilled over his forehead so to give growth to his brows making a hiding place for his eyes. "Come sit my friends." A hospitable Dahour motioned them to gather around a large table set on top of short wine casks with stools to sit upon. "Now friend tell me what have you brought to wet my appetite?" and again that deep throated guttural laugh almost a twin to Giants own. Barabbas shrugged his shoulders, sighed deeply telling Dahour he had nothing for him although he would ask a favor. "Anything for the son of my true friend Y'hanaton; your fathers treasure' continue to flow my way and we make many deals." He slapped Barabbas' back with a force that would have floored most men.

Barabbas leaned into the face of his friend whispering his wants. He asked, "Where would I find a buyer for some very rich items a friend has come across?" Dahour whispered names and locations where other receivers of stolen properties could be found. He then poured each of them a drink from a large carafe wrapped with a wet cloth then raising his own cup toward them then drank it down. They in turn saluted him in the same way as they drank this rich tasting cocktail. As they were leaving Dahour handed Barabbas a leather wallet, which he quickly put into his tunic pocket. Their work done here they were on their way.

Outside, Ayoub could not help but remark upon the foul odor of the underground and how he could not be there another moment. They all nodded their agreement.

****

As instructed they waited in the clearing for their boss to return. An hour and a half later they heard a strange noise coming from the west. Although the sound they heard did not register immediately until they peered out of their hiding place surprised to see Giant leading an ass pulling a small cart. He led the jackass around the rear of the cave stopping at the opening of the den, "Now let's load the entire cache into the wagon." Schmuel asked, "Are you sure all of it will fit into this small wagon Barabbas?" Barabbas smiled as he lifted the back off the wagon revealing a deep chasm of a wagon with ample space for the entire cache of goodies. They loaded everything in short order Giant laughing said, "Follow me; Schmuel take the lead rein." He did not tell them of their destination for some time but as they left the Jericho area Majheed did ask, "Hey Giant where are you taking us where are we going?" They all knew when Barabbas did not answer it was best not to ask again.

They followed the Jordan River north three days arising very early of a morning for traffic was much less and they could make much better time and would stop in the late afternoon to rest. They arrived at the small town of Salim where they found a resting place near the river, Barabbas told them, "We will rest here for it is a very relaxing area and beautiful, we will jump off early in the morning." Once again Schmuel knowing he might be pushing his luck standing straight and winking at his bud's, asked "Where are you taking us Giant?" Giant studied them for a moment shaking his head pretending to be irate squeezing his dark brows hard shadowing his eyes then smiled and answered, "We are going to Bethsaida Julius on the North shore of the Sea of Galilee; Dahour told me we will get the best prices for our loot. It is another hundred mille before we get there so now get your rest."

****

The afternoon of the second day found them in Philateria at the south end of the Sea of Galilee. Giant told them they were to take a boat across the Sea to the city of Bethsaida Julius (House of Fishing). This city was the home of Peter, Andrew and Phillip. Other than Barabbas they had never been on a boat and this was quite an adventure for them. They watched in awe as Giant led the ass pulling the wagon aboard when Aboud asked,

"What if the animal gets spooked or something he's never been on water has he, well neither have I, wow I don't know how to take this?" They decided this was the greatest adventure they had ever had until the ship pulled out of Philateria, and Ayoub and Majheed were looking a little green. They did not say anything until the ship was into the deepest part of the Sea when their color came back. Schmuel and Giant were munching on some fruit, now when Ayoub and Majheed saw them they ran for the rail and leaned over the edge of the boat. Soon all was well and they sat down on the deck their color slowly returned to their faces. Dusk was wrapping her arms around them as they debarked and Barabbas told them to watch for a sign that said Inn of The Moon. They left the docks and began their trek to the city less than a hundred yards away. The walls of this City looked newer than most others they had seen. They did not enter the City for the Inn where they would live while here was just outside the east gate so they circumvented the northwest part of the city and soon saw the lights of the Inn of The Moon.

****

The first night at the Inn in Bethsaida Julius, Ayoub and Majheed slept fitfully for they were very uncomfortable sleeping inside out of the wheather. They had become accustomed to a grassy bed and the sky for a ceiling, so sleeping inside closed quarters was not to their liking. The following night was worse; after an hour of uneasiness

Ayoub awoke seeing Majheed drag his pallet outside into the night. He smiled and followed, pulling his bed out the door. They pulled their beds around the corner of the Inn to a grassy spot near a tree and dropped to their pallets. A huge sigh escaped them both as they fell upon their pallets pleased to be in the open air and fell fast asleep.

As always the sun's warm fingers touched their eyes awake beckoning them to greet this day. They stretched, rose, dragging their pallets, entering the inn to wake the other two members. As they walked near the entrance of the inn they could smell the aroma of Turkish coffee, seeing them the owner said, "Come my friends, come in, welcome, partake of the coffee fresh brewed; come, come, my good wife has just baked some fresh hot camash (pita bread), lavosh and lubana (drained yogurt), olives, figs, come in look at the fresh fruits; ah yes and of course olive oil for one to dip the bread into and fresh boiled eggs." They were all smiles for this was a feast of a lifetime. This breakfast of course reminded them of their homes and as Barabbas said, "I could eat everything in my sight, but we will not cast rudeness upon such an azema," (invitation). He would offer to pay for the breakfast but that would be rude for when one is invited then to even offer to pay would be a slap in the face of your host. When they were satiated and smiling with the contentment of a full tummy Barabbas rose saying, "Many thanks to you and your wife for an excellent feast fit for kings we are in your debt and pray we may have the pleasure of some day repaying you for your kindness, yes you are a true Canaanite; come men we must be on our way south." Not a one of his men flinched for they knew if anybody asked after them they would be given a facetious direction.

****

Bethsaida was a bustling City with clean streets and neat and tidy houses. Barabbas stopped a friendly looking man asking for directions to the bowels of the city and as the gentleman was giving directions they heard a swelling din as a crowd approached.

Four askaree leading a tall thin man with black hair and brown sad eyes, yet with a smile that enlightened all who saw him. They suddenly stopped directly in front of Barabbas and his group and the sergeant of the guard turned to the man they had shackled and slapped him hard across the face saying, "Don't lie to me you are he who calls himself John the Baptizer and you have been preaching that another is coming who will be King of all, am I not correct." John answered sadly, "I am he whom you say, although I have not broken any of your laws for I prophecy He who comes after me I am not worthy of walking in His shoes for He is The King whom other prophets have spoken of for hundreds of years." The sergeant turned to the crowd that had gathered saying, "See it is as I have said and for that you will be taken to the dungeon to be transferred to the large Herod jail in Jerusalem."

Barabbas did not know what stirred him to step forward but he did somewhat forcefully, saying to the soldier, "Why do you treat this man thusly he has done nothing to you for we can see he is a preacher and a prophet and he is only doing what is intended of him." The soldier stood up to Barabbas and told him to mind his own business and not to stick his nose into the soldiers business or, "I will take you to jail as well." Barabbas laughed his usual guttural guffaw smiling large and shouting, "It will take more than you four to take me anyplace for if you put your hands on me you will *suffer* the consequences." The soldiers face reddened and he frowned at this huge man whom he would arrest adding another feather to his now flowered helmet so the Praetorian would take notice and he would receive a promotion, his ego growing. While holding onto the ropes around Johns wrists he turned to the three soldiers commanding them, "Arrest this man now!" As the three soldiers approached Barabbas stepped back saying somewhat softly, "I don't think you want to do this but if you insist I will be tempted to wrap them into small pieces than," turning to the Sergeant, "I will come after you!" The head soldier laughed arrogantly, "These are experienced Roman Soldiers, my best men and they will bind you and take you into custody." He turned speaking to a large soldier who stood above six feet weighing over two hundred and sixty pounds. "Take him into custody!" The soldier grabbed one of Giant's wrists to bind him while one of the other guards took hold of Barabbas' other wrist. Giant relaxed, his muscles seemed to slack, hence the guards would believe they had the upper hand. A confident laugh came from the largest guard who began fastening a strap to Barabbas' arm. This fake relaxation carried over to the Roman guards who now assumed this would be an easy arrest. One soldier held Barabbas' right arm and another his left and now like a flash of lightening Barabbas grabbed an arm of both men and fell backwards the weight of the soldiers keeping him on his feet; as he fell backwards he flailed both arms and before they knew what was happening the soldier on the left of Barabbas went flying to the right while the other went flying to the left. The one on the left flew hard into the wall of the city while the other landed upon a boulder nearby. The third soldier came running toward Barabbas diving at his legs thinking he would floor the big man by rolling into him. The soldier did not know what hit him for Giant stepped aside and as the man flew through the air to tackle him he brought his huge fist down hard upon the soldiers head and his entire body went limp as it hit the ground. Barabbas then turned toward the Sergeant arms akimbo not saying a word. The Sergeant's expression soured as he released the ropes around John's hands politely handing the shackles to Barabbas shouting, "You have won this battle big man but I will be back with the Praetorian guards and more soldiers to arrest you." He then broke away at the speed of a gazelle, turned and looked back shaking his fist at Barabbas.

Barabbas turned to John, "My friend you must leave the city for they will be after you." John suggested Barabbas do the same but the Giant just laughed and clapped John on the back saying, "Go prophet and do your job and if you get to Nazareth look up my father his name is Y'hanaton, my mother is Shifra." John waved a blessing back at him thanking him as he turned toward the road south out of the city.

****

This is one way the big man gained his reputation. Yes, he was a thief never a murderer and having the same compassion of his mother and sister one could see it in all his relationships with others. His buddies asked, "Are we now moving on," and he shook his head in assent. "We will find the buyer for our goods now to make a deal," as he walked into the city and turned south. Soon they approached an area emitting a mixture of so foul one could almost see wisps of black floating upwards 0as if attempting to escape that gross area below. Ayoub looking at the other two, "Why does each city have a place like this, I wonder are there many who make up the underworld which sometimes I hate to admit we are part of? Oh well." He remarked aloud the other three looked at him questioningly and Schmuel asked, "What?" Ayoub answered by shrugging his shoulders. Out loud but quietly he said to himself, "I guess you could call me a thief, oh well that's how I make my living and I love being with Giant."

There in front of them was a wall with a large gaping entry way and like other cities inside that opening another huge dumb animal type human with a dirty smile his teeth pointing in many directions. The brute had no hair on his head although the hair grew over the rest of his body and his face was the color of a red apple, under the dirt, and pockmarked. This was the first bald man they had ever seen up close. The guy stood up towering above Giant and his body blocked the entrance; then he smiled and horror of horrors they thought, is this an ogre? He looked at Giant saying in a deeply graveled voice, "What you want big boy, want to see somebody?" Now as the creature spoke a sick stink flowed from his mouth engulfing their spaces and they leaped back almost retching their noses screaming for redemption. Barabbas coughed and spat to the side of him saying, "Yes I want to see a man by the name of Spaspirios I am told he is a short man of Greek heritage with red hair and beard and a large curly-cue mustache." "You know Spasy?" "No but he will see me for I have rock and paper for him." "You wait here I go tell Spasy, you not come in or I get berry mad, O K?" Curious the three young men with Barabbas asked, "Why did you say you had rock and paper." He told them it was a code to tell the Greek he had valuables to sell.

They waited less than a minute when the huge barn door returned pointing in the direction of stairs going down into a dungeon like area. Barabbas told them to watch their backs and be alert for this looked like an area where anything could happen for he had been warned by Dahour thieves will steal from thieves for here there is no honor among them. He told them that he had a note from Dahour to the Greek that would open doors for them. They walked through a sea of noisy and strange humanity and in most instances reeking of a mixture of strange odors so strong at times they would hold their nose resisting retchin. There were eating establishments, all types of shops one might expect in any bazaar and much activity from all around them. From the many languages that meld together none could make out what any others were saying. This then was mass confusion that is until they came upon a clean and orderly bazaar of some five thousand square feet. Everything in sight was designed to show clearly each item in its own setting to give value to that item.

    Suddenly before them stood another giant of a man saying, "Aha stranger I see you have something to sell huh, well this time you will give it up to Waqhash or I will take it from you and make it my own, for nobody can compare with me." The three of them were surprised to see Barabbas genuflect toward the hulk another seven foot tall mountain of a man; one could see his face for the black hair falling from his head partially hid his face although as the hair cascading down merged with that of his brows and face. One eye could be seen pocking through the black seeming impenetrable, dishevelment growing on this animal, yet the most noticeable was a proboscis of unusual proportions seemingly seeking daylight. They watched as Barabbas seemed to become a servant to this man for he bowed to the floor and his challenger snorted with glee, "I have you now rich one give me what I ask for or I will make mince meat of you!" Now the foul smelling one relaxed himself completely, for he knew, at least he thought he knew, he controlled this action. Unexpectedly with a charge forward Barabbas dove for the feet of this man jerking his legs from under him. The sound this man's skull made upon the hard floor echoed throughout the area, he was down for the count and probably would never awaken. Barabbas pulled himself up off the floor and sprang upon the man's chest looking down as he said, "This is the ugliest face I have ever seen for it looks as if it belongs on the rear of an elephant." A humongous outburst of laughter met this statement and they all cheered Barabbas pleased at this surprising outcome, for there were those who had seen Whaghash take down many men and strip them of their belongings and they hoped but never imagined it would happen yet Whaghash' time would come and now was and again the crowd cheered raucously. Whaghash eyes opened slowly as he looked up at this defender mumbling, "This never happen before who you anyway?" Barabbas laughed, "You needn't know who I am but you should remember my face for if you ever cross in front of me again I will finish the job I have just started, now do you cede, oh I'm sorry, give up and vow to attack only those of your own ilk?" Barabbas stood over the top of the man's chest then slowly stepped backwards allowing Whaghash to rise. Although he tried several times he could not raise himself off the floor until finally another man who had witnessed all came to help the fallen animal. Whaghash finally stood on his feet although glassy eyed saying to Barabbas, "You only guy ever do that I don't tink you win in fair fight." Barabbas chortled, "You'll not get that chance for I make it a habit never to allow that for the only time I did," at this he leaned into the shagginess where the face should be whispering loudly, "that person was laid to rest, but if you ever decide you want more just let me know, that is if you ever see me again."

From the back of the large area stepped a clean well dressed young man whom did not fit into these surroundings at all. Smiling he spoke to Barabbas, "Sir you must be the man my master Spaspirios has been looking for, please come with me." As they walked toward an area clean and neat with everything arranged and displayed and easy accessible from that area walked a pleasant looking red haired man with a very pleasant smile about five foot seven inches tall not over one hundred and eighty pounds, hoisting a large barrel over his head and walking toward them effortlessly. They were surprised to see the five foot seven red haired Greek walking toward them with a fifty gallon barrel hoisted over his head. He grinned at them setting the barrel down then with a deep bass voice said loudly, "I think I know who you are, I have received a note from my friend Dahour telling me of your coming, you must be the one called Barabbas." He extended his arm as they clasped hands in greeting Spaspirios said, "I did not expect to see such a giant of a man." That thick accent one would expect from a Greek in this part of the world inviting them to sit at his large long table. "We will discuss your offer and hope to fix it to our mutual satisfaction." While the three others satisfied their thirsts, snacked on delectable finger foods and strolled throughout the store browsing the Greek and Giant transacted some type of deal.

It seemed the meeting lasted an eternity until he called to them and waved for them to follow him. They went back to the inn where Giant paid what was owed and retrieved the wagon, which had been placed in a secure area. They moved into an area over the large hill on the west side of the city leaving Schmuel and Majheed with the wagon. He stood in front of them showing them a sword and asked which of them would like to carry the weapon. Schmuel said he would take it for he had learned from his father how to wield a sword. The animal pulled the wagon into the forest as deep as possible. Barabbas cut a three-inch branch from one of the trees and hammered it down through one side of the spokes on the wagon into the ground then did the same on the other side of the wheel. He did this with three of the wheels and told them to take the ass out of harness but tie him to a tree and hobble him. He and Ayoub then began a hunt for a forest hideaway.

This was a wooded area reminding them of their own hideout in the Wilderness of Judea. Barabbas had told the Greek they would move out of the inn for they enjoyed the outdoors. He suggested they might find a place to stay inside that dense forest. Barabbas knew if Spaspirios knew of this place then others had probably used it so now he was determined to find another place if they were to remain in this city long.

The deeper they moved into the forest the harder for them to move forward. He pulled a sword from its sheaf and began hacking his way deep into the jungle. As he went he bent a twig on a tree, or made a small mark in large limbs or trunk of trees. These indiscreet markings would allow him to find his way out. He knew the deeper they went the less problem they would have of others finding them. He turned to say something to Ayoub but he was nowhere to be found.

A moment of extreme anxiety washed over him and he walked back to where Ayoub was walking just a few seconds before. He did not want to shout for if someone had taken Ayoub he did not want to telegraph it. Barabbas traced his steps back to a humongous oak, stopped, leaning against it and using his eyes hoping to spot any unusual movement. He would circle the tree to inspect the other side. He looked at the monster tree knowing the trunk had to be at least ten feet in circumference. He rounded the tree and stopped for there was no place to go. He had never seen such a thick overgrowth of vines in his life. Following the growth around, he began counting his footsteps. Counting out loud he was saying, "thirty-five, thirty-six" then he stopped for out of the corner of his eye he caught a movement to the rear of his peripheral vision.

Surprised he was somewhat startled for as he turned he saw Ayoub sitting on the ground smiling and chewing on a juicy pear. Barabbas smiled with great relief asking, "Are you O K what happened where did you go?" Ayoub's face beamed with pleasure and Barabbas knew that surreptitious look of a secret for the slight grin and the sparkle in his eyes was that of a child hiding from a mother. Ayoub stood up motioning for Barabbas to follow, "Come my brother." They walked about fifty or so paces then Ayoub pointed in the air and Giant looked up to see absolutely nothing but when he looked back Ayoub was gone. Without thinking Barabbas shouted, "Where are you, you little imp, what kind of game are you playing?" He turned looking to his rear then spun slowly around in a circle his eyes searching. When he turned back there was Ayoub sitting on the ground in front of him. Frowning and scratching his head in disbelief and for the first time in his life stuttering, "Uh, uh Ay, oh uh," those were the only sounds coming from his mouth as he gaped and his eyes had grown large for he

Two Men Named Jesus

did not understand what was happening. Ayoub was laughing rolling on the ground for he was enjoying this immensely. When finally he reached his composure he walked directly into the overgrowth and through it. Barabbas watched unbelieving, "Holy Methuselah, he cried how did you get through there, what's on the other side, how can I get in?" Ayoub pushed his hand into the growth and moved the heavy vines revealing a small entrance through the vines. "Here is our new home Giant." "Yeah, yeah I see wow this is better than the one in the Wilderness, stay here and I will return with everything!"

Ayoub separated the vines to enter the opening. The ground a soft carpet of thick grassy moss and it seemed he was walking on cotton. He looked up toward the sky where the light was shining through a ceiling of vines grown up the trunks of trees then stretching their tentacle like fingers from tree to tree clinging to branches as it scaled first one then another limb it's kin emulated others until finally they wove a ceiling just thick enough to allow old Helios to reach in his fingers of light. This resulting act of nature erected a cathedral like ceiling and a circular clearing large enough to house an entire family. Once inside the only light came from above for the density of the wall of vines made it impossible to see out. Ayoub sat down thinking, "We must design a warning system." As they arranged their quarters Ayoubs thoughts remained on that idea. Soon the pleasure turned into work and when they finished they looked at one another and all fell onto their pallets and soon were fast asleep.

The next day Barabbas told Majeed and Schmuel they would accompany him into the city to accustom them to the surroundings, "It seems Ayoub has his mind on other matters so we will leave him with his thoughts, Ta, Ta little one will bring something special to you." He could not wait to set up the things his mind had dreamed of the night before he had it almost all worked out. He took a coil of rope and some soft wire, not knowing what he would use to make the noises that would announce intruders yet he set out on a search for what he did not know. He found a growth of bamboo and cut several stalks and put those in his drag bag. As he walked he kept his eyes open for anything that might give him a clue. Another loud cracking sound echoed bouncing off the wall of trees as he stepped upon another dry twig. Aha he would get his thoughts together for now he had the beginning of an idea.

He peeled the green protective cover from the bamboo and set them aside. He did a double take as he peered at those stalks and his mind reverted to his childhood. Out loud he said to himself, "I remember now when uncle Daveed made lutes out of bamboo." He measured two hands long on each of the shoots then marked them with his knife while others he made longer others shorter. When he finished he had twenty-eight pieces in various lengths. Ayoub sat looking at them not knowing exactly what to do. Seeming to be in a trance for some time he suddenly grabbed one of the shoots and with his knife put a hole through the end and out the other side. He slowly did the same to the rest of the shoots then began unraveling a piece of rope ending up with a long piece of string which he cut into various lengths and threaded through the ends of the shoots. He took them outside the clearing putting them into his tunic then began scanning the ground for a small rock. Finding a rock to his liking he climbed a large tree. High above the ground he twined his legs around a large branch then tied a piece of cord around the rock and the other end to the rope. He stood facing another large tree about twenty feet his back up against a large branch extending up from the one he stood on; tying a rope around the branch and his body would give allow him to throw the rock across to other limbs on other trees. He lowered the rock with the twine tied to it then began swinging it so it could gain momentum. After several throws he knew that may take all day so he tied the end of the rope to a smaller limb on the tree then tied several of the bamboo pieces to the rope about twenty inches apart. He tied a cord to the end of the rope that would stretch across to the other tree and dropped that cord to the ground. Climbing down he tied other bamboo pieces to the rest of the rope suspending them in the air. Then taking that end of the rope tying it to his waist climbed the other large tree at about the same height and tied it firm. He tied a cord to that end and dropped it to the ground as before. Walking back along one of the paths they used in and out of the clearing he brought the cord around one of the hundreds of vines then pulled the cord along the ground to another vine on the opposite side and tied it off. He did the same thing on the other side thus protecting the only places one could walk getting into this area. He stood surveying his handiwork and smiled for he was happy with his invention. He was tired now, "I'll lie down for a few minutes," he said out aloud, then stretched his weary self out on his pallet.

****

Ayoub awoke startled to the deafening clanging of the bamboo tubes resounding thorough the clearing and beyond. He did not realize what was happening then recalled his new alarm system. As he sprang to the entrance of the clearing he heard the voice of Barabbas, who had just returned from scouting the city, shouting, questioning the unexplained noises. The racket, made louder by the hollow area, staggered the three of them. Ayoub stopped at the opening laughing and enjoying his handiwork. He stepped out of the den smiling as the din subsided saying, "How do you guys like my invention, now if anybody enters this area we will know immediately and we will capture them." They could not believe what this great little guy had done but were so pleased with him they applauded his work. Giant picked him up, placed him on his broad shoulders and they all danced around singing a happy song. Later they sat around enjoying their evening meal he informed them they would spend two more weeks here in Bethsaida then we must move on. Soon they sold all their treasures to one of the fences in town. The buyer handed him his money asking, "Where are you headed big man?" Barabbas put his hand in the air and circled it over his head shrugged his shoulders and shouted for everybody to hear, "We are moving south into unknown territories." Anybody that might wish them harm would be misdirected.

****

NORTHWARD BOUND

He led them north out of this city which had given them much ill gotten gains. They nodded and smiled their thoughts alike. Toward dusk as they trudged northward along the river they wondered where they would stop. Pleased the master director Schmuel smiled, "We have trudged speedily for we have moved at least forty mille and if I am not mistaken," looking to Barabbas for verification, "We can stay the night at Thella, is it not a small town near Lake Senichonitis?" "Yes," replied Barabbas "we will remain here as long as you like. This is a to bathe and cleanse yourselves, now get on with it I'm going into town to buy our dinner and I will return shortly so find a comfortable resting spot for the night."

He returned soon with speeiha (meat pies) luban (yogurt), & mitta (cucumbers).

Two days later tired from their trek they were happy to see on the Southern slope of Mt. Herman a beautiful City Barabbas smiled saying, "This is Caeseria Phillipi which is a great city and we will find many marks here for this is a somewhat wealthy city. Remember what you have been taught for tomorrow we will case the City and find a now listen, if we take it slow we could be in this area for a couple of years."

They located a really plush area inside the oasis set at the head of the city and made that a home they would utilize while in this area. They tied ropes to two corners of a large tarpaulin letting it hang to the ground then tied the ropes onto limbs of two trees on each side of their clearing; on the other side was a row of large trees where the grape vines had weaved in and out over and under the limbs of the trees making a natural wall around the clearing. After they had eaten they fell fast asleep for the trip had tired them.

****

They were awakened by singing of hymns of praise and all moved to the top of the oasis to see two men standing at the top of the large hill facing a huge crowd of people below them. The songs were coming from the people and the crowd was swelling around the hill and soon covered the entire slope. At their position they could see everything very clearly for they too were on the top of a hill. The hymns ended and the throng quieted to a point of total silence, it was an unbelievable experience for them. One of the men stepped forward raising his hand in the air and signed a cross first to his left then to the center and last to the right making sure he blessed the entire crowd. Almost to the last person they bowed their heads in acceptance of the blessing given. Barabbas and his small band watched in awe never having seen anything like this. The quiet was unnerving for they did not understand what was happening. The other pleasant looking man came forward and blessed the crowd. Both of the men were almost six foot tall, ready smiles, almost white hair and beard, and although when they smiled one could see sadness in their eyes.

"I am James of Nazareth and this is my brother John. We bring you the love of our Savior Jesus Christ and His blessings. Our Master has taught us that we must be faithful to those things which he teaches of Our Father in Heaven." James then recited the Beatitudes to the crowd; then, lastly he gave them more words of Jesus saying, "For He said you are the salt of the earth; but if salt has lost its taste, how shall its saltness be restored? It is no longer good for anything except to be thrown out and trodden under foot by men. You are the light of the world. A city set on a hill cannot be hid. Nor do men light a lamp and put it under a bush, but on a stand, and it gives light to all in the house. So, as The Master has told us, let your light so shine before men that they may see your good works and give glory to your Father who is in heaven."

After the two had addressed the crowd they each drank from a water pitcher then James and John stepped forward so the entire crowd could see them clearly and together they blessed the crowd again and many of those in the crowd knelt to receive that blessing. The crowd became totally silent and an air of respect and awe permeated the entire area as a cloud of happiness and admiration engulfed them as the gathering walked silently closing in behind the two Apostles as they with the crowd following disappeared into the evening mist.

Quietly Barabbas and his friends walked back to the clearing none of them talking for they were all struck with an overwhelming feeling they did not understand. They did not want to shake their thoughts for the quiet unexplainable feeling of peace was a pure comfort and in that serenity soon were all fast asleep; a tranquility they had never known before. Years later they spoke of it to each other they all dreamed of floating in the air upon white clouds and when they awoke it was with a calm and pleasant feeling. Later they talked of the previous evening and how the two men spoke quietly but the entire crowd heard every word and they truly felt something good from the two men. This was another encounter with The Masters Words.

****

The souk in Philippi was similar to that of those other large cities but the occupants here seemed friendlier and the market most as large as the previous. Barabbas told them they would do a walk through and possibly buy something. "Do not take a thing," firmly, "only look, this will be our first look but we must know the size and the layout of the souk, locate the back exits used by the merchants." They were to follow him from store to store in pairs or more as if they were on their own ignoring the others. They made their way from the east gate of the city north for four hundred yards then back along the other side of the souk. As they made their way around Ayoub noticed they continued running into a short fat man and his entourage of four slovenly looking men. The young inventor took note of this and he would inform Giant later. Each aisle was wide enough that seldom there was a slow down. They turned out the east gate they had entered approximately an hour later then walked down the grassy hill to the oasis.

****

The short fat man, cohorts following, talked to them as they walked. He whispered to his men, "We will follow these four I believe the big man is carrying something of great value. Now when they stop we will take the four of them, it should be an easy pick he is the only one we must be worried about the other three are of no threat at all." Those words could come back to haunt them and more perhaps to slap them silly.

****

As Barabbas' group entered the area they had marked off for their stay while in Philippi the fat man who had been following them pulled up his five foot four inches sporting a head of hair black as the blackest night, why were there so many pock marked hirsute faces in this area. This guy had large ears resembling those of a gremlin as he came into view of Barabbas. Looking at them Barabbas shook his head for the four misfits dogging his heels were men with huge physique's being muscle bound perhaps professional wrestlers possibly from southern Turkey, but none of them were very clean and they all resembled each other possibly because they and the clothes they wore were so grimy and grubby the acrid odors emanating from that direction wafted across the beauty of this lush area; the two at battle. "If the odor moved lower it seemed it would change the color of the grass to dark brown", thought Ayoub. The short fat man stepped directly into the center the Patriots had claimed for themselves standing arms akimbo his legs spread to hold his folds of adipose tissue folded, seeming to roll over each other.

Giant who was sitting down rose to his full height and quietly spoke.

"What is your business here stranger either move yourself and your grimy lot or you will be sorry you ever saw me." The four muscle men stepped forward, smiling broadly a counterfeit confidence certain they held the upper hand. Before they knew what hit them Schmuel sprang from his position and moving at breakneck speed launched himself into the air turning himself ninety degrees his legs extended firmly meeting the two knees of one of the animals directly. The shattering of the bone was unnerving obviously his leg fractured screaming as he hit the ground how he made his way up hopping on one leg while holding the ruined was anybody's guess. One of the big ratty men stepped into one of Ayoubs rope traps lying on the floor of their clearing, and seeing this Ayoub grabbed the rope and yanked with all his might on the rope which by now had locked itself around the man's ankles and with a sudden jerk of a released taut limb he flew into the air dangling upside down. Majeed leaping from his position in the rear of the clearing came past Barabbas like a gazelle running as hard as he could throwing himself head first into the midsection of the third man surprising the big oaf and knocking the air out of him while Schmuel finished the job with a club. Thier surprise was extremely advantagious.

Barabbas laughing made short work of the fourth with one punch to his midsection and a left-hook to the chin, so, another log like human hit the deck. Their leader stood his eyes unbelieving, his visage red the blood rushing to his head. Barabbas looked down at the little fat man who now was speechless his mouth open but nothing came out and Barabbas stood there now *his* arms akimbo. The little man rose looking furtively around then commenced backing out of the clearing very slowly, when he knew he was clear he made a hasty departure away from the city and one by one as the others awoke or were released followed their leader straightaway. They were all concerned for Schmuel for he was lying on the ground sobbing, or at least they thought he was. All three of them ran to him and Majheed reached under Schmuels body turning him face up. The Canaanite was laughing so hard it sounded as though he was crying.

They stood for a few seconds attempting to comprehend what made Schmuel so happy. Realizing what they had accomplished with slight effort glanced at each other and soon they were all rolling on the grass laughing hard and tears streaming from their eyes. As soon as things quieted down Barabbas told them he had a treat for them; "We are going up the side of the mountain to visit a site the likes of which you have never seen come," he said, "follow me, we still have time to enjoy the view and I know you will be surprised and."

They were almost running to keep up for, this was somewhat beyond his normal gait, but again, his pace increased. They zipped past individuals and groups of people. "Gosh," masheed showting breathlessly, "the crowd, the crowd, where are they all coming from?"

Above them approximately thirty-five yards on the right was a huge outcropping, a natural parapet forcing the path to the left and it looked as though the side of the mountain was swallowing them up, but when they arrived at that point they were again surprised to find a large plateau and the mass was meandering around visiting giving one the feeling of a huge family reunion.

The largest group was standing admiring a most beautiful waterfall coming from high above and splashing into a natural pool, seeming to be the same color as the sky, the pool seeming to drink the cascading waters in as though never sated but completely absorbed. And as they looked, almost awe struck, the water suddenly pouring over the opposite end of the large pool and falling fifty feet to the top of a small mesa slopping over the side of the drop, once again cascading down into another large fall.

It was the most amazing sight they had ever seen as they ran from one side of the plateau to the other attempting to behold the movement of the waters. Barabbas waved at them to follow him as he fell behind a line of people moving slowly toward the pool. Several women were standing next to the pool and as they moved closer they were each handed a cup. Watching others ahead of them they dipped the cup into the pool and drank. As they did they were surprised, as all who drank were to find the water the most refreshing and best tasting they had ever had. They listened as a gentleman who looked to be a scribe or presbyter was explaining that this was the Head of the Jordan River, which had been flowing for ions and always known as the purest of waters. Barabbas had no idea how to answer the question the others asked; "How could this water taste so sweet?" Giant just shook his head and suggested they listen to the teacher talking. Being somewhat reserved they hesitated to ask him.

They sauntered to the opposite side of the large plateau invisible and aromatic fingers from the opposite direction tickled their noses inviting them to another crowded area. As they looked they could see a large vat sunken halfway into the ground with hot coals burning below several spits holding large pieces of various types of meat cooking on spits, youngsters boringly turning the cranks ever so slowly allowing the rising heat to lick at the meat making it to snap and crackle as it dripped it's life source into the fire.

Giant waved them to follow and licking their chops at the odor they fell in behind him as they slowly made their way toward a long table holding dishes of the broiled meat. He pointed toward those behind him as he gave the lady his order. They received the dishes of meat, watercress, bread and a bowl of dipping sauce. Following their leader to a small area near the edge of the plateau away from the crowd they sat and enjoyed one of the finest meal they had ever eaten.

When they finished they heard the crowd near the pool applauding. Schmuel asked, "What is going on, do you hear the laughing and singing?" Curious they turned to see what the fuss was about. Handing their plates over to a waiter they drew closer and heard the presbyter speaking to another tall man with beautiful features, his face and hands tan, conveying the fact his life was spent in the open. He had almost pure white hair that flowed around his face neatly and into a long beard. The presbyter turned to the crowd holding up his hands to quiet them. When the sound subsided he climbed natural rock steps to a small landing with a large boulder protecting it and spoke to the crowd. "Brothers and sisters," he began, "we are so happy to have Father James Bar Zebadee, Bishop of Jerusalem, with us today. For those who may not know, this man was chosen by Our Lord as one of His Apostles and we are so blessed to have him here to speak to us." The crowd applauded politely, no shouting for they would welcome this Apostle of God, as they knew they should with great love, admiration and respect. The Disciple stepped up to the small platform as the crowd quieted. For those who knew him James' smile was infectious and the mass smiled back at him. James raised his hand blessing the crowd then began,

"My dear brothers, take note of this: As Our Lord has told us, "Everyone should be quick to listen, slow to speak and slow to become angry, for man's anger does not bring about the righteous life that God desires. Therefore, get rid of all moral filth and the evil that is so prevalent and humbly accept the word planted in you, which can save you. Do not merely listen to the word, and so deceive yourselves. Do what it says. Anyone who listens to the word but does not do what it says is like unto a man who looks at his face in a mirror and, after looking at himself, goes away and immediately forgets what he looks like. But the man who looks intently into the perfect law that gives freedom, and continues to do this, not forgetting what he has heard, but doing it—he will be blessed in what he does. If anyone considers oneself religious and yet does not keep a tight rein on his tongue, he deceives himself and his religion is worthless. Religion that God our Father accepts as pure and faultless is this: to look after orphans and widows in their distress and to keep oneself from being polluted by the world."

He spoke on of the Glory of God's love for all asking them to take the Word into all nations. He closed by again raising his hand blessing the crowd.

The crowd moved slowly forward to greet the Holy Man and possibly speak to him but more so that they might receive a blessing from him.

Puzzled, Barabbas with his three friends stood looking at the happenings around them curiosity filled their eyes. They were not prepared for what they were witnessing as those in the crowd edged forward to the Apostle. Some of those in the crowd, took his hand, some kissed his hand some genuflected but all showed their happiness at meeting one of Gods messengers. They watched silently until the last person spoke to James. None of the crowd left but remained watching the others giving respect. The four Patriots exchanged glances still not knowing who this man was or what his message meant. Yet something struck them for the mass of humanities enthusiasm still enveloped them and not realizing what was happening they felt gracious warmth they had never experienced until now.

Suddenly a noise from below announced a cadre of Roman soldiers who marched up the hill lead by a Centurion. They moved directly through the crowd moving the mass aside and closed ranks around the Presbyter and the Apostle. stopping directly in front of James, the Centurion began questioning him, demanding, "Are you James the Apostle?" He asked. James, smiling acknowledged he was the same. Shouting in a voice loud enough for all to hear, the Centurion, "You are hereby arrested by order of King Herod and will be returned to Jerusalem where you will stand trial for preaching falsely against the King." The Presbyter stepped forward saying, "You are mistaken this man as well as all Christ's Apostles have never broken the law of Herod, how," at that point he was struck down by one of the soldiers knocking him to the hard ground. Barabbas and his buddies watched, Barabbas breathing deeply concern showing on his countenance his demeanor changed as he breathed heavier and faster than normal.

The soldier stood over the religious man telling him to stay down. The Centurion motioned for two of the soldiers to take charge of James telling them to fall in between the others. Barabbas could no longer contain himself for this went against his grain. He felt the warmth that had surrounded them and knew, without truly knowing why, this man was an unusual person.

He stepped in front of the moving cadre and held up his hand stopping them. The Centurion glared at Barabbas telling him to move out of the way or he would be forced to use his sword to remove him. Barabbas did not move and the crowd gasped at his courage. Unlike himself he spoke softly to the soldier asking, "Sir what exactly is the crime this man is charged with?" The Centurion looked at Barabbas saying, "This does not concern you, but if you continue with your harassment I will be forced to take you in as well." James smiled at Barabbas raising his hand in a blessing and saying, "My good man thank you for your well meaning assistance but I implore you please abide by the soldiers wishes for I will be in the hands of my Lord God and He in His infinite wisdom will take care of me." Barabbas had no idea what James was talking about but he felt something that told him to respect this man's wishes and as the Holy man blessed him Barabbas felt that same warmth come into him again as he stepped aside not knowing he was fulfilling Gods desire.

His three buddies had stepped forward to be near him and they watched as the soldiers took James down the hill and away from the crowd. They followed dejectedly still not knowing the reason for the warmth and now the feeling of a dear friend's loss. At the bottom of the hill they stood watching the soldiers accompany their new found friend away from them. They followed their leader back to their lair and fell into their own thoughts as nothing was said as each withdrew into their own little cocoons, minds racing to understand these last few hours.

The sun was seeking its resting place in the western horizon and they were all tired from the pressures of the day, of course not realizing what caused their fatigue and as they lay heads down they were almost instantly asleep.

****

They awoke one by one as bright fingers of light walked their way across the clearing softly pausing momentarily above each of their eyes attempting to brush their eyelids awake. They were thankful for the extra hours of sleep for it brought them back to their own reality. The events of the day before were subdued inside their minds eye and allowed them to return to their daily habits. They chatted during breakfast all being in a good mood, he surprised them saying, "We will move today! Now! Pack everything you have, when everybody is ready we will begin a new journey."

Barabbas having packed everything on the small trailer pulled by the ass began a westward trek toward the Big Sea. They crossed a small feeder stream that flowed into Lake Semichonitis and there spent the next night under the stars and their last day climbing these low mountains. It was a pleasure not to be in a hurry.

He told them they would be going into Phoenicia,

the land of the Canaanites and explained he had learned all this from his Great Uncle Tysier. He continued, "These people were called the Purple People for they had invented purple dye as well as the alphabet, art, (whatever that his he thought), music, drama and many other things, oh yes they are the greatest ship builders too." They looked at him as if he were crazy and Schmuel being the most intelligent; at least on the surface asked, "What is a ship?" He told them they would soon find out.

Afternoon was upon them as they climbed the last very large hill and stood on the crest looking west shading their eyes with their hands and all of them gasping in awe. Schmuel was trying to say something but it would not come out of his mouth. Aboud and Majheed were standing with their mouths open gazing at the expanse of The Great Sea. In unison they said, "Ya Allah!" (Oh my God), I've never seen anything like this in my life. "Giant," said Aboud, you have shown me more this day then I would ever dream I would have seen all my life." Majheed could only say, "Me too, me too!" Schmuel shook his head in agreement and they stood there hours passed, looking across, as well as up and down stream for they wanted to take in as much as their eyes could behold eating up the seascape hoping it would never end until slowly the moon rose and they proceeded down the mountain arriving at a small footpath which lead them to a grassy spot where they made camp, eating their evening meal and babbling about this new adventure.

****

A totally new freshness in the air awakened them with a coolness they had never experienced. They stirred, changed positions, then fell back to sleep another few minutes until they realized they were in a very different local than they were accustomed for their was a new feeling in the air which carried with it a soft cooling unfamiliar temperature not really cold yet very comfortable.

Majeed, Aboud and Schmuel awoke to an aroma summoning them. There not far was Giant turning a spit upon which a leg of lamb was cooking over red-hot coals. They did not ask questions but hurried to take advantage of these aromatics and later filled themselves on figs, dates and pears.

Pleased, he led them out toward the Big Sea where their eyes gazed out upon a natural beauty of a large cove open to the great waters as they looked into a huge City. Their eyes settled on a large gate, humanity streaming in and out toward the souk. A strong odor wafted it's way to them; a smell of which they knew, for most souks had large and small fish tanks where customers could pick the desired fresh fish. This was somewhat different from other souks they had been to. Aboud slowly meandering into the first area of the souk turned a corner with, "Whoops," he shouted, "What the heck is this?" He stood looking up into the glassy stare of a humongous fish hanging by its tail from a pole crossed over four others to hold it up. The rest of them ran to his voice, stopped by what they saw and began laughing. Schmuel said, "That is the largest fish I have ever seen," and turning to the fisherman asked, "Sir is that edible?" The gent laughed answering with a nod of his head. "Wow it's as tall as you Majeed and must weigh four times as much."

Giant's shrill whistle brought them out of their momentary gawking, they shook their heads, following the sound out to the pier where he was standing. "Look at all the boats, have you ever seen so many and look over there at the size of those surely they would hold an army." Aboud queried. Barabbas explained the large ones were called ships then he pointed out to sea toward a very large ship and told them it was a warship. He pointed out the cannons peeking out doors in the side of the ship. They were happy to increase their education and enjoyed it all.

They made their way up the gangplank of one of the ships and a sailor stopped them, "Who are 0you and have you permission to come aboard our vessel?" Barabbas stopped stood erect saying, "We have never been on a ship and would like to experience it just this once if we are allowed." "Wait here, I will see if the Captain will permit this." Soon a large man dressed in strange but somewhat fancy garb approached asking, "Good day Sir's whom do I have the pleasure of addressing?" Stretching tall Barabbas answered, "I am Barabbas and these are my friends we are from inland and have never had such an experience, could we ride on it?" He looked them over circling them making mental notes to himself than winked at his Ensign saying, "Ah yes my good gentlemen we will be happy to host you, be here when the sun rises tomorrow and we will take you aboard." That night they moved their sleeping bags near the water that they would be near the ship as the sun rose, "We don't want to take the chance that the ship might leave us if we are not on time." Barabbas told them.

Having moved their camp nearer the water they awoke to the waves slapping against the shore and the sun's rays diving toward the water and bouncing off into their eyes as they stood to take in the sight of the Big Sea once more. They were still awed at this sight and as waters of seas and ocean's do for us humans it gave them such a great feeling of contentment.

****

WHAT PRICE SLAVES?
A MAN FEEDS THOUSANDS!

     Barabbas and his men were welcomed on board and began their tour. They watched as huge items on deck were tied to a platform by huge ropes hanging down from a forty foot by six inch round pole held to the side of the ship by a swivel steel ring. They watched as men on deck pushed down on the pole raising the loaded raft to the floor of the deck by slowly easing up on the handle end of the pole. Large ropes were tied to each corner and those were linked to the pole. They were told this was another invention by the Canaanites. He stepped over a 36" round hole in the deck covered with a lattice cap. Barabbas asked, "Is that how you capture rain water?" The sailor told them, "That is how we get air into the hold of the ship." The sailor pointed to a huge round pole twice as large as the girth of Barabbas buried into the deck of the ship reaching into the sky and through that pole smaller poles injected into that extending out over the ship holding huge pieces of papyrus tied around the smaller poles. He explained the use of the large sheets saying, "When we are ready to put out to sea the oarsmen who are located below this deck will pull their oars through the water to turn the ship either into the wind or alee, back, of the wind then the papyrus will be lowered and as the wind catches and opens the sails the ship will move."

Wow amazement shown in their eyes. They heard shouting from the Captain then from the Yeoman as sailors scrambled up the mast releasing the drapes to the wind. As the wind caught the sails they extended out over the ship and the large ship moaned and groaned, its planks creaking to move its mass into the wind and they could feel the ship move forward. Barabbas and his friends were holding on to whatever was handy so as to not fall down for the deck was heaving and weaving up and down rolling with the wind and the waves. The Yeoman led them aft saying, "Do not look forward into the waves for the swell of the ocean will make your stomach churn and you may become ill." When they reached the open sea they then began to walk around the deck under the direction of the Yeoman. The Captain shouted something to the Yeoman in a language they did not understand. The Yeoman turned to them asking, "Would you like to see the lower deck?" Schmuel answered for them all, "Yes we would." The Yeoman answered, "Come follow me."

They climbed a steep ladder down into the lower parts of the ship surprised to see water on the bottom deck. The officer pointed out the stacks of various items piled upon pallets with long legs underneath to keep the merchandise out of the water. They knew there were spices of all kinds for the aromas floated over them as they came nearer. He led them to an area aft, which was like a cage he extended his hand inviting them to enter and he stepped back and suddenly slammed the door and locked it. He laughed and explained that this was a place they placed drunken sailors or anybody who might threaten them. He teased them for some time walking back and forth in front of them, pretending it was just a farce.

The Captain arrived laughing, and that is when Barabbas and his buddies knew they were in trouble. Looking at them the Captain spoke to his aide, "Aha Jumboot they will fetch a fortune especially the big one." His friends looked at him for direction but Barabbas' face had grown into a fierce glare, which they knew would eventually grow into big problems for this Captain and his crew. Suddenly a calmness entered him, as he smiled then sat down on the bench behind them and they knew he was again setting the stage for his attack later. Soon they were alone; and they gathered around Giant as he whispered, "I should not have trusted them but I was sure they were good people, have hope for I will get us out of this mess you can bet on that." They would wait.

Fresh water and food, or it was designated as such, was brought to them after several hours. They could see through the latticework above, the sun was waning and soon dark would creep upon them in this murky, muddy hellhole. Barabbas spoke to them softly telling them not to worry for there would be an opening soon and they would pay and dearly for this erroneous imprisonment. Thanks there were enough bench spaces above the water that they could sleep, and they did although uncomfortably and fitfully.

****

They awoke, the sun streaming into the sludge pit warming the waters increased the stench of the murkiness. Giant, "Stay on the benches for as you can see the water rises and there are dead animals in it." They would bide time waiting for the ship to stop. When they woke they were brought up unshackled for the Captain told all, these men were a submissive group; this was exactly what Barabbas would have them believe. They were lead down the gangplank to the wharf, rushed toward a shack on the edge of the waters some one hundred yards away. They could see into the shack for the large door, hinged at the top raised outwardly and up with a tall post holding it open.

Inside a large man sat at a table with four guards standing behind him and at the Captains elbow were two large seamen. The Captain and the stranger began haggling over the price of the four men for sale. Barabbas asked quietly, "Ya zalama (Gentelman) may we sit down please?" The Captain nodded toward the two sailors. Barabbas signaled his men to stay quiet.

The haggling continued for a half hour in which time all of them including the guards were bored with the proceedings and they were stretching their hands over their heads to exercise themselves. The hostages and their two sailor guards were napping on the floor. Giant had signaled them to pretend to be fast asleep and winking at them Barabbas lipped directions to await his cue. Time wasted on for another three or four minutes then suddenly Barabbas' body exploded out the door jerking the large post holding the door open at the same time shouting at his men, "Nayum, nayum." (Sleep, sleep) he shouted and they dove for the floor lying as flat as possible. He turned back inside holding the pole horizontally and as he knew the guards and sailors would charge him he bound forward holding the post as a battering ram spun around and caught the four of them across their chests throwing them off the walkway into the water. Still holding the post and with the two sailors charging

him he waited then swung the pole hard again knocking the two to the deck of the wharf. Dropping the pole he turned toward the Captain and the stranger who had been bargaining for them.

Both gaped at him flabbergasted, the Captain turning red as they both looked for a line of escape, but that only line was being blocked by this enormous man with a frown and they could see the heavy door had fallen when Barabbas pulled out the stopper. The Captain tried to smile saying, "Sir I am sorry please take it easy with me." Then the stranger reached into his tunic bringing out a large bag of silver and gold coins saying, "Sir I will give these up to you but you must understand this is my business I buy and sell slaves," Extending his arms holding the bag saying, "Take all of this and please do not hurt us." Barabbas took the coins and the leather bag at the man's waist and pointed to a coil of ropes in the corner of the room, "Tie them together and hobble them." Stuffing the purse into his tunic he waited for them to be tied, then told his men to raise the door. As they stepped out of the shack he told each of them to pick up a limb from the stack beside the hut, and said, "We will use these for weapons and now let us get back to the ship."

They were a strange group four men leading two others shackled and boarded the ship. He told the Captain, "Try anything out of the ordinary and I will crush your skull now do as I say." The yeoman approached with his men armed with spears but the Captain shouted, "Drop your weapons and ready the ship for sailing, now!" He gazed at Barabbas with a questioning look and Barabbas said, "You have done well Captain but wait I may have other orders for you." Barabbas led them to the ladder leading to the steering platform. Standing over the Captain his club held high they tied them to the mast while instructing the Captain, "Now you will sail the ship back to Tyre where we will leave you. I warn you, do not try to follow us for I will watch for you and find you then feed you to the fishes." One could tell the Captain was teriffied yet resigned himself to the situation, which he could not control.

As soon as the ship docked Aboud left the ship while Barabbas directed all the sailors off the ship telling them, "Do not be concerned for you will not be harmed I only want you men to remain unblamed for your Captains actions. As the last happy sailor disembarked Aboud returned with a Centurion and cadre of soldiers.

Boarding the ship the Centurion questioned Barabbas at length then satisfied he took the would be flesh peddlers into custody stating, "This Captain has been suspect for several months finally somebody has outsmarted him, thank you my good man." Aboud & Majeed was signaling Barabbas to hurry. When the Romans finally left the ship Barabbas heard a simultaneous great sigh from them with Majeed whispering quiet loud, "It's a good thing he did not know who you were for he might have arrested us!" Barabbas' answered, "Who might know us here in this part of the world do you forget we are not in Jerusalem now?"

The following day Barabbas lead them on a tour of this magnificent City. They saw the Rectangular Theatre, The Roman Columns at Al Mina and the Triumphal Arch, which took their breath away. They strolled to the causeway connecting both parts of the city. He told them this was as much a joy to him as it was to them then he shaded his eyes and told them to look at the walls of the Island City. A stranger, proud of his City, watching them smiled saying, "The walls are one hundred and fifty feet high built to ward off any enemies". As they approached a small hill just outside the east gate of Tyre they heard the murmurings of a huge crowd sitting terraced on the side of the hill. Something was going on here but what, they did not know, so they stood watching the crowd and waiting for what action might take place. Barabbas told them this could be a crowd they may be able to fleece for it looked as though they were all city dwellers from their dress.

They watched as a large man with coal black hair and beard, his skin so suntanned it looked to be leather. He rose from the row of people closest to the top of the hill, standing he raised his hands over his head and the crowd quieted. He viewed the crowd as his eyes searched for any sign of soldiers and when he was sure he again raised his hand and blessed the crowd making the sign of the cross over all. He spoke, "For those of you who do not know I am Barnabas of the new Apostles and am traveling with the beloved Paul of Tarsus." At that the crowd applauded. A gaunt man his white hair reflected the sun along with a short beard stood smiling at them turning from left to right blessing them all. Barabbas and his men were surprised for, yes the man Paul looked to be that of Saul the tax collector but what a change in his demeanor. For this man smiled and there was no arrogance in him. So they watched and listened.

Paul spoke of Jesus and the things they were taught by The Saviour. He repeated some of the parables The Lord spoke. He sighed and told them that this would be the last time they would see him for this would be his last trip. When the crowd heard this they were dismayed. Then the questions came some almost shouting for they wanted to know the answer to that short announcement. Again raising his hands in the air he quieted them shaking his head no saying, "It is not for me to explain but remember Barnabas, Tesilius and many more have been ordained and will help you on your way. The crowd quieted for they knew he would speak to them.

"I speak the words I spoke to the elders in Ephesia; "now a prisoner in spirit I am going to Jerusalem knowing nothing of what might befall me. As I go on from city to city the Holy Spirit assures me that bondage and affliction await me." The crowd stirred but with raised hand he quieted them and continued. "I care nothing for all that, for I do not count my life precious, compared to my work which is to finish the task which the Lord Jesus Christ has given me, in proclaiming the good news of God's grace. I told them to keep watch over God's Church and over yourselves in which the Holy Spirit has made you Bishops. This and more I told them and the letters will verify. Be on the watch for those who would vilify and bring you false messages for I bid you farewell for you will not see my face again." Now there was much weeping as they came forward to embrace the Beloved Apostle. They began singing softly as they escorted him down to the ship where he would begin his final journey. They watched as he boarded the ship then as it moved away from shore he stood waving at them while most of the crowd wept softly and continued weeping and quietly singing hymns of praise.

Barabbas and the three with him watched and wondered for they did not understand the devotion shown to this man Paul. Once again they had a feeling of loneliness although it was a totally different feeling they knew not how to explain, they turned and walked to the camp they had made for themselves near the Big Sea.

****

They awoke to a bright sunshiny day. After breakfast Barabbas rose stretching saying, "Do not ask where we are going for I hold it as a surprise for you." Their faces mirrored the curiosity of children awaiting a prize. Knowing the day prior was somewhat of a letdown he wished them to leave the events of yesterday behind. Since they were near the Great Sea he would travel along that route for the quiet slapping of neap tide as it flowed was like unto a pill of tranquility relaxing them and this would continue for almost two days when they would reach their destination. They spent that night near the water and once more the splashing and flopping of the waves upon the shore eased them into a deep comfortable sleep.

****

Approaching Ptolemais from the north Schmuel remarked, "Look look will you how the City seems to reach out into the Big Sea?" Aboud, "Yes look how tall the walls are and the walkway continues out to where the ships are loading cargo." Schmuel always the watch dog, "Perhaps we should ask permission before venturing out onto the walkway." That made Aboud and Majeed stop, turning their heads toward Barabbas for understanding. Barabbas smiling answered, "Schmuel don't be a naysayer follow me for I do not lead you into a den of snakes," laughing he strolled onto the walkway knowing they would follow. It was further out then it looked and almost twenty minutes later and the walkway widened greatly into a bustling area filled with sailors and merchants loading ships along the docks which reached out into the sea each pier accommodating several ships. A man approached dressed in white and wearing a strange looking hat he spoke with an unusual accent, "Step back away from the loading area!"

A well dressed merchant smiled shouting to them, "Ahllaen, (welcome), I can tell you are strangers in our City, come with me." They followed him turning south along the walk warning them not to get to close to the water for this was a very deep part of the Sea. Another one hundred yards later the gentleman pointed to an arm of the city only about twenty yards wide jutting into the sea some two hundred yards creating a half circle seeming to hold a portion of the Sea inside another large bay. Looking east they could see how the walkway curved slightly with yet another very small stub of land reaching out into the sea creating a small bay inside the larger one. They continued east around the bay which turned south reaching around that end of the City. As they made their way around, the Merchant introduced himself as Tahir Maalouf telling them he owned several Merchant Ships bringing Spices and vegetables from a Country of Yemen, where most of his own Tribe The Ghassanieh lived and had developed a type of planting along the side of mountains which they named terracing and explained it fully. Barabbas thanked him for guiding them around then asked, "Where might we find a comfortable place to make camp?" He asked, "Do you prefer an Inn or..?" Barabbas said, "We love to sleep under the stars." The gentelman pointed south where he said they would find a forested area with lots of water. He stopped saying, "It would be my pleasure if you would partake a meal with me." And without waiting for an answer walked into a sidewalk café to a large table inviting them to sit. He spoke to a server telling him what foods to bring and soon the table was loaded with many types of foods.

This day they ate their fill of Kafta, Kibbe, Yabrat with laban and of course olives and goats cheese, all accompanied by maharrout (tissue paper thin bread) and camash (pita bread). When they thought they had eaten all they could they were served Turkish coffee along with sweets such as mahmool (butter cookie), shredded wheat cookies with varied fillings, and of course bitlawah, (Arabic) or baklavah, (Greek). Schmuel whispered to Barabbas, "Perhaps we should offer to pay for the meal." Barabbas shook his head for they knew that would be an insult to the Gentleman. As they rose to take their leave they thanked the Zalamah (gentleman) for his hospitality. He assured them it was his pleasure then suggested if they had time perhaps they would like to see some of the famous sights such as the Villa of the Four Seasons Mosaic or the Palace of the Governor and there are many more. Also going south he suggested going by Cana only a half-day from Ptolemias. They waved thanks to him as they continued their journey.

Talking it over they thought it a good idea to stop off at Cana, also called Khirbet, to see what a smaller city offers having seen so many large cities.

****

As they approached the outskirts of Cana they heard music & singing, the happiness of revelers coming from the most magnificent home they had ever seen. "Wow,uh, gosh look guys," Schmuel pointed out, "that house has another house above and another above that, and look at the beautiful gardens on top, wow that is beautiful." They strolled along the road and stood at the gate of the domicile open wide to see the magnificent courtyard abounding in lush flora interspaced with palm, date, fig, pear, apple and many other trees. "Look," shouted Majeeb, "look at those short bushes that look like cedars wow and I've never seen so many flowers in my life!" Meandering along a mosaic walkway bordering a world of flora they stopped and looking into the courtyard captivated by the dazzling scene, "Wow," shouted Ayoub that's what I call a party!"

A gentleman handsomely dressed in the finest clothing they had ever seen stepped down from the porch waving welcoming all the passeerbys to come in. Glancing toward them and waving them inside he bade them, "Come in, come in all of you for this is the day my child will marry and you are all invited, yes, yes come in and share our excitement partake of our fare, please, please!

They walked nearer still on the path never had they seen so many people wearing such finery. Once again looking directly at them the Gentelman reissued the invite. He asked, "Are you hungry join us?" Barabbas somewhat embarrassed answered, "Oh no Sir we were just watching the celebration and we have never seen such a uh," a man near him filled in the blank for Barabbas saying, "a Palatial home", Barabbas finished his statement, " it is the most beautiful house ever!" The gentleman happily explained, "My son is being married this day! They thanked him and stood there as he walked toward the house. They moved away from the gate to observe. They turned to leave but hearing concerned voices from the portico they watched as the servants stood waiting instructions. They watched as a gentile six foot tall man smiling, talking to a lady. The Lady asked a question of Him and he asked her, "What have I to do with you for my time has not yet come?" The beautiful Lady smiled and turned to the servants telling them to fill the jars with water, which they did. As Barabbas and his crew watched the servants dipped wine out of the earthen jars and into their serving pitchers. Seeing this they gasped at the wonder of the miracle.

Aboud looked at them asking, "Do you see what I see, they filled the jars with water and that man waved his hand over them and the water turned to wine." Schmuel said, "He must be a prophet of God I have never seen one but I remember my grandmother telling me about prophets and seers." Barabbas to said, "I have never seen a person with such a presence that gave me such a feeling I cannot describe." They all agreed then moved on not knowing they had seen the One True God.

If they only knew they would be a part of a small group of people privileged to have been blessed just to be that near the edge of the universe. Schmuel asked a

Two Men Named Jesus

gentleman walking by, "Pardon me sir can you tell me where might there be a place we can lay our heads and rest?" "But of course just around this hill you will find a large inviting oasis with an overabundance of room," looking the big man up and down approvingly, "and your brothers." The couple smiled, and Barabbas raised his hand toward his partners. "We thank you for your hospitality Ume."

Motioning at his bud's to follow he headed south up a small hill. Soon they saw the tops of huge date trees as they came to the crest of this hill. Looking down they could see an exceptionally v0erdant oasis; as they approached there spread out into this valley lay lush green as far as the eye could see. Looking east in the center of this valley a small lake gleamed back. At the far end of the lake was a group of wagons half circled facing the lake and as they looked beyond more caravans grouped their wagons near the water and along the shore they beheld many more such groupings. The first three camps were full up but as they approached the next one there along the shore was room for many more. Majheed twisted a rope into a halter for the animal and staked him out near them that he might graze. Majheed spoke to the donkey, "Ya hammarrh, (donkey) eat and sleep for we will have need of you tomorrow." Aboud spread a large napkin on the grass then pulled the containers of food from the wagon placing them on the napkin saying, "Futhalow, (help yourselves)." When they had satisfied their hunger they spread their napkins upon the ground under and around the wagon and as always Barabbas climbed onto the bed of the wagon, as was his habit legs hanging over the end. Schmuel lay on his pallet, yawned and said, "I am sleepy I hope we all sleep well tonight I bet you have something good in mind for us bookarra (tomorrow) Giant." The big man just snickered leaving them wondering.

****

Two days later found them on the road to Bethsaida. As they neared the City the larger and larger the crowd of travelers grew moving toward Bethsaid. It was as if a magnet was pulling them forward. When they reached the periphery of the city the sun was racing for the western horizon casting its gray pall upon them. Aboud asked, "Why are there so many people, it is like a sea of bodies ahead and around us, something extremely important must be taking place here." Barabbas seemed to be deep in thought for he did not answer but said, "Aboud take the donkey and tie him behind that large tree behind those bushes, were he cannot be seen then join us for I want to move ahead of the crowd." Aboud was back very soon and ran to catch up with Giant; as he did the big man swooped him up into his arms saying, "Majeed grab onto my waist and try to keep up stay at my back as I push through the crowd; hold on to each other." They formed a single file with Aboud hanging on to Giants

Two Men Named Jesus

girdle and reaching his hand out the other two held on. They made their way around the edge of the lake Barabbas pushing people out of his way. Some thought to say something to him but when they saw the size of this man they smiled and gave way.

Barabbas pointed to a group of men standing away from the crowd near a huge boulder talking as if something was very important. Barabbas' curiosity bested him so he moved closer and listened soon he turned to them saying, " Do you remember the man we saw at the wedding in Cana who made wine from water, see there He is the one standing with his back to the rock this is the third time I have seen him and He is always with this group of men. There is something about Him that, unlike any other I have ever seen, gives me a feeling of warmth, do you guys feel it." They nodded their heads as they all smiled. Then that leader turned to the crowd of thousands and seeing Him quiet engulfed the entire area. As he began to speak Majheed said, "How can they hear him for there must be thousands; look see across the lake and all around us." But as Jesus spoke softly his voice carried over the top of the multitude and each person heard him as clearly as if he were standing next to them.

They heard the Leader say to the big man, "Peter what are you saying?"

"This is a deserted place, and already the hour is late.

Send them away that they may go into the surrounding country and villages to buy bread, for they have nothing to eat." But Jesus answered and said to them, "You give them something to eat." They answered, "Shall we go buy two-hundred denarii worth of bread?" But he said to them, "How many loaves do you have? Go and see."

When they found out they said, "Five {loaves} and two fish."

Then he commanded them to sit down in groups on the green grass. So they sat down in ranks in hundreds and fifties. And when He had taken the five loaves and the two fish, He looked to heaven, blessed and broke the loaves, and gave them to His disciples to set before them all. So they ate and all were filled. And they took up twelve baskets full of fragments and of the fish. Now those who had eaten the loaves were about five thousand men.

Barabbas held them back saying. "I thought we would not eat for I knew there was not enough food but look how much food is left, wow, who is this man?" Then he and his men stepped back toward a large group of bushes near the twelve where they could hear all.

Mark 6: 33- And Jesus when he came out saw a great multitude and was moved with compassion for them. So He began to teach them many things.

Matt 11:21; "Woe to you Chorazin! Woe to you, Behsaida! For if the mighty works which were done in

Tyre & Sidon, they would have repented long ago in sackcloth and ashes. But I say to you that it shall be more tolerable for Tyre and Sidon in the Day of Judgment than for you. And you Capernaum who are exalted to heaven will be brought down to Hades; for if the mighty works which were done in Sodom it would have remained until this day."

The leader looked as if he were tired He sighed then turned and with all the Disciples walked around the large boulder and they were gone. The crowd drifted away as people do toward their homes mulling the words of the Master.

****

Aboud found the donkey and released the guide arms then staked him out near where they were to sleep. Again they laid their napkins out under and around the wagon and fell asleep. Most of them slept comfortably but Barabbas dreamed a continuous dream which he could not figure and whatever it was it held his attention for he continually saw the face of the man who fed the multitude. He knew he was being told something in his dreams but continued shaking it off for this feeling was uncomfortable. When he woke he shook it off blocking it from his mind.

The excited braying of the donkey and stomping of his feet trying to walk out of his hobbles woke them.

Releasing the donkey Barabbas led him to a grassy knoll so he might graze then back to his brood. "Come now sleepy heads get up for today we go south to Tiberius where we will met up with an old friend and possibly grow our numbers." Schmuel asked, "What do you mean grow our numbers will we take on more partners?" "Let me worry about, that my young friend, and remember no matter how many may join with us we four will always be a family." He laughed roaring, his voice echoing around the clearing. "Are you all ready, I see you have packed the wagon with our valuables now let us move on to another new beginning?" They would follow the sea south to Tiberius.

****

As they entered Gennesaret their eyes were drawn to the high hills set back from the Sea of Galilee. "What are those statues on the high hill, they look like frozen men standing there, and oh look, that one is only the top part of a man." Aboud seemed mesmerized and before any of them could speak again a man who had been watching and listening heard them and explained, "Those on the hills are statues, not frozen men." and he smiled a friendly smile. "Yes they are statues of Herod Antipas who built this city, notice if you will the streets cross each other just as those Hellenistic and Roman cities are designed, now look behind you past the hot springs see that building, it is a large stadium, also built by Antipas and see the Synagogue near it, have you ever seen anything so beautiful? Do not forget before you leave the city be sure and place your feet in one of the hot springs for it will make you feel as if you are re made, now enjoy our city of which we are proud of."

Majheed sort of crept toward the hot spring nearest the stadium; when he got to the edge he slipped his sandals off and lowered one toe to the water. As his foot touched the water he drew it back with a jerk, then pleased at what he felt sat down on the ground and dangled his feet in the spring, almost shouting, "Hey guys this is great, what a nice feeling I feel as if somebody is rubbing my feet, gosh I can't really explain it, its, its, uh, uh golly I don't know just *WOW, WOW!"*

Barabbas would not partake of this for he thought it was a childish thing to do until he saw an elderly man come forward and climb down into one of the larger pools. "I wonder what makes the water bubble up it's as if there is a fire under the earth." Schmuel not usually surprised by much just smiled. Soon they all four had their feet dangling in the hot springs. "Your right guys", said Giant, "this is great." The crowd was growing as the day began and from behind them they heard, "Hey you, big man, with your huge feet in the water do you think you are a small boy, do your dogs hurt, wow what large feet?" Barabbas turned his head somewhat amused for he could tell the voice speaking to him was a smiling teasing one. He sprang from the water to see who was shouting at him. "Jameel you old no good thief what are you doing here how did you find me?"

"I waited, keeping watch so I would not miss you and as you entered the City I told my gang not to say anything; we followed and saw you talking to the City Magistrate you must be an important person for him to talk to you." Barabbas seeing a great opening here took advantage of it. "Well Jameel, you see that man is an uncle of my father and he asked us to stay with him, he said he had a large compound above the city and we would be welcome." Jameel was impressed and yet he was doubtful of his old friend for he knew it was Barabbas' nature to pull ones leg from time to time. So Jameel said, "Well my friend shall I direct you to Judge Abdullah's home or did he tell you how to get there?" Barabbas thought he had Jameel so he continued with the tale. "Uncle Abdullah said for me to ask anybody and they would point out his home or probably lead us to it." He thought, "I've got him now I will go along with it until we get to the Magistrates home." They stood looking around and Jameel pointed out more points of interest as they talked of old times. "Barabbas buddy, I hate to tell you but the Judges name is Tanell Habeeb and he is neither related to you nor me," now he burst out laughing, "you are a credit to the liars club, you cutheb (liar) you would never have stopped if I hadn't trapped you." Barabbas wrapped Jameel in his arms saying, "Come meet my men," loudly he said, "men come meet this poor excuse for a man who looks mean but he is a kitty cat and I could floor him with one punch for he has a glass jaw."

They took turns introducing their gangs. Jameel introduced his four, Tannoush, Haleem, Kallil and Fouad. They were all well built men as most who live their lives in the weather just as Barabbas' group did. Barabbas was surprised at himself as he compared his four buds with Jameel's four. They were all strong men and other than Majheed could make their own way. They found their way up the hill and would seek a cave or a place to spend the night and, "Tomorrow" Barabbas thought, "I will present Jameel with my men." So they began their climb seeking the ideal place to make their new home. As they climbed the brush seemed to grow denser.

Half way up the hill they heard Schmuel shout at them and turning they scanned the area from which his voice seemed to come yet as their eyes searched the area from which came the shouting Schmuel was nowhere to be seen. Finally only fifteen feet away he rose seeming to come up out of a huge bush but as they came closer he was standing some ten feet back of it for it was as large as a room. They approached the bush and just stood there for they saw no opening.

Surprisingly Schmuel came walking out from under the bush for it was so overgrown the opening could not be seen from that spot. "Come follow me to our new home!

The cave Schmuel found was large enough for fifty or more people. They could tell the cave had been used by a large group most likely robber gangs or hiding place for soldiers hiding from their peers. Looking around they came across spears, swords, mace and all types of weaponry although it was all old and mostly rusted but by cleaning they could be very well utilized. Schmuel was charged with the management of the hideaway and he doled out areas for each of the seven others to care for.

"Now those rooms I have laid out and numbered will be yours to care for and keep clean." The three with Jameel looked at him as if to ask are we supposed to follow those orders. He said aloud, "Barabbas and I have talked about this matter and it has been decided we will combine our groups as one, Barabbas as leader this is all for the best!" This was an ideal home for it had several rooms with passageways worming back into the hill some one hundred and fifty feet. In two of the largest rooms were marble like tables set upon legs of rock and benches of rock attending the tables. They continued cleaning the entire cave until the sun was going down and Barabbas said, "Let us go out of here and down to the beach where there are café's, tonight we will eat well." This pleased them all and when they returned two hours later they were all ready for a good rest.

Two Men Named Jesus

That night while the others slept, Barabbas and Jameel set forth their plans to attack caravans coming from the south headed for Asia Minor for these were well known to be the richest of all caravans. They would pay a lofty price if need be for information as to those caravans carrying such riches as Frankincense, Myrrh, (one of the most desired and costliest spices), gold, silver and of course incense. They knew no caravan Master would give that information out readily but Barabbas had a plan to loosen tongues. "We will begin tomorrow to search out such caravans and you will see they will be the largest with the finest wagons and many horses." Jameel asked, "Will they not have camels?" "Yes of course but only as pack animals; you see that is one of the marks of a wealthy caravan, as you should know, only the wealthy have horses and we will soon have them ourselves." Jameel yawned saying, "Goodnight my friend."

****

THE PATRIOT ARMY IS BORN

Majheed busied himself in the cave moving some of their belongings from the floor to the shelves in the wall of the cave. Enjoying what he was doing, singing and whistling soon became loud enough to awaken the others. He heard a rustling behind him and turned just in time to duck the fast flying sandal making its trail past his ear. Laughing Majeed said , "Ok guys rise and shine for this is the last time I'm going to clean up your messes from now on you will put your things where they belong or I will toss them out." Laughing he limped out of their way for he knew there would be other missals directed toward him. Jameel speculated, "Oh now that we have a leader do we also have a director of cleanliness?" His noisy laugh encouraged the others and they joined the chorus.

The Giant stood studying the activities of his newly formed group smiling pleased at himself and his 0new band. He walked around and over them as he strode the cave in deep thought. Finally he stopped in the large front room, "Ok gents I think Majheed has it right; there will be no one person to tidy up your messes for if you cannot keep things neat and clean then we will have discipline for that. From this point on you will be fined for just such infractions and, Oh yes, guess who will decide your fates?" Barabbas said nothing but he tapped his favorite buddy on the head and smiled looking toward his charges. He smiled and nodded his head, "Majheed you are now *Director of Hygiene*, ha, ha, ha!" The rest of them could be heard mumbling and grumbling although in much fun.

"Come now gather around and learn how we will handle our organization." They all dropped to the floor or on one of the seats anticipating Barabbas' explanation. At first some of the ten thought he was pulling a joke as he was known to do but when they saw his countenance they decided he was serious. He stood for a moment looking at them, "We must now put together our own form of organization. As you know the Romans have their levels of authority. We will have a similar structure. As Jameel was the leader of his group I think it only right he should now be my next in command." Pausing he checked the eyes and mien of those of his own group as well as the others. "Are you all OK with that situation or is there any disagreement's with this move."

Giant paused and waited while he sipped a drink of water yet watching all of them closely hoping he had made the right decision. He was relieved for he noted there was no unhappiness in the faces of his own group and he was hoping the others would go along as well.

Schmuel rose from his position on the floor of the cave. They all held their breaths uncertain as to what he was about to present. Ayoub and Majeeb knew the insight of their older partner so were not worried in regard to what he might have to say. Barabbas said, "I would expect you to be the first to make suggestions for we all know your expertise." Schmuel waited for quiet, "There is no doubt in my mind that we all will agree that our leader be Barabbas for he is knowledgeable of the workings of the Roman Guard and has traveled over the territory even into Asia Minor; I say we agree on that while also giving our support to Jameel as second in command." Ayoub and Majheed rose to stand next to Schmuel and at the same time Tannoush, Haleem, Kallial and Fouad rose and applauded. When the applause died Jameel stepped forward, "Thanks for your vote of confidence I hope I can live up to it. I would like to suggest that our legal counsel, if we have one, should be Schmuel, what do you guys think about that?" That was met by a roar of approval for Schmuel was a young man who presented himself knowledgeable, well liked and most level headed keeping himself informed on such things as the actions of the Romans and their laws.

Barabbas stood, now smiling happy with the outcome of his band of rebels and somewhat proud of himself. "Now it seems that our numbers have grown and we are a group to be reckoned with. I shall plan our activities much more thoroughly and we will become the wealthiest band around. We will be known as Barabbas Patriots and many will want to join our group for we shall endeavor to drive the Romans out of our Country." Jameel raised his hand and Barabbas nodded for him to speak, he rose saying, "Ahshurrty, (old friend) I have five other pals who have helped me in the past when I needed additional help. They are trustworthy and very hard working men. I suggest you talk to them and question them to see they are worthy of your insight. We can meet near the springs and you can question them for verification. I know they will be good for our cause."

Barabbas' eyes fell on Schmuel and knowing his thoughts said, "O K Jameel locate them, explain the next move that they will be tested through a training program, if this is not to their liking then excuse them." "A good idea Barabbas," turning to the others, "now you all understand why he is our leader."

****

The following day Jameel left the camp early and returned two hours later accompanied by four young men their ages near all the others of Barabbas Patriots. As they came nearer to the cave Jameel stopped and waited. Barabbas' voice broke from behind them surprising them all. "Hello Jameel it's nice to see you what's up?" "Oh hi B," Jameel answered not wanting to give away anything saying, "Hey guys this is a very good friend of mine."

Still not mentioning Barabbas' name he pointed to each of them saying their names. "The two big guys with no beards are Ezra and Jodan," standing over eight hands both had black hair neatly dressed light skinned and blue denoting them either Greek or Phoenician. Then Jameel pointed to the others saying, "This is Judah he is from Palestine and Jonathan from Trans Jordan." These two were heavier weighing in over two hundred pounds mostly muscle each standing much over seven hands, dark hair somewhat darker skin and roman noses. All four of them had ready smiles and looked to Barabbas as if they were con men for he knew their type well. Barabbas questioned them at length to determine their intentions and strengths and insure his leadership and with a very stern look in his eyes making sure the entire gang noticed his change in demeanor, "The four of you put out your hands and now we will mark your palms by cutting a dot and a dash in the fat of your flesh." Not one of them hesitated as they extended their hands for the initiation. Taking a small knife out of its sheaf inside his tunic he spat upon it then wiped it clean and turning to the four he took the hand of Jodan, than putting the knife on the fleshy part of his hand below the thumb slightly pressed the sharp end of the knife into Jodan's skin. Jodan kept his eyes up and straight ahead attempting to pay no attention to Barabbas actions while the other eight watched closely holding their breath not knowing what their leader had in mind. Barabbas put more pressure on the knife and they could all see a very slight tinge of red on Jodans skin. Barabbas stopped, taking Jodans hand in his own and shaking it saying, "This proves to me you and your pal's loyalty; huzzah for you all for this will make a great start toward our goals." Barabbas' approval of the four swelled their ranks to thirteen, twelve of them being very ably built and yet smart.

Was this even more than Barabbas had dreamed not knowing his personal evolution had just taken a step up the proverbial ladder of power, for here in Genneseret on the Sea of Galilee would become their headquarters and they would operate from this point throughout Israel?

"This will be the first official meeting of Barabbas Patriots. Majheed you will lay out the kitchen area to your liking and will make a list of things you need for your pantry then we will see that it will be stocked with whatever you need. Listen now for this is of the utmost importance; it will be necessary for all of us to make sure our location is not discovered; it *will* become a habit that before entering or leaving we *will make sure* we are not seen. No matter that we are hurried or not, our first thought will be to maintain our secrecy."

****

Sitting on a high tor Barabbas looked down at the caravan approaching from the south. He had gotten word through the usual scuttlebutt regarding the various movements of rich caravans. Through that thieves connections would come, sometimes erroneous, they would hear of wealthy people moving across the miles with all their valuables moving from one country to another or from another community to another. Along with this Kallial and Fouad were becoming experts at identifying the wealthy through a crash program by their leader. He made sure all the members sat in on this instruction course. "Always look for the finest dressed people around the souk (market place). Always be casual as you can, do not allow yourself to become too interested in your marks. Walk around outside the walls of the city and watch for those caravans their wagons being pulled by asses or camels but having several horses in tow directly behind the last wagon. Always look for a Caravan Master who always rides a Hassan and flows in and out of the caravan subtlety checking . Now this is one of the keys, identify the personal servants and try to make friends with them and speak to them each time you see them." He paused to take a drink. "You must make yourself as invisible as possible as you walk through the souk pretending to shop for some item of need, remember this, by keeping your head down you will not be easily recognized in the event something happens. Continue to watch those rich people who may live within the area of the city. Allow yourselves to be seen in the souk by all *but* those marks for at least three days before you make this next move. On the third or fourth day you are to shadow those servants to their homes." He paused holding his finger in the air as if to admonish them and continuing, "Another key; if we are working from our headquarters *do not,* I repeat, *do not* return to the cave but seek refuge in other places that will keep you from being identified with the rest of us. Each evening make sure you are not being followed; take a covert direction home."

****

After an almost three day trek from Gennesaret they were well rested upon their arrival in Saida (Sidon). They were happy to see this old City for as Barabbas explained the value of being here for this was the most industrious City in the entire area. Barabbas taking a deep breath said, "Hey guys smell that clean cool air we must sharpen our minds and our talents cause we will remain here for sometime as this is a virtual goldmine, once more *stay alert!*

This port was the largest of the industrial ports of the world for the Phoenicians' were the first to venture beyond their own shores and navigate the Great Sea. These first designers and builders of ships sailed the Aegean Sea on the northern coast of Africa to Carthage and braved West and beyond the Great Sea to Sicily, Corsica and established their first colony in Espanola. This would be Barabbas' greatest escapade and as he planned it in his mind the largest robbery ever. He was already well known and thought as he smiled to himself, "I will be the king of thieves and the Giant Barabbas will be known and feared throughout the world." Of course none knew how large the world of this day really was.

They stood on the shore overlooking the sound and the beauty of Sidon captivated by this most beautiful and exceptional port. Although this was not his first visit Barabbas loved this port for its most relaxing atmosphere. They were brought out of their solitude by a gentleman's voice interrupting their tranquility. He came nearer saying, "Welcome to the Chief City of Phoenicia as we call it Saida; it is beautiful no, perhaps you would be interested to know that Noah's great grandson Zidon built this City hundreds of years ago. But you see I am a proud Phoenician myself and I love to report to those who will listen for we are a wealthy Community and a highly commercial area." His chest seemed to grow as a wide grin of happiness enveloped his face. "We produce gold, silver and manufacture embroidery, dies, metals and especially glass. We are christened by the Greeks as the purple people for we invented that color which we developed from an oyster. He paused anticipating questions but only quizzical looks came his way, "Ha, ha, ha, ha," his pleasant laughter rang out over the water, "rather interesting wouldn't you say? And now listen to this; as close as we are to the Israelites we have never been possessed by them. At one time this area belonged to the King of the Israelites Asher but he did not want to drive us out for we were his wealthy neighbors and he knew from his ancestors that the Sidon's had oppressed

Israel. But then I prattle on and have not yet welcomed you to our city. I am Hiram called after he who was king that is my great, great, great grandfather of the line of the tribal family El Ghassanid. I live not far from here if you look upon that hill above the city you will see my home which was built by my Grandfather," he pointed toward the Mountains of Lebanon and a high peak upon which one could see a beautiful palace built upon it, "So if the need arises be sure and seek me out for I love to talk of my dear Saida. Enjoy your stay gentlemen and welcome to our fair city." He turned and meandered off toward the city his hand above his head waving a pleasant farewell.

Barabbas turned away from the water seeking a place to sit. Seeing a large rock he sat upon it, "Come gather around I will lay out your assignments. "Majeed, Aboud you two will be the guardians of our den. It will be your job to find a hideaway near or inside the city where we will headquarter. Majeed, since you have found our permanent home I know I can count upon you to find a local spot for us the rest of you will begin your stroll through the souk and the city. Take your time for we have much of that, we will meet here on the beach later. Do not walk together or even near each other and when you see one another do not speak in fact you must pretend you do not know the others. Study, study, study select the better shopping areas of the souk and check out each of the gates into the city. We may find there are three, four or more gates for this large a city will have a horse gate or similar named for that will be where all stock is brought for sale. Now go and use your eyes and brain; you will find me here later I will be watching you!

Indeed Barabbas would be watching them but unbeknown to them for he was a master of disguise which he had picked up from an older thief some years back.

****

The man's back was bent and his neck askew to the left; a growth of beard covering his face and wrapped in sackcloth that covered his head and trailed down his side. He held one corner of the sackcloth in his left hand but under it was hidden a battering ram three feet long. The patch over one eye made him very conspicuous but most took one look at him and walked away avoiding the odor. This was the Giant in his best camouflage as he meandered around the city watching his men as well as spots of interest where wealth was obvious.

Barabbas allowed himself and his crew a week to study the area in and around Sidon then called them in for a meeting at the new hideaway. When Majheed led Barabbas to the cave he walked past three extremely dense and unusually tall bushes. He stopped and turned smiling at his mentor saying, "Well Giant we are here how do you like it?" Barabbas frowned looking all around then said, "Do you expect us to sleep in these Burberry bushes, how do you expect us to get into those they will tear our clothes and our skins very badly;" he then caught the grin on Majeed's face, "All right my little house keeper quit messing around and let's find a place to hide ourselves." Majeeds impish face broke into a huge grin, "OK boss we are here and you nor anyone else can see our den from here but watch me." Barabbas and the others watched as Majheed walked to the corner of the mountain wall and turned left as if going around the corner. They waited for thirty seconds or so then Majeeds voice came from the area behind the Burberry bushes surprising them all. "Here I am guys can you see me, walk to the corner of the mountain then turn left and walk through the dense growth of grapevines hanging down?" They followed his instruction and soon found themselves inside a large cave which would accommodate them all. "Wow," Jameel said, "I don't know how you do it but you must be some kind of a sorcerer Majeed, this is great." Schmuel agreed, "He has a knack for finding these places; O K guys settle down now I've got things to talk about."

Barabbas stood. "I've been watching a particular family who owns a large group of servants and live in one of the largest homes I have ever seen it is located above us. It is a castle of sorts and they ship loads of merchandise out of a warehouse near the east gate of the City. I have found the family name to be Ghalaloumy, an extremely wealthy family with very intelligent security and the worst thing for us is most of the security people will not be known for they are undercover, they do not dress as guards. Schmuel and Jameel, you will apply for a position at that business and learn all about the shipments in and out. Find out where they ship to and how often. Keep track of the destinations of the caravans and report back to me every day." Kallial, Fouad, Ayoub, Ezra, Judah and Jonathan will begin casing the markets. Split into teams of two and begin bringing in gold, silver and copper items. One on each team will wear the large smock with pockets inside; when your pockets are full leave; *do not be selfish* when you have a load take it home." They worked the souks of the city meanwhile making friends of several of the merchants.

****

One day Barabbas, Schmuel, Ayoub and Kallial were thrown together within the east souk not knowing the others were there. Barabbas was watching a young lad whom he guessed was about ten strolling through the souk looking at the fruits, vegetables and other food stuffs with a starved longing. Barabbas could almost feel the pangs of hunger racking this youngster; his mind flashed back to a time when Barabbas himself had these same pangs. He watched as the young boy walked slowly around several different stores eyeing those delectable foods. As he watched this youngster those ancient pangs hit Barabbas' stomach and eager pains of hunger coursed throughout his veins and his unused fatherly urges nailed his ego as feelings he did not know welled up inside him.

He did know what or why the feelings were there

but suddenly he felt as though he were looking at himself as a child. He looked aside and noticed a seller with a work apron around his middle and a Roman soldier walking together watching the youngster. Barabbas pushed past the two as he quickly reached the young boy grabbing the small hand and in one movement lifted the lad up into his arms. "Boulis" (Paul), the big giant said, "I have been looking for you my son have you not found the food you want yet; OK I'll let you down now and you pick out all you want to eat," as he did so he winked and smiled leaning down he whispered, "Pretend I am your father," He spoke to the ash haired, blue eyed youngster with a dusty face as if he were his guardian. "Oh come now sonny here is a bag to fill full of whatever you want." He laughed as he set the youngster down on his feet directly in front of the largest store within the souk. The store owner let out a huge sigh thinking how close he had come for he was about to arrest the wrong person and genuflected in front of the huge person facing him. "Sir is there anything in particular the children need, is not that the boys sister sitting in the corner? I am so glad you are here we have been uh, uh keeping our eyes upon them for we knew, uh, uh, uh or thought they might need help?" The store owner wiped knowing how close he had come to err. He turned to the guard, "It is all right sir why don't you pick up the girl and bring her here to her father." Assuming the big guy was their parent the guard strolled over to the corner and picked up the blond haired beautiful six year old somewhat odoriferous for she, like her brother needed a very good washing.

The boy, who by now was answering to the name of Paul, was loading up a bag of more food than he could eat in a full month. The guard handed the girl to Barabbas who took her saying, "My sweet Angelina where have you been you have worried Papa and I have been looking for you since early this morning." He turned to see Schmuel walking toward him and without missing a beat, "Here young man I hire you to take this child and wait for me outside for I need you to assist me." Schmuel followed the tacit game to a t taking the youngster from Barabbas' arms and walking outside and with forethought reached down and helping himself to a peach, pear and some figs nodding at the storekeeper who acknowledged Schmuel with a big grin for this was going to turn into a fairly good profit for the young child's bag turned into another. Barabbas laughed aloud with all those around turning to see what the joy was. Barabbas picked the child up in his arms and Ayoub who had been watching the entire proceedings said loudly, "Sir I will help you with your packages just lead the way." Barabbas tossed the store keeper more money than the items were worth and shouted, "Thank you my good man, may He who is God bless you." Quickly the answer, "Please come back any time for I will remember those uh, uh poo', uh, children." Here was a lesson learned by the Patriots; to help those who are needful! The young boy Paul and his

Two Men Named Jesus

sister Angelina, who did not know their own real names, became the children of the Patriots and were good help for Ayoub and Majheed keeping the den neat and clean.

A gorgeous sunrise met them as they sauntered out of the cave stretching to get the kinks out. This would be a day of rest the previous two weeks had accomplished a normal months work. Walking around the city studying and observing the people dressed in their finery some going to Temple some to the shore and others setting up picnics under the shade. They were fully engrossed when they heard the loud mumbling of a crowd which became louder as they approached the next house. It seemed a crowd was gathering around a woman who was seeking out a man of the same age of Barabbas who was being followed by this woman pleading with the man. She was telling Him that her daughter had an unclean spirit within her and she was pleading with the man to help her. (*Mt 7-26) Orthodox Study Bible) "The woman was a Greek, a Syro-Phoenician by birth, and she kept asking Him to cast out the demon out of her daughter." But Jesus said to her, "Let the children be filled first for it is not good to take the children's bread and throw it to the little dogs."

Barabbas gasped saying to his Patriots, "Look, look it is the same Teacher we saw at the wedding in Cana the same man that fed the 5,000, watch and listen see what happens; that lady is asking him questions about food crumbs I think."

(Mt 7-28) And she answered and said to Him, Yes Lord yet even the little dog's under the table eat from the children's crumbs." Then He said to her, "For this saying, go your way; the demon has gone out of your daughter." And the Teacher left. The crowd along with Barabbas and his group followed the Lady to her house watching and listening.

(Mt 7-30) "And when she had come to her house she found the demon gone out and her daughter lying on the bed." They all heard the gasps and awe of the crowd and heard them saying, *"Oh look the daughter is healed and now there is nothing wrong with her,"* and they saw the mother bring the daughter to the door of the house to show her to the crowd. Barabbas and the Patriots were awe struck as was the masses. Then Schmuel shouted, "Look guys The Man is gone where in the world did he go so fast, did anybody see which direction he went?"

Barabbas pulled his group aside as they walked away, "Yes that is the same Rabbi that we saw before do you remember Him for wherever He goes the Romans seem to watch Him for they want to arrest Him for making Miracles; be sure and let me know if and when you see this Man because I like Him for I am drawn to Him and maybe we can protect Him. "Have you noticed everybody calls Him Lord?"

****

It was almost 8:00 A. M. and they had just finished their morning meal of crackers, grapes, figs and Turkish coffee. They were all smacking their lips and complimenting Majeed. Barabbas dipped his hands into the wash basin sitting on the table then wiped his hands on his napkin saying, "Ok Schmuel, Jameel let's have your reports as to the caravan trade. You have worked there now for six weeks so tell us what we want to hear." Jameel answered, "I will let Schmuel give the report for he is now the chief checker for the company." He turned to Schmuel and nodded. "Well guys I will do my best. It seems a large caravan of at least ten wagons pull out of our warehouse each Monday morning for the area of the Marib Dam in Southern Arabia (Yemen). That is about five hundred miles but they take merchandise with them that will be distributed along the way in Southern Israel, Syria in the Provence of Houron and other small Provinces. They will travel to Southern Arabia; the Romans call it Arabia Felix or Happy Arabia, and leave such things as marble from the Island of Cyprus, brick from the Provence of Galilee, and bales of hemp. Times we will load Cedar Trees from Canaan, Tyre and Sidon. But let me assure you except for the marble the most expensive things are those that are returned from that region that come to them from Africa. The capital of Yemen is Sheba where the Marib Dam is situated. Jameel is familiar with this area for he is from The El Ghassanid Tribe residing in Sheba near the Dam. Frankincense and

Myrrh is the most expensive items brought back from the Arabian Peninsula. This is the only area which produces frankincense, myrrh, cassia and cinnamon. I have learned that the trees bearing frankincense are guarded by winged serpents of small size and various colors to keep thieves away from them, for it is a most valuable medicine." He laughed and laughed for this was quite a story.

Barabbas broke in, "Ok Schmuel, wow what an orator you have become, I know, for you study constantly; but now tell us what is your plan?"

Schmuel began, "Here is my plan. As you know it is only about seventy mille to Houran in the South of Syria. This is a small town but does a flourishing business in many of the products the company handles. There the caravan will rest. Now, when we leave Sidon you will follow at a safe distance. There will be many other caravans, most much smaller than ours, as well as families following the same trail, some of them will stay right with the business caravan mostly for protection as an additional small wagon you will not be noticed. The main caravan will rest there. This will give you cause to set up your tents and rest. There will be guards around the wagons and you will know the value of the merchandise within the wagons for the most valuable will have the most guards. Make a mark on the right side of the wagon inside the wheel area to denote these. Take note and study these and make yourselves aware of the area around you. This is most important for you will not relieve any of their wares until the return trip. You will settle in Houran until the caravan returns with the more valuable items such as the frankincense and myrrh. Are we all clear and are there any questions?" Barabbas waited for a moment then stepped up, "Well done my faithful assistant I believe we all understood fully." Barabbas was proud of his growing organization.

The caravan slowly made its way into Houran with a line of followers, small caravans and families, traveling near the large caravan for protection. The twenty large carriages pulled into the outskirts of the small city and circled themselves near an oasis where they would have access to water for the oxen, camels, asses and horses. This particular rest stop was reserved for the Ghalaloumy Company.

Barabbas and his crew were three or so mille behind the head of the caravan and arrived some time later but settled across from the oasis near a community with several Inns for the demand here was always high. Barabbas found he must pay to enter the area even though they would camp outside rather than in an Inn being accustomed to an outside venue, laying their napkins out on the green grass they pillowed themselves opposite of each other. The first one facing north the second with his feet at the others head facing south and so on around a circle; thusly they could watch every direction for as most thieves know detection must be immediate.

S. Eugene Cohlmia

****

A week later the caravan of the Ghalaloumy returned. Ayoub woke the Giant, "Here they come and they are loaded." They were slowly limping into the oasis for they had increased their number of carriers by four now totaling twenty four. Barabbas intelligently stated, "They must have found a bargain because they have increased their weight returns considerably." Ezra, Jo Dan, Judah and the rest were licking their chops for Judah reacted with, "Hey boss it looks like we might make a haul here right?" The uh'huhs, and the agreeable mumblings from his buddies awoke Barabbas' intellect as he gave them a steely look with, "Whatever you guys do remember what I said about getting over confident. This will probably be one of the toughest jobs of our lives and we've gotta be smart and careful remember some of their security guards are dressed just as warehouse workers you cannot pick them out, so again, and again be damn careful!"

That night Barabbas gathered his crew for the final briefing. "Jonathan as soon as this meeting is over you will go to the area behind the smallest gathering of their wagons. Find a place to tie your steed close by then about every 200 feet building large stacks of dry kindling, dry cedars and leaves that will ignite quickly. Find another location further away from that point and build a much larger fire stack; bide your time until the only movements are the guards. At that time set the fires lighting them about five minutes apart. After you ignite the third one wait several minutes before lighting the large one. Whatever you do not get caught; when you have finished go to your steed and wait for us at the junction of the two roads north of us at the large boulder off to the side of the Y in the road." He paused eyeing the balance of the group and they knew he was deep in thought. Then, "We will wait hidden near the wagons until the first fire awakens them. The teams will be, Tanoush and Haleem, Kallial and Fouad, Ayoub & Schmuel, Ezra & Jodan, Judah and Jonathan, Jameel and Majheed. The first six wagons will be your assignments they are carrying the most valuable properties. I will inspect those beyond that number and take what I deem valuable. That will be the extent of our treasure hunting for this night. If any of you are caught we must not rescue you immediately for as you know that would jeopardize the rest of us. You are to explain you were hungry and needed something for your family or any story that comes to your mind but remember whatever story you tell stick to it and tell it the same each time otherwise you will slip up." He sat down for a moment taking a sip of water than began again. "They will question you as to the fires but you will deny knowing anything of them and they will know you are telling the truth for you will not have any smoke odors on you. If they take you with them back to Sidon stay comfortably relaxed and do as they say for if you relax and seem to accept your incarceration they may relax the guard on you. If that happens wait for an opportune time and make a break. You must plan ahead what you will do; do not be rash and try to escape without a plan. Now get some sleep and I will wake you when it begins unless the shouting wakes you first! I have purchased three extra wagons which are hidden just outside our sleeping area and as you rise they will be transferred nearer the wagons of the train. Throw all the treasures you steal into one of our wagons, as you know they are marked with a p, hide them under the canvas and the last man will take the wagon back to their hiding places. I will tell you when we will retrieve and move them." They all stretched out on their pallets to rest. Slowly the day dropped its eyelids and accepted the coming of the night as the night birds began their serenade and the fire in the western sun seemed to slowly ebb to accept its eventuality.

The Patriots knew there were times Barabbas did not sleep. So it was usual for him to take a walk during that early hour of the night but as always when they awoke he was back in his nest. This night Barabbas walked into the small town just before sundown and moseyed along the outskirts of the souk. He strolled for some five minutes then found four youngsters giggling telling stories having fun. He walked up to them and stood still until finally silence from them. Barabbas smiled, "Hello my young friends I hope you are enjoying the cool of the evening?"

"Yeah you bet." Spoke the tallest of the four who seemed to be the leader of the group. "Boy you are a big guy Mr. how tall are you." This youngster asked. Barabbas laughed his usual raucous laugh which seemed to please these four young men. "Ha, ha, ha," he said, "I am taller than some trees but shorter than most houses." And he paused as they burst out laughing. He sat down on a boulder near them and whispered, "How would you boys like to each make three Dinar this evening?" The youngest one with a large nose and black hair and cleaner than most of the others said, "Yea man we'd love that how, just tell us what do we have to do?" Another gasped, "I've never even seen that much money we'll be rich." Barabbas motioned for them to follow him as he walked toward the tree line. When they were in the thickest part of the trees he stopped and said, "Now listen to me *and listen closely;* if any of you ever speak of this I personally will come back and cut your tongues out then give you to the Roman Guard, do you understand?" Their eyes narrowed and crossing their hearts then spitting on the ground they all locked their hands in his. Barabbas had no need to look back for he knew these youngsters would follow his instructions perfectly and *never, ever* speak of it again for they had felt wealthy and yet frightened down to their toes and they would never even speak to each other of this experience! He gathered them around him whispering his instructions. When he had finished he stood stretching to his fullest height glaring down at them. They knew this look of severity and once again made a cross over their hearts.

****

They awoke to the shouting from the caravan, "Bring water now; see there, a fire back in the woods." Another voice came from closer near the back of the wagon train. "Hurry, bring sack cloth, water and shovels." They rose and slowly scattered toward the direction of their assignments. The shouting came from near and far. Mostly eager voices shouting and running and pounding of feet resounded in the night air to a crescendo. The teams took their positions and soon there were only one or two people at each of the wagons noted. The Patriots stealthily moved from their hiding places near the wagons some having hidden themselves under the wagons waiting to make their move. Again the voices louder this time but the identical actions as before and more of the train's people joined those others to fight the fires. Each fires glowed as its fingers jumped into the night. The last was huge and it burned extremely rapid and brisk and began to fall apart scattering fire outward from itself which made it almost impossible to fight. Then from the train master came, "Aha look there," and he pointed toward the east, "I see youngsters fleeing the area they must be the ones who started the fires; you four come with me to catch them." He signaled four of the men trying to fight the fire and they all five lit out to follow the youngsters. They ran hard for almost half a mile then slowed seeing it was useless. They had lost them for the youngsters had curved in and out of the thickness of trees and undergrowth being accustomed to the area they knew their path of flight. The train Master realizing the chase would lead to naught shouted, "Pull up, forget it get back to the train." As they returned they could see the fires were almost out except for the big one. He issued the order, "Those of you who are not needed at the fires get back to your wagons."

Worn and tired they returned to the wagons. The train Master along with his assistant began their trek from the last wagon toward the front of the train, its headquarters. Halfway to the front of the train he heard, "Ieeahh; look, look come and see my wagon has been trashed only half of the gold and silver is left!" From another wagon somewhat further back, "Ya Allah" (My God) Master, Master come see my wagon is in shambles some of the spices have been taken for I can only count fifty of the hundred I left Yemen with; what has transpired here?" The Wagon Master ran from wagon to wagon shouting at each of the drivers and guards, "Count your load against the manifest count closely to make sure, let us gain a sure accounting. The fire, the fire, we have been duped with those fires and those children were simply an added diversion to pull us away from our wagons. Oh my, oh Lord never before has this happened to us, I was negligent as were we all." His employees tried to soothe him, "Blame us Lord for we should have been more guarded but when it," The Wagon Chief interrupted his employee, "Do not take the blame it is my responsibility but when this happened we all knew we had to jump to the fire!" Then from another direction came a shout from the Officer of the guard, "Sir we have an injured man here." The Chief approached a litter being carried by two men and on the stretcher was Schmuel dried blood on one side of his head and splotched with mud and dirt with bruises on his arms and hands as if he had been in a fight. His Chief reached him questioning him, "What has happened Checker tell me what?" Schmuel tried to pull himself up on his elbow it seeming to hurt him. "No, no said the Chief lie back, relax. Now, tell us what transpired?" Schmuel shook his head as if to clear the cobwebs from his brain.

"I was in my wagon at my accounting when I heard an unusual noise in the next wagon. I shouted to find out who it was and what they were being so noisy about. When I received no answer I jumped out of my wagon and stepped over to number 12. As I looked in I saw a stranger ransacking the merchandise. He was transferring the most valuable gold and silver utensils from our own bins into his sack. I must have surprised him for I asked his name and what division he was with for I yet do not know all the employees. Without answering he hit me over the head with a bat or something and I began fighting with him when another person came behind me and began pummeling me with his fists and then it was all over for I passed out. I do not know who they were the one looked as though he may be a light skinned Nubian and the other I never saw. I am sorry My Lord, I am sorry." Then Schmuel dropped back down upon the litter seeming to feint. "Take him to his wagon and make him comfortable I will send the company doctor to care for his wounds. Stay with him, tend him until he is well." The wagon Master turned to his aide, "Come let us make an accounting to see what is missing and we must better protect ourselves that this does not happen again. Alas, alas, this is the first time in ten years this has happened and we have not a clue as to who they were or what they look like. I do not look forward to the report I must make to my beloved employers, how can I tell them of my blunder, my oversight not to have taken better caution with their merchandise? When we arrive I will throw myself upon their mercy for they are the finest people in the world." His aide put his arm around the shoulders of his Chief comforting him. "My Lord it is not your fault it is for us all to bear with you."

****

Barabbas and his men stayed out of sight two days until the large wagon train left, then they left the area and began their own trek up the coast. Unlike the Ghalollomy train they would follow the coast all the way subsequently not going near the line of return of that large train. It would take a week or more for the wagons were over laden. After three days they arrived at Azotus near Judea continuing north near the port of Jamnia Harbor through Joppa, Appolonia through the Plain of Sharon then directly east to the Jordan River they would circumvent the Sea of Galilee taking their time through the back roads making their arrival late at night and transfer the loot into their hideout. By the time they lay their heads down upon the pallets it was past midnight. Barabbas told them, "We will keep our hands clean for a while and I will make contact with some of my buyers. We will not trip our hands here in Gennesaret."

****

Schmuel and Jameel walked into the cave as Barabbas was talking to a huge man with extremely dark head and facial hair with an exceptionally large hooked nose protruding from a weather beaten countenance with two slits for eyes bespeaking untrustworthiness they swelled open and shut as he talked. As if his expressions did not give forth enough of a story he accentuated everything his voice bellowing through his hands. The overgrown bush did not even look up when the two walked in. Barabbas held his hand in front of the man's face to quell his speaking. "Schmuel, Jameel this is our fence Zubbacki Dundoonie; I have introduced him to the others and now you all know him. Zubb is the man you have never met for I have seldom had much to sell to him or others but now that we are expanding our business he will take all our treasures and convert them into massarri." This brought rousing pleasures from the gang. Schmuel did not shake the hand of Zubbacki for inside his heart Schmuel felt no trust for this man and he could tell Barabbas' eyes held the ugly Zubbacki at bay.

Zubbacki, his tongue swelled as he spoke with a thickness for his words were, at times, slurred and saliva trickled from his lips the slick moister ended on his sleeve where he was wont to purge them, "Have you heard Giant we have a new Governor Agrippa who is the nephew of Herod Antipash," the slur again, "that dog who has tried many times to slow me and those of us who are in this business to a halt. One of Agrippa's first acts was directed against us who he called bandits? Agrippa our new Governor did this in Galilee and Peraea when he took over that territory. Beware now Agrippa is a worse threat to us than was his uncle who tried to steal his nephew's royal title but Caligula the King of Gaul intervened and exiled Herod to Gaul. It is rumored Caligula is losing his mind; yes history will bear me out! But now we must watch this Agrippa for it is common knowledge he is going to try to put us out of business for it seems he is the greatest of thieves himself but *he* does it legally." Barabbas made haste to finish this business with Zubbacki who turned to leave then said, "Be careful when you send for me for they are watching the lower levels of the city and the Roman guards make three turns through the bowels of the city daily they are groups of two and they take their time. Come to me in three days and I will have finished the count of your spoils and will expend you your dues." Barabbas started to speak but Zubbacki said, "Yes, yes I know slip the blindfold back over my eyes and lead me out." He laughed a most unusual guffaw that sounded more like a taunt and waved as Jameel put his hand over the man's head so he would not crack his cranium on the cave entrance. As he left most of them frowned and shook themselves as if trying to shake off an unpleasantness.

****

Barabbas' fame grew within the underground of thieves and many wished to join him but he was extremely particular who he allowed into his group. They became known as Barabbas' Patriots for when he saw unfortunate's with personal problems he saw to it they were taken care of utilizing whatever made them better off and none knew the derivation of the aid. The reason for the name Patriots was the fact they had defended families, and individuals ,without compunction, for the Roman guards accused them undulley.

****

Their numbers grew until they were almost a hundred. At Schmuel's urging when they had grown to fifty they divided into three groups with the main headquarters remaining at Gennesaret. Schmuel himself found a cave north of the main headquarters near

Agrippina south of the main cave. Then later another in Decapolis and one near Jericho, all of them well hidden from the naked eye all near as much room as the main one in Gennesaret; later as they grew another two were found, one in Masada, on the Asphaltitus (dead) sea in the Judea area, some twenty five miles south of Jarusalem. Barabbas found four bright young Nubians whom he purchased from the estate of a wealthy land owner who had just died, he made them runners and full participation in the Patriots. Knowing their loyalty they would rotate from one hideaway to another carrying messages given only in sign language. The Patriots were never to travel in one group.

Schmuel was the second in command and Jameel the third. Aboud and Majheed were in charge of the hideouts to keep them in order with each having four assistants as well as the two youngsters they had adopted. Those who were his commanders and assistants met with him once every two weeks to verify all procedures. They were proud of this operation for it ran smoothly and similar to an army; thanks to Schmuel his mind was like a trap and he maintained the organization.

****

Barabbas sent word to all they were to meet in Jerusalem for there was to be a huge circus performing for one week. The Souks would be loaded and small caravans would be located within a mile radius of the city.

Barabbas sent word to split into teams of eight to twelve so as not to be suspect. Schmuel designated their sleeping places in Jerusalem as well as Bethpage and Bethany the three city's less than two to five miles apart.

****

As they and thousands of others were on their way to the circus near Jericho and Taurus, the Herodian Fortress, a crowd of hundreds was growing around and upon a large hill looking down into the Jordan River.

Barabbas and those closest to him, slowed then eased closer to the shore where a tall thin man with white hair and sad eyes yet face smiling was speaking, "Repent for the kingdom of heaven is at hand! (O.S.Bible Mt. 3-1.) (Mark 1.7) "There comes One after me who is mightier then I, whose sandal strap I am not worthy to stoop down and loose. (8) I indeed baptized you with water, but He will baptize you with the Holy Spirit." He baptized any who would step into the water with him. The man's deep bass voice resounded across the waters as he put his hand upon their heads and bowed them into the water, "I baptize thee in the name of The Father." One by one men, women and children walked into the water and waited for him to bless them with the waters while the huge crowd grew and grew. Barabbas and his men watched, some near, others within shouting distance watched and wondered for they knew not what this strange phenomenon was. After a long while, off in the distance came the unmistakable sound of soldiers marching toward them.

Barabbas motioned for his men to fall back to a safe distance and watch. The unit of Roman soldiers arrived pushing the throng back, the Lieutenant shouting, "Disband this meeting for it is illegal, we have orders to scatter you, now move, move, hurry or I will be forced to order the soldiers to take you captive." He stood looking at the man, who was John the Baptizer, "You, water man, come out and stop this nonsense this dunking people in water what is the attraction?" John smiled looking up from his stance in the water saying in a loud yet peaceful voice, "Sir I am about my Lords business and if you will I would baptize you." The leader of the soldiers scoffed raising the short whip he carried saying, "I give you one more chance to come out of the water and stop this foolishness!"

Barabbas raised his hand in the air circling it and immediately the Patriots had encircled the soldiers. He then pointed to Jameel then raised his hand in the air and brought it down in a chopping motion and suddenly the soldiers were split into two groups, now ten each. Jameel pulled his sword raising it in the air and at the same moment there were forty other men with swords raised in the air threatening the Roman unit.

Barabbas' booming voice said, "Retreat Romans or be destroyed for this man John is doing nothing to bother neither you nor your leaders. These people have a need for this thing they are doing so retreat or I will order my men to attack!" The Roman Lieutenant within the circle of the Patriots glowered at Barabbas, "I will have your name big man and you and your men will soon be in the dungeons with the other Christians." Barabbas frowned back at the Roman leader, "Oh yes I see the power you have Roman, me and my men are sorely afraid," jesting now as he faked a cowardice stance, "please do not turn us in to your leaders." Then he glared at the Roman Lieutenant saying quietly, "Go now Roman and take your men with you before I change my mind and do away with you, feel lucky today for I give you your life." The Roman officer commanded his men to, "Close ranks, fall in and march!" as he led them off at quick time. The crowd, roaring their approval of Barabbas, shouting (unfortunately for now the Roman guard knew who was to blame) "Barabbas, Barabbas our rescuer. Hurrah, hurrah, hurrah!" John strode to Barabbas holding his hand out to him and thanking him, "My dear man although you do not realize it you have become a servant of The Lord for now you have helped in His work." Barabbas face became a picture puzzle of quizzicality for he did not know what the man meant by it. He asked, "Sir, I have seen this man before once in Cana at a wedding where I watched Him turn water into wine, and two other places, please tell me of this man!" Before John could answer the crowd praised him in loud voices surrounding him separating the two and John disappeared over the hill.

****

Barabbas and his Patriots became famous to some yet infamous to the Roman Authorities for a price was put upon his head and theirs for the Romans offered huge rewards for any information that might lead to his arrest for now Agrippa the newly appointed Governor vowed to his Court, "I will seek out this man and put him on a cross closing down his operation." Agrippa selected fifty of his best soldiers assigning them the sole duty of finding Barabbas and his band of cutthroats, as Agrippa licensed them, and bring them to justice. Month after month the warrant grew until it was one hundred Dinares. This was a great amount and Barabbas knew he must be cautious now with whom he made friends. Schmuel confided in his boss and friend that he, Schmuel, would keep watch in their own group to see that none became more than hungry for the reward, "From this point I will interview any who would join our ranks. They must come to me for verification, so Barabbas, my brother; you have no say in these things for I have lifted them from you." Barabbas laughed a pleased laugh and a warm relief like that of a cloud lifted from his countenance.

****

Jerusalem was a thriving active city with caravans, Jewish & Christian families, robbers, thieves and many others crossing this Center of life for so very many. Barabbas met with his men before sending them to their criminal acts, "Remember who we steal from. We *do not take from those who* are earth people, I call them that for they are the salt of the earth and work hard for what they earn. In fact you may find it appropriate from time to time to invest in those who are worthy." A couple of the new men, one Strendam, and Proppa looked at him as if they thought he was out of his mind. Noticing this he addressed them, "For those of you who are new and for some reason have not heard we donate to those who are poor but clean and honest. If you cannot determine it leave it alone for others to spot your Captain Schmuel is the instigator of this program when this assignment ends speak to him."

****

Fifty members of the Patriots were mingling among the masses of people enjoying the circus. In a large cage far from the entrance were two lion tamers showing off their skills snapping whips noisily over the heads of lions and tigers making them jump over large buckets, over the top of chairs and other tricks. Close by was the large coliseum where races took place various and sundry races of men against men, men against animals, horse and chariot races and so much more. The noise level seemed magically to hold all in suspense for there was much to see and one's mind could only fathom just so much and if one studied faces one would notice the eyes darting from booth to booth watching the magicians, jugglers, wrestlers, men of strength and many other actions that went on and on.

This kind of spell is exactly what the Patriots were counting on for they moved stealthily in and out of the crowd picking the pockets of the wealthy as well as stealing items from the very booths nearby. Barabbas insisted they always work in teams of two or sometime threes for if they were accused of something they would be able to pass off the item in contention.

This day was becoming a very prosperous one for the teams had collected over three hundred and twenty five pounds of silver, several hundred shekels and dinary and clothing which they had handed off over half to the unsuspecting needy.

Late in the afternoon as they busied themselves they noticed the crowd was slowly shrinking and Barabbas standing away from the crowd noticed the mass was slowly walking away and those left in the crowd was *them*! Jameel who happened to be in the vicinity of some thirty of his men was bent down picking up a shekel he had dropped but when he rose he saw his group and it looked to be about seventy people whom were surrounded by a huge cadre of Roman Guard. He cleared his throat loudly giving his men notice that something was taking place. They all looked up to see what was happening. The Romans were moving the lay people out of their circle and that circle tightened around the Patriots. "Hold you thieves, hold in your place or we will be forced to cut you down!" From one of the Captains of the Roman Guards, Jameel spun slowly trying to count his men while searching the outer parts of the crowd for direction hoping to see the face of Barabbas or Schmuel but nothing. Taking a page from Barabbas' book he walked uphill to the Roman Captain saying with force, "What is it you want Sir why do you pressure us?" "Ha, if you do not know then you are indeed in need of a brain Sir." Jameel stood his ground with, "And pray tell Roman pig what am I being charged with?" Jameel hoping to gain time for his men who may need more time to pass off any merchandise noticed at the same time the circle slowly tightening with the guards pushing some of the crowd outside that circle yet at the same time attempting to gird those left into a smaller and smaller area.

Then Jameel caught a glint from the top of the small hill behind the Roman Captain; looking up he saw the face of Barabbas for a split second then it was gone. Now he knew the Giant was aware, as always what was happening. Jameel slowly moved his eyes across those faces of his men and they knew what he was asking, "Have you passed off the heavy merchandise." They all but one returned his gaze with nods. He knew by that they were in trouble with only Justinium who now would be arrested knowing he would be rescued somehow. Jameel knew he must take solid ground attempting to divert the Romans either by irritating them or keeping them busy.

"Well Roman Pig why do you not search me and see that what I have can be proven to be my own." This was well and good for Jameel being a Lieutenant was not allowed the luxury of stealing merchandise his job was to watch and be helpful. Barabbas had planned this, months ago, and would not concede to his officers to steal for then they could be arrested and they must be free in order to lead. The Roman Captain motioned for two of his men, one on each side of Jameel, to take his arms and hold them up while he searched. When he had searched him thoroughly and found nothing of the unusual his countenance changing colors said, "Release him, we will search each of these others one by one. While half of the Roman unit stood guard the other half cautiously searched the garments and bodies of the rest of the Patriots.

When they came to Justinium they found several gold keys, some silverware and many other coins. "What is your name and who do you work for, is that," pointing to Jameel, "not your boss of thieves?" Justinium looking as stupid as he could asked, "Who that guy, no I don't know him and I didn't steal anything from him and if he says I did he's a liar." Jameel made a motion to hit Justinium but the Roman caught his arm saying, "Go, leave my sight take those others with you for I can tell they are employed by you." "Ha, ha, ha I do not know most of them but there are six who are my helpers." Methodically six of the Patriots followed Jameel out of the crowd that had gathered and grown to huge proportions as his other men disbursed throughout the crowd. As he left and not to be noticed Jameel winked at Justinium who, to make it look good, shook his fist at Jameel shouting, "I hope you fall in a tub of dung, ha, ha, ha, ha!"

Later several mille from the circus Barabbas' words to Jameel, "You handled that very well and I must say I was extremely surprised at the cool way Justinium followed through, good for him. I followed they took him to the dungeon on the third level where our man Ambullah is in charge." Jameel laughed saying, "Aha he will pay off his Captain and Justinium will be released within a fortnight."

****

ROMA CITY - THRONGS OF CHRISTIANS

Barabbas, Schmuel and Jameel were so happy with their last months work they could hardly contain themselves when they were told they would go to Rome and work Circus Circus, the largest in the world; yes Rome, wow now they would have a chance to see the largest city ever, even bigger than Byzantium, yet most of them had never been there. At last count they had dwindled to fifty members for some had resigned, some returned to their homeland and others who had grown older simply quit, advisably not to be affiliated with anybody. Schmuel made sure those who were leaving were sworn to secrecy and given a stipend; they were all surprised and pleased at the gift which assured the Patriots of loyalty even outside their organization. Barabbas was extremely proud of Schmuel who had turned out to be an extremely sharp business person. He knew how to keep employees happy and of course this made it easier for everybody.

****

It was Barabbas' intent to travel as though they were wealthy which would allow them to steal from the wealthy while on their journey to Rome. They would leave from the seaport most familiar with, Saida or Sidon which would take them around the Island of Crete with a short stopover and on to Athens Greece where they would spend one night then begin a new morning onboard ship each day their enthusiasm for the sea grew their smiles evidencing it. Now into the Great Sea which would take them to the center of the World and to Rome their destination and upon arrival it would be Schmuel' job to find a headquarters away from the crowds where they could stash the loot they took from this wealthy city.

****

Barabbas met with his entire crew to discuss the trip to Rome. Twenty of the crew who, for various reasons, did not want to go after discussing it with Barabbas, "I know several of you do not want to make the trip for you, John, Sandlianos, Treantinous and several others have women whom do not want to see you go. That is well and good and I have been told that some of you are not prepared to travel on board ship; fear not for I approve of your decision and will see you when we return. See Schmuel and you will be given enough money to live until we return. I warn you do not operate any scams or thievery on your own, for you know I will hear of it upon my return and if you are captured I will not rescue you. We may be gone for several months but *we will* be back; now let's all have a good time this night for our trip begins tomorrow." The Patriots to make the trip to Roma would be thirty, still a goodly number of men traveling toward the same end.

****

As they boarded the ship that would take them across the Great Sea to Rome they, like most of those who would be boarding, were eager and awed of the Sea. Barabbas stood at the gangplank helping those elderly people board for the ropes were not exactly taut. The huge crowd standing on shore watching those whom they felt was lucky to be taking such a great trip, suddenly made way for an entourage of six men moving toward the ship. Barabbas feeling a need to do so but not knowing why, said, "Make way for this group!" As he stepped back sereneness engulfed him and the white haired gentleman smiled at him. The finely chiseled features of the first man on the right whose beautiful white hair flowing down his face in a cascade and haloed that face in brightness yet sad eyes, was speaking to another smaller version of himself, "Andrew please return to Antakya and relieve James so he can make his trip. I hope to return soon unless Our Lord talks to me from above. Although I was Patriarch of Antakya for a while I will now return to Rome to face the duties there. James will return and take the reins soon but until then protect that City where we were first called Chrestians." (Antique spelling). The man called Andrew hugged Peter, "God go with you my Brother and you will enjoy Bartholomew and Hristos {two of the second 20 Apostles} (Christos) as your aids, and to you both stay close to Peter and pray for our work," turning to the other two who accompanied them saying, "come Mathew, Leonis give Peter your blessings then we must be off for we have a far pace to go." They gave each other kisses on each cheek as Andrew walked away to return to his own destination. Barabbas looked questionably at Jameel and the crew asking, "This man looks familiar have we seen him before; they called him Peter; I think he was one of the men we saw once in Bethlehem with that Rabbe' Jesus and the one called Andrew was he with him also?" Schmuel answered, "I think you might be right Giant I do recall seeing both of them but not where, after all we have traveled over the entire area of Israel and Phoenicia for years."

After all these years unusual circumstances have brought Peter and Barabbas to the same point in time and neither would suspect the directions their lives might take from this point on; especially the turn of events that would take place in the life and heart of Barabbas and those around him.

A full day later the ship Antilles pulled into port Iraklion on the Isle of Candia or as the Romans liked Creta (Crete) for just an hour to load an order of marble destined for Rome. They had very little time as they strolled around Crete for awhile and marveled at the structures of the buildings how marvelously laid out the city was. This was the first city they had ever seen that was configured in even distances between streets being a city platted.

It took three days to arrive at the toe of Italia as they entered then left the Ionium Mare (Sea of Ionia) south into the Great Sea and west again where the ship plied through a small slip between Cicily on the west and Messana on the East. This was so very thought provoking for them for it looked as if they could reach out and touch both coasts. It would be the next evening they would arrive at the port of Ostia where they would unload then move east to their final destination; Roma! Oh what anticipation, this city all had heard of through the years and now they are *here!*

There was little to remember as they walked off the gangplank to the wharf at Ostia for this was a bustling port and the huge amount of dock workers trying to get on board almost outnumbered the passengers attempting to land who most carrying their own luggage if any. Now they would depend on Barabbas to direct them as they hit the wooden pier he pointed away from the ship toward what looked to be an oasis area at least it was green. They moved away from the sea toward the point Barabbas directed; when he felt he was far enough away from that crowd who were now dispersing he motioned them to take a seat.

"It is nice to be on dry land again." One of the youngest Patriots remarked which broke the ice helping them to relax. "Take a drink of whatever you have in your skins, stretch and breathe in the air of Italia. Soon we will be in Roma and of course the first line of business will be to find a home we can work from; I am told you will be amazed at this City". After only ten minutes they decided they were ready for they were eager for this new adventure.

The Patriots climbed a large hill on the west of Rome and stood on the crest looking out over a huge expanse of a city. From this vantage point they could see rows and rows of wooden homes next to each other and in front and behind each line of homes were passageways with people, carts and all kind of conveyances moving back and forth. "Wow," from one of them, "I can't believe what I am seeing this is really a great way to set up a city." They all agreed as they began their downhill trek. As they neared the bottom of the hill glancing to their right was a large open area void of trees, grass or any vegetation. Fifty or so feet away two Roman guards sat facing a large entrance into a huge sunken area of the grounds and the huge mouth of a cave growled ominous sending a signal this was indeed a danger area. Schmuel and Vittorio curious moved toward that area but one of the guards blocked their way, "This is a forbidden area, a poisoned place where healthy humans cannot go!" They stood gazing into this huge pit with gapping mouths looking out of the side of the hill and darkness inside. No movement could be seen inside the caves and Schmuel asked, "What is inside, why can we not see, is it dangerous, are there demons or what?" The guard pushed them back further away saying, "From where do you hail stranger, have you been under a rock, do you not know of the sin of Leprosy?" They stood awe struck their eyes searching the darkness of those cavities hoping to see that which they knew nothing of. Curiosity having taken over, the entire group gathered together near Schmuel and Vittorio quietly asking questions wanting to know what was going on. Barabbas ambled to them, "Come men." As they walked away Schmuel explained what that dreaded disease was and how it affected humans for he had seen the same forbidden area outside Jerusalem located in a desolate area where most humans would never near.

They moved away and up another hill looking down upon Circus Circus the largest arena any of them had ever seen. The hustle and bustle of movement within a half mile of that huge amphitheatre staggered their imagination. No matter where they looked up to a mille away from the arena, there was tent after tent large and small and near each tent were carriages, chariots and animal tied to stakes surrounding the tent. They could see animal trainers working their lions and tigers, huge warriors dressed in the armor of war, magicians practicing, barkers shouting, jugglers and all practicing their various trades to be shown soon inside Circus, Circus. Barabbas motioned them closer to him. "You will move throughout the crowd in your usual twos and threes and remember to move slowly and deliberately. Take what you can but do not load yourselves down. When the need arise hand off your take to the runners and they will return them to Schmuel and our headquarters. *Once more, DO NOT GET CAUGHT!*" Barabbas had no idea what he was now up against but a cool creeping sensation like hairs on the back of his hands. As one is wont he brushed his hands ignoring the telling from his id to his ego which inevitably over rode all.

Schmuel found another ideal location for their hideaway. It was an old home built among a forest like growth of trees hiding it from a worn lane circumventing the trees. Schmuel could not find who owned the broken down house so took it over saying he was borrowing it. The take was so very good the runners who carried the loot back to the headquarters were worn out by the time the shift ended sometime after the sun had slid behind the seven hills into the western horizon. After almost two weeks they sat around munching their evening meal Schmuel suggested, "Barabbas my friend I hope you have found a fence to move this merchandise cause as you can see the loot is taking over the house." "Do not fret my little auditor Humphemia the Syrian is on his way here now with two large wagons to relieve us of our problems. When he arrives I want all but three of you to hide nearby. I do not want him to know our numbers for as you know some of these types become jealous and will turn us in if it be to their advantage. Schmuel and Jameel will remain inside the house with me and they will make the deal as I set to the side pretending to be deaf."

Those who were to hide themselves had done so a few minutes prior to the arrival of the buyer who was a typical fence, typical that is for this gent purchases only quality, well dressed with fine clothes and clean. As he entered he genuflected toward the two leaders who were ignoring the Giant setting in the corner. Humphemia browsed the merchandise and spent more time looking over the money, silver and gold. After thirty minutes he looked around the room they were in saying, "Gentlemen you have spent your time well and I will make you an offer on the better items and….," at that point Schmuel turned to Jameel saying, "Well partner I guess we must accept the previous gentleman's offer for did he not say he would take all the merchandise?" No hesitation on the part of Jameel, "Of course we must do so." It took less than a minute for Homephemia to answer what he heard, "Well now if that is the case gentlemen if I must I will make you an offer on the entire load, would that please you?" Jameel and Schmuel looked at each other ignoring

Two Men Named Jesus

Barabbas who up to now was not needed at all, then from Schmuel, "I haven't heard a figure partner what do you think?", Before he could answer the large well dressed fence opened with a figure which made Barabbas frown and grunt as he picked an apple apart with his teeth. Schmuel knew what that meant and gave the fence a look of regret saying emphatically, "If you are going to continue to offer such low bids we must offer you the door!" and Jameel opened the door wide standing there as Homephemia backed himself up looking over the loot again. Jameel said, "Come now we don't have time to mess with trivialities such as you, goodbye Sir, we are expecting another offer." The gentleman jumped forward saying, "No, no Sir please forgive me," then immediately made an offer that made Barabbas almost choke on his next bite of apple as he smiled toward his Lieutenant and Captain for the offer was much more than the Giant anticipated. They accomplished their goal and enjoyed their stay here in Roma but as they all felt, it would be great to get back home knowing they would return much, much wealthier than when they arrived.

****

The following morning Schmuel would book their passage back to Phoenicia preferably near Sidon or Tyre if possible for then it would be much less of a trek to Gennasaret. "Guess what my friends," Schmuel voiced his pleasure as he walked in, "I have found a ship that will take us to Plolemais which will give us less than a day's trek home that is unless you are in a big hurry to return for the ship does not leave for a week so we can enjoy our visit."

On the fifth night of the seven before they would leave Rome deep into their slumber Barabbas and Jameel being the lightest of sleepers awoke to hear a piercing roar from the Inn a few blocks away. The noise grew immediately noticeable which urged them to go outside to investigate. As they stepped out the door they could see brightness in the heavens over the city a mille away and suddenly realized it was a great fire and they saw preceding the fire and running were two people in seconds the two grew to a multitude of humanity and a few minutes later that multitude grew to a sea of people screaming rapidly moving away from the fire. So many words shouted across streets and roof tops only those hollering could tell what they were saying. Of course the words seemed to float on the air, broiling, blistering heat that seared the normally cool air as it moved closer, ever closer their way. Barabbas lost no time for he realized they were in the path of this great man consuming monster moving toward them. The fire engulfed everything in its path for most of these homes were built of wood. Only the largest of them were made from the clay's of the area.

"Move men, now; forget anything you would take with you and follow me." Barabbas looked back to make sure all of them were with him as he climbed the hill above the Inn. When he came to the top of the hill he summoned Schmuel to him. "Now my brother what direction must we take to outrun this ravenous cannibal and reach a safe haven." Schmuel stood on top of the hill and seeing the smoke and flames not far off leaping like hyenas in their direction shouted, "We must find a spot above these flames." He turned looking toward the higher hill near them, "Come let us climb higher and seek shelter there, see the places in the side of the mountain showing darker spots, those may be caves were we can be safe." He began to climb and they followed him up, up the side of the mountain. Soon they could hear Schmuel's voice, "Follow the sound of my voice you are not far from me and I have found safety."

They all crowded into the cave which was large enough to hold them all and watched from this vantage point as the fire crawled like a monstrous fire dog reaching out its tentacles of blistering, blazing fingers ahead, right and left touching, igniting everything in its path and moving so fast at times it caught an animal or human unawares of the rapidity of its movement. Yes it was like a ravenous, starved ungodly visceral with a multitude of legs ever nervously moving in all directions so very hungry it knew not its own appetite as though it was captivated by its own animal instincts. "In my life time this is not something I want to see again, nor is it something I want to see even now." Schmuel was almost shouting over the din the burning twisting animal made as it seared its way in, out and over everything in its path. "Look, lord look, how far it has come it is moving so fast it is remarkable anybody can move out of its way." Barabbas putting his hand over his eyes, "I can feel the intensity of the heat coming closer and closer even from here. What could have caused this combustion that it moves so fast?" A voice came from below shouting, "Run, run faster my children we must find a safe haven." Barabbas shouted, "Come we must save those youngsters." As he fled the cover of their cave running downhill at breakneck speed careening down the side of the mountain being slowed only by the bushes along his downhill route reaching out their limbs to support this body as it moved toward the fire. As he reached the bottom of the hill still running several of the Patriots were narrowing the gap between him.

Barabbas almost plowed into the family of four small children being pulled along by their parents. Seeing what was taking place, Barabbas shouted, "Follow me *NOW!*" as he scooped up two frightened screaming tots pulling his precious cargo nearer his chest in order to protect them. Barabbas' feet never stopped as he turned digging those big sandals into the side of the mountain as he rose slowly higher and higher. He raised his eyes to see where he was and there not far was a chain of humanity reaching boldly to relieve him of his frightened priceless treasures. He heard a voice, "Take my hand

Giant the smoke has clouded your eyes." He reached out to the voice not realizing the tearing of his eyes closed them for fear of endangerment. Directly behind him came the others carrying two additional young ones to match the two Barabbas had cuddled to his chest.

Never was anybody so gratified as the father and mother of these fine four children. They wanted to thank the Patriots, "My name is Toufeet Shamira this is my wife Adelia and our four children Evagenia, Mousha, Haleem and adeeb, I wish there was a way to repay you for surely you have saved our lives this night but we have nothing to offer you for our home is gone with all our possessions." As he voiced his love tears began streaming down his face which brought tears to his wife and children as they huddled around their loved one. Adelia took Schmuel's hand and kissed it, embarrassed he tried to pull his hand away but the children took his hand and they all hugged him then hugged each of the Patriots in turn, she added, "You are angels of the Lord," said the woman, "We are followers of the New Christ and we prayed as our house came down around us engulfing us totally in flames, remarkably we were not touched by the fire, then when we thought we were caught again by that beast you, you saved us from a horrible death and we can do nothing to repay you for your bravery."

Her words pleased them and gave them a loving feeling such as they had never had, it was something that made them smile as they dipped napkins into a small rill suddenly trickling down the side of the cave and washed the faces of these four young tots and as they watched the crawling flames lick the bottom ledge of the mountain but it was all earth. Haleem shouted, "Look at the fire it turns and goes back into the town it cannot climb into the earth for there is nothing to burn there." Their eyes were glued upon the tentacles of the fires then still looking down they saw something else that caught their eyes.

Here was the man Peter who had arrived with them on the boat from Jerusalem very animated and discussing something that must have been of extreme importance for the other two with him were just as excited as the gray haired Peter. The one called Hristos said, "But Peter why do you want to stay in Rome, it is burning and there is little you can do here for our worship caves will surely all be under fire soon." Peter smiled at Hristos and took him in his arms saying, "All the more reason my Brother why those who are left will need my support; you and Bartholomew must return to Israel for that is where your work is." Bartholomew reached out taking his leaders arm saying, "Peter, I see no reason you must stay for there are those who are doing your work for you here." Peter soothed them by saying, "I have returned to Roma for it is our Masters wish that I be here," pausing he choked and tears pushed themselves from his eyes as they slowly found a rivulet down his cheek forcing a slight smile, "and now I ask your prayers for this is my pleasure that I answered Him who has chosen us for this will be my end and I wish for you to return to Israel that you may continue His work; when you return give my love to all and say that it is His will, Goodbye!" They watched from above as the three men gave each other the kiss of Love taught to them by The Master. Then Hristos and Bartholomew tore out of Peters grasp sobbing and turning toward Ostia where they would catch their boat.

Those watching from above were touched in many ways for some were sobbing others shaking their heads in disbelief and yet Toufeet and Adelia were smiling with tears in their eyes for they had witnessed that act of sheer unselfishness and abiding love of those whom they knew were already Saints. As they watched Peter make his way back into the City they suspected his plight; they squeezed hands in that knowledge.

Barabbas said to Toufeet, "Would that we could take you back to Israel with us for I feel I have known you all my life and it would be a pleasure to have you near." Toufeet laughed, "I understand fully for it is He who has saved us and now made us brothers and it is a mutual feeling, I thank you for your kind words but we must find a way to rebuild for we are Romans and this is our Country."

****

GOOD TO BE HOME

"Ah," breathed Barabbas as he stepped onto the land of his ancestors, "It is a most welcome feeling to be back, Saida looks great I look forward to getting back to Gennesaret. One of the things I have missed most is the sweet taste of the waters of the Jordan. "Yes, yes," Schmuel agreed, "but I long to return to Phillipi for the sweetness of that same water and to taste the glorious flavor of that sheesh (charcoaled meat)! " You are making us hungry let's get home we will ask Majheed cook up some of that very food." Barabbas piped up, "With fruit and cheese for desert," said Barabbas, then feeling these were his family, "come my children let us tarry no longer let's get home."

"It has been a great week for we have taken much from the city of Jericho. I must tell you we have given that much and more to those in need. As we travelled between Jericho and Jerusalem, by the count of our good accountant Schmuel, twenty eight families are now able to support themselves for what you have given them." It was a happy

Two Men Named Jesus

time for the Patriots and now they would relax in Jerusalem where most of them had lived previously. Coming to his favorite café now located just inside the east gate of the city they waited until there was seating for all of them. The owner, Najeeb Mahneam, knew this would be a great day for when he fed this crew his friend Barabbas would pay him a bonus almost as great as the bill of fare. "Come in, come in my friends, Nasheem," he shouted toward the back of the room, "come serve our friends bring the wine we have been saving after that the scheeshed lamb while it is hot, the ba ba gunnoush, hoomose, salata and all for their pleasure." They ate and drank into the early hours of the morning then took themselves back to their cave to rest for this would be as Barabbas told them, "A couple weeks of vacation and let none know of our movements before this day; if curious simply tell them we are visitors from the north, if they want more info just say we are from Asia." "Ha ha," from Schmuel, "that is a big continent, ha, ha, ha."

****

One beautiful morning Barabbas and a few of his men were strolling around Jerusalem enjoying the spring day. "What a great breakfast Majeed, you and Ayoub have been doing a great job." Majheed waved his hand in the air then pumped it down saying, "Boy it must have been good that's the first time you've complemented anybody for a while." "Yes, yes I do feel good today and

I am enjoying this time off; it is good for we have enough laid aside to last us for quite some time," then thinking he said, "don't get any fancy ideas were not retiring from work for we all love our jobs too much and it would not take long to run out of money." That brought a laugh from them all. They were all very quiet for some time when Jameel said, "Look guys that is a new building since last we were here, do any of you recall this being here?" None of them could recall and all thought it was a very new building. They stopped to look for it was an imposing building.

"Look," remarked Majheed there is that man we saw with Peter in Rome, do you remember I think I heard them call him James." Schmuel answered, "Yes I am sure that is the man they call James and I have heard he is the Bishop of Antakya." "What does that mean?" came from someone in the crowd. Schmuel explained, "He is the boss man of this particular area for the Christians and this the headquarters he operates from. Do you all recall when the man Peter was speaking to his aides in Roma telling somebody to return and help James in his Church?" There was some mumbling as to their understanding of this but not much for it was such a casual day and they were very relaxed. They paused studying this stucco building which rose taller than most others throughout the city and they watched as people were streaming through the doors crossing themselves and genuflecting as they entered.

****

While strolling around the city, unnoticed to them, a Jew Simon Antropidous, having been appointed by Herod as a Magistrate, accompanied by his Senior Centurion was not far away watching Barabbas and his group. Simon Antropidous would make a name for himself for he wanted to become the Governor and had for several months now been watching what he surmised might be the actions of Barabbas and his group for he had a score to settle with this Barabbas. The two of them met several years prior when they were both young. Simon and some of his peers had been playing a game of kick ball when one of the opposite team had an unfortunate accident that took him out of the game. The Captain of that team was looking around the crowd to see if he knew anybody that he might substitute for his injured player. As his eyes roamed the crowd he gasped and smiled seeing Barabbas standing at the edge of the crowd. He shouted, "You, large man there may I speak to you?" Seeing the Captain pointing in his direction Barabbas looked to his side then behind him and he was the only large man there; turning his finger toward himself asking quizzically, "Who me?" The young Captain came abreast of Barabbas reaching out his hand saying, "Who are you big man and have you ever played kickball?" Barabbas somewhat miffed at the question replied, "I am called Barabbas; of course I love this game." Captain Hunna (John) answered, "Good would you fill in for my injured man?" Barabbas could hardly wait for he loved running, bumping others and kicking the ball. Simon seeing his friend recruet this huge youngster shouting, "I object Hunna this guy is not a part of our class he is just a poor man's son and should not be allowed to play with our crowd." "Phew on you Simon since when do you make up the rules and what is wrong with poor people your parents have hired many of them! This is my man and you have no say in it." It was settled although Symon did not approve and designed several plays and attacks upon the big man. As hard as they tried Symons team could not throw this big human for when he was hit one simply bounced off of him. Then Symon called time gathering his players around him. "Listen closely guys. I will start this quarter myself and kick the ball directly toward that horse," and he stopped for effect while the others chuckled as he would expect them to do for he was the son of one of the most powerful men in the Sanhedrin as well as being the most powerful bully in the boys club, "he will concentrate on the ball so I want all of you to attack him with all your strength hitting him on one side. Watch for me as I will dive behind his legs, that force will topple him and should hurt him." As Barabbas kicked off rolling the ball between his legs gaining speed as he did headed right toward Simon. He saw the opposing team behind Simon stretched out in a line heading directly for him. Barabbas had never seen this tactic before but his mind shifted into high gear suspecting what they had in mind so he increased his speed and as Simon neared him he kicked the ball as hard as he could then smiled. Like a menacing projectile the ball careened forward so fast one could almost see a trail of blue smoke on its tail. The bullet of a ball hit Simons mid section solidly and his gasp rolled across the playing field as a tremor might. That sound stopped all of them in their tracks as the wealthy man's sun plopped to the ground his lungs attempting to return to normality but try as he might Symons breaths came in huge gasps. Barabbas reached down pulling the stunned man onto his feet and holding him up. "Are you alright Symon you don't look so good maybe you should take a rest." And turning to his Captain he asked, "Maybe we should take a recess or make a substitution, right?" A pleased roar from the crowd then applause perhaps this bully has met his match. Smiling Barabbas offered Symon his hand to help him up but the scowl that met him told Barabbas that Symon wanted no part of him; smiling Barabbas walked away while the crowd gave him a round of applause. Symon would never forget that beating taken from Barabbas whom he made his arch enemy and vowed to best someday.

When he took over his duties in this province Symon knew Barabbas had given the Roman authorities much trouble suggesting to his Captains of the Guards to watch out for a giant of a young man and told them he might have a large group with him not knowing his guess was partially correct he was grasping at straws for the beating he had taken from Barabbas was painfully etched in his memory. He had put out feelers sending spies among the people in an attempt to gain any proof or indication toward Barabbas' illegal movements although he did not know that would be fruitless for those who knew of the band of Patriots were recipients of Barabbas' kindness and would never give him up. Symon Antropidous had set himself this goal which he hoped would boost him toward a seat of prominence which would eventually spring him into the Governor seat or even King. This was not the first time he had spied upon this group nor would it be the last.

Enjoying themselves the Patriots continued their stroll and later were approaching the North gate of the city and decided to take a seat at one of the Café's for a refreshing drink. As was their habit when in and around crowds Barabbas, Schmuel and Jameel always kept their ears open in that they might glean something of importance toward making their life easier, in other words, an indirect invitation to some treasures some place or news in that same vein.

Once again Schmuel and Barabbas were having a conversation, or at least Barabbas thought, but as the Giant looked toward his Captain Schmuel was not listening for he had his head down leaning to his right to better hear two gentlemen at the next table, and in order for him to hear better he held his hand, palm up toward

Barabbas to quiet him. Schmuel held his finger over his lips forming the word, *"LATER,"* with his mouth. They all sat quietly sipping their drinks. A few minutes later the two gentlemen rose and departed and as soon as they were out of sight Schmuel rose moving toward the outer gates of the city signaling them all to follow to their home place.

When they were all assembled Schmuel spoke, "Well gent's I have good news. It seems next week in the Judea area there will be a huge shipment of gold and silver. The boat will dock in Joppa a week from today. If we move to Joppa right away with as many carts as we can we may be hired by the shipping firm to haul some of the goods back here; now here is my plan, Haleem, who is a writer will furnish us with company papers stating who we are and any other information pertaining to our company. I have given some thought to this and I am giving the name of our company, "Haul Right Trucking," what do you all think?" A roar of approval would have pushed him into another room being that strong & loud. Barabbas said, "Wow you are something else Schmuel, I swear your mind moves faster than anybody's I've ever known, that's great." Schmuel continued, "Haleem we will meet later and I will detail the inscription.

Joppa was built upon a hill and could be seen from several miles away. It was after all only thirty mille from Jerusalem and took them a full day to find their way to the edge of the City. Several months prior Schmuel proposed they unitize themselves into something similar to the corps of the Roman army. As most knew in those days inside a city the Roman guards traveled in pairs. When called upon to make an arrest of a single person two guards were ample. Depending upon the need units could exceed fifty men. The Patriots numbered seventy men half of them stationed in and around Judea near Jerusalem and the others stationed at the original headquarters in Genesaret although they would be called together as and when needed. For them all to arrive in any city where they intended to do their thievery en masse would be a catastrophe; so under the direction of Schmuel their numbers were split into units from four to ten men and would be given directions into and out of a given city and always if one came into a city in a particular group one would not leave with the same group. All these things had been worked out months ahead by their director of operations Schmuel.

"Good day Sir," intoned Barabbas through a newly grown mustache of huge proportions and in a thick Greek accent, "I am Genendo Spaareeky, owner of Haul Right Trucking." The giant of a man looked down at a meek and mild person sitting at a desk perusing and sorting stacks of papers. This intelligent looking gentleman's nose peeked out over the top of one of the papers, "Oh yes sir we have been expecting you and I am to usher you into the owner's office immediately." The young man rose motioning for Barabbas and Schmuel to follow him.

They were ushered into a room with open windows on four walls allowing the light to enter making this a very inviting room. A very well groomed gent stood up from a high back chair bowing, "Welcome my friend I am so glad you are early it is much appreciated for it tells me you are well organized; I am Fareed Mooseeny the owner of this shipping company." The six foot gentleman with salt & pepper hair yet clean shaven, light skin and extremely happy smile saluted Giant and Schmuel in the Roman tradition. "Thank you Sir, may I present my Lieutenant Samir Daloomaak, Samir will present you with the contracts and provide you with all the necessary papers from our Company." In a like salutation Schmuel saluted Fareed as they sat down and began their negotiations. "My first question sir is how many wagons have you for it will take many with strong and able bodies to unload this ship?" Schmuel smiled, "Sir we have ample I am sure but in case we need more we have that availability at close proximity." And so the deliberations began Fareed seemingly happy with the smiling Samir and Genendo who genuflected, turned and walked away for it was Schmuel who would do the negotiating.

They waited in line, four loaders and a driver on each wagon emblazoned on the side of each wagons tarp was, "HAUL RIGHT TRUCKING," below that an axiom reading, "FROM HERE TO THERE AND BACK AGAIN." Ten wagons hugging the dock awaiting their turn to unload the precious Cargo and standing as close as possible to the unloading and watching to see that everything moved as it should was Fareed the owner along with Samir & Genendo (Schmuel & Barabbas). After fifteen minutes of standing in the hot sun Fareed turned to his truckers, "Gentlemen would you join me in my office for a refreshing drink?" Schmuel holding a checking board full of page after page of duplicate way bills answered, "I am sorry Sir but please excuse me," then pausing for effect pretending to count, "72, 73, 74," uh, oh, I must remain here to insure continuity, Gi," coming close to calling Barabbas Giant, "Genendo you go with our host." Then immediately turning his back and sighing heavily he lowered his eyes back to his work board. Tanoush, the driver of wagon #1 eased up to his boss Schmuel almost whispering, "Let me make sure I have everything right. As we load our wagons we are to secrete every *eleventh carton*, right, setting it to the side and hiding it under a tarp O K, but how do we know what is in the cartons?" Schmuel, "How many times must you be told just do as you are told and not to worry what is in the cartons! Now go!" Schmuel was almost irate for this Tanoush was a good worker but always afraid of making a mistake. The wagons unloaded from the ship then traveled up the hill a mille and one half toward Mooseny Distributing Co. where they unloaded each wagon without a hitch.

****

It was after midnight at the headquarters of Barabbas' Patriots near Jerusalem when they all awakened. "Ok guys let's get started we've got twelve wagons to move to Genneseret, Jameel will lead five and Schmuel will lead seven. Jameel's group will take the hardest route southwest to Lydda through Emmas south to Gabath Saul as if going to Jerusalem but will continue south laying rumors you are headed to Saba (Sheba, now Yemen). You will move west across the Jordan River at Archelais then north skirting Perea across the Jabbok River, through the Region of Decapolis staying on the plains and skirting as many towns and cities as possible, on through Pella north to the Sea of Galilee east around the sea north to Genneseret." He paused taking a deep breath smiling for he was proud of his organization, he turned to Schmuel, "You will take the other route north to Joppa around Antipatis in Samaria then directly north around Yishub, Gitta, Norbata west around the Mountains of Carmel to Scythopolis north to Agrippa; be sure and stay on the west side of the Sea of Galilee then through Tiberias Bethmaus again skirting as much traffic as possible then the short hop to Genneseret." He smiled at Schmuel his eyes asking, "Did I do Ok?" Schmuel smiled nodding assent for he knew this was another area Barabbas would love to be rid of in fact a conversation between the two three days prior spoke of many things and Schmuel asked Barabbas, "Then Ashirrtie (my close friend) it seems you are throwing more and more my way is it that you have too much to do or are you getting lazy in your old age?" They had a great laugh on that one but Barabbas flushed somewhat saying, "You know how much I trust you Schmuel and after all we are not the small five we used to be," he paused his eyes seeking the past, as we all do from time to time, remembering what we think of as better days, "but I must say I will not recruit more men for we now move in five Tetrarchs as well as the Province of Syria to the North." Schmuel and Barabbas knowing each other now as brothers hugged, "Take care of it my brother." Barabbas walked away as Schmuel rose, walked out of the cave watching the Patriots wrestling, throwing spears and knives and just keeping in shape for whatever comes up.

He watched as two of the men, brothers, very muscular both the same age, twins, of Greek descent tumbled over in over doing acrobatic stunts. None of the men watched them for they had seen the two and knew most of their moves; if they stood side by side there was none among the group other than Schmuel who could tell them apart for if they stood blue eyes sparkling their smooth, fair skin gleamed and the same ready smile caught all off guard. Not only were they great acrobats they were of all things even greater pick-pockets. These two were invited to join the Patriots after a run in with not just the two of them but with their cousin as well.

This is the story of the two Greek's as they linked up with The Patriots.

Two Men Named Jesus

It was a bright sunshiny day as Barabbas and Schmuel were returning from delivering a large treasure to their favorite buyer in the bowels of the City of Nazareth. They were at the north gate of the City when Schmuel remembered Ayoub had asked him to pick up some fruit and cheese. The souk was crowded to a point where there was little room to maneuver Schmuel looking over the foodstuffs and Barabbas behind him some eight or ten feet. As Schmuel reached into his tunic for one of his money bags Barabbas watched as a blond headed Adonis bumped into the records keeper and simply brushed his hands into the other side of Schmuels tunic taking the other money bag. Barabbas waited for Schmuel to look back or say something for he must have known he was being picked yet nothing was noticed. Barabbas hung back smiling thinking, "This kid is as smooth as fresh Labana (drained yogurt) I've never seen anyone so fast and slick." He watched while this young man continued fleecing the crowd with nobody aware. Looking across the crowd Barabbas saw a look-alike doing the same thing on the other side of the souk. Barabbas followed Schmuel out the gate toward their own destination and was happy to see the two young Greeks following Schmuel, not knowing he was one of the person's they had just stolen from.

Barabbas would make sure they would not leave his sight and seeing Tanoush and Kallial heading toward he signaled them not to say anything but to fall in behind him as he pointed out the two young men. He signaled his men telling them to stick with the two at which time they stopped not far from the entrance to the oasis. Barabbas sat down nearby seemingly paying no attention to them. Schmuel watching Barabbas knew his actions were covert sought out Ayoub, Majeed, Fouad and Jodan bringing them to the clearing near the oasis signaling them to circle the two young men not knowing what to expect. Schmuel and the others watched as another young Greek walked up to Barabbas saying, "Sir would you like to see me turn this five dinar coin into ten dinar?" Not waiting for Barabbas to answer the young man held up the five dinar coin between his thumb and forefinger flipping it into the air then catching it and immediately showing Barabbas the coin between his fingers and yes it was now a ten dinar gold piece. Barabbas showed his child side hoping the young man would do it again and of course he tried but as the coin was falling out of the sky Barabbas reached up grabbing it and at the same time taking the young man's hand squeezing it hard. The hand opened revealing the ten dinar coin. "Very good youngster you are fast, in fact one of the fastest I have seen." Turning toward the other two Greeks, "Won't you three join us as I have a proposition for you?" And so the three Greeks, the twins Corythus and Cleothus along with their best friend Magnes were inducted into the band of Patriots.

UNFORSEEN TWIST OF FATE

Ezra a man of 32 never to be married for timidity had clutched him in its arms at birth which made him accept his plight in life assuming this was happiness; a man complacent as was his father one who could walk through a mass of people unnoticed yes that nondescript. Though as Ezra's life span increased a yearning for something more attempted to rise to the top of his ego. Importance was not an adjective familiar to him and motivation was not part of his vocabulary until one day his ego rose and began pushing against his thoughts, so after months of dispute Mr. Id gave in to that enormous push and suddenly Ezra found himself in front of Schmuel asking, "I would like to go home to Hippos for my Father is turning elderly and he needs me to tend him for there is none to do so." He knew not why he asked of his release for he could not foretell his egos hidden desire to be free. Schmuel knew if he granted this man's request he must remind him of his pledge of fidelity to the

Patriots, he asked, "Ezra do you realize your pledge to never divulge any information or movements of the Patriots during the time you were with us; under penalty of death?" "Yes, yes," Ezra verified remembering his pledge he put his right hand over his heart then bowed. Schmuel studied his face and actions for a while adding, "Await in the outer room and I will call for you." Schmuel thought long and hard recalling the assignments Ezra had been a part of: he followed directions implicitly but was never given an assignment on his own. Schmuel knew he was a follower and nothing more. Calling Ezra in to his office he rose took Ezra's hand and said, "Then go now Ezra and once again think hard and true before you mention your life with the Patriots for as of now we do not know you and will deny your existence with us ever; have a good life, wish your father well and oh yes take the back way out of the cave through the thick part of the forest."

Arriving home in Hippos was a pleasurable experience for both Ezra and his father. They stood facing one another unsmiling not knowing what their next move might be for their relationship had been nil since his Mother had died several years previously. They finally shook hands and both laughed nervously then sat down to a meal prepared by Ezra's father and for the first time in his life Ezra drank wine. It was a cheap version of wine yet gave him a great buzz something of which he was unaccustomed for suddenly a new sensation engulfed his being and for the first time in his life he felt important and feeling of superiority coursed through his veins. Suddenly Ezra sat up straighter and the alcohol became his master as he downed his fourth glass of wine. A knock at the door brought him back and he arose a new man. Swinging the door open to a familiar face yet one he could not attach a name to. Momentarily his Id took over and he burst out, "Maaka my old friend I can't believe it's you, you old culab (dog) you haven't changed a bit you look the same as you did when we were 10, yeah and that's the last time I saw you." "Ezra, the color of your hair has changed, I can't believe and look how heavy you have become wow you have muscles where I have fat, ha, ha, ha." They suddenly embraced then just as suddenly broke away embarrassed and giggling like children. "Come in Maaka sit down, eat something, you remember my father Shariff, have a drink." It wasn't long before both of them were three sheets to the wind each lolling upon one of the tattered sofas and neither of them hearing Shariff say, "Enjoy yourself boys I am going to bed I need rest."

Ezra and Maaka spent their days in the lower parts of the city as well as out near a grassy slope not far from the gate of the city. Not having anything else to do they spent most of their days drinking and going through the savings Ezra brought home from his days with the Patriots. One evening with the alcohol content higher than it should have been, Ezra unintentionally spouted,

Two Men Named Jesus

"Oh yes Maaka you should have seen me when I was with *my gang*, we were the best thieves in Israel or Phoenicia and never were we caught." As he laughed the alcohol commanded his brain as euphoria crowded out his sense of loyalty giving him a sense of importance. Unbeknown to Ezra, Maaka's uncle was a guard in the service of the Roman Magistrate Simon Antropidous.

So although unintentionally the die was cast and Maaka was telling his mother of the antics of Ezra bragging about some of the gold pieces Ezra had claimed to steal. Her brother Zeptha, the guard, was cap napping on his sisters lounge and overheard the telling. Zeptha would never have carried the information directly except that this day his Captain was extolling the necessities of reporting any information that might help their Magistrate who was now offering huge rewards for the correct information. During a meeting on a Monday morning a bell went off in Zeptha's head and pictures of dinare's and other monies danced in his mind. Upon the completion of the meeting he asked for an audience with his Lieutenant who after hearing what the man had to say was ushered into the Captains office. After hearing the story the Captain congratulated Zeptha, "Thank you for bringing this information in Zeptha, I know you will be rewarded for His Eminence Antropidous will himself pin the medal on you!" Oh what a proud day this was for the Roman guard; if only Barabbas could know what dangers lurked behind corners yet to be examined by him or his crew.

S. Eugene Cohlmia

Simon Antropidous called his Chief Centurion into his office. "Daminion, seek out your man Zeptha a guard in one of your units who has brought us information possibly regarding a ring of thieves. Question him thoroughly perhaps he can give us more information." Antropidous felt fortunate to have this Centurion in his employ for this Centurion was an extremely truculent brash ogre like personality and mere appearance brought fear into those under his interrogative control. His was a massive body over six feet weighing in at two hundred and sixty five pounds. His entire body was a mass of muscle a hirsute being that looked out through black irises beneath eyebrows connecting to both sides of his temples and continued across the top of his oval face. Very little skin peeked out of that face for once again it was mostly hair that flourished upon this man's body. He knew his own men referred to him as "bear" although they would not mention it to his face. Immediately Zeptha was brought into the office of Daminion who began, "Zeptha, tell me where you received the information and from whom; it is of utmost import. I take no pleasure in pressuring you but I must know all." This would be a new experience for Zeptha. Terrified and intimidated under the gaze of his superior's capacity for rough harsh treatment in gaining information Zeptha' mind worked faster than ever and he knew if he were to mention Maaka's name it would go badly for his nephew but then on the other hand if he did not come up with something substantial his own life could be in jeopardy. Upon hearing the shrill harsh voice of the Centurion his mind bounded back. "Now Zeptha," the Centurion speaking softly urging the man to speak, "tell me everything you know as to this information." Zepthas face changed colors like a chameleon and before he knew it he was telling all he knew. "I overheard my nephew speaking of a friend of his who he has known since they were children. The friend has been gone for several years and has just returned from where I do not know. My nephew was telling his mother that this man had a gang of thieves and they had stolen for years and never been caught." Zepha stopped for that was all he knew and could give no further information. The Centurion said, "Go on, go on what else can you tell me?" Zepha was now fearful of a terrible option for him, "Sir that is all I know, I swear I know nothing more." Without more discussion the Centurion waved Zeptha away making motion to his guards to release the man. When the office was void he told his chief guard, "Find the nephew, his name is Maaka, and bring him to me *NOW!*" The office emptied most speedily.

The following day Maaka was brought before the Centurion and as usual no time was wasted in his questioning. Maaka knew of this man's reputation and was petrified for what might happen to him. It began, "Young man I shall not waste your time nor mine, understood?" The Centurion put his malicious screwed up face into the face of Maaka which brought a surge of terror through the Patriots veins and his face turned colorless. The Centurion shouting, *"From whom did you receive your information and do not lie to me as I will not hesitate to cut your hand of?."* Anxiety, dread and panic raced through the man's entire body and without hesitation hoping to clear himself instantly he blurted, "His name is Ezra and he is friend of mine I will take you to him, please don't hurt me that is all I know!" Maaka drooped to the floor in a dead feint his body limp and lifeless. Once more Chief Centurion Daminion as always gained the information he desired. Now finding this Ezra would not be hard for they knew Maaka would lead them to him straightaway.

Maaka stepped onto the front porch of Ezra's house and knocked then stepped back and ran for he had done as he was told. When Ezra opened the door there stood three Roman Guards. "Ezra Maloon," the guard questioned, "Yes," said Ezra, "I am he what do you want?" "You are asked to accompany us to the Magistrate's office for questioning." Ezra thought nothing of this for he knew that office had nothing on him for he had never stolen anything in this region and he was not being arrested so he suspected nothing and went with the guard voluntarily. On the way to the City offices the guards, having been instructed thusly, socialized with him making him feel there was nothing to worry about.

Ezra was taken to the office of the Chief Centurion

and was invited in. "Ezra Maloon," began Daminion, "would you like something to drink while I ask you some questions?" Ezra sat down relaxed answered, "No thank you Sir I am quite content." "Ezra" the Centurion began as pleasant as possible, "some while back in speaking to a friend you mentioned that you were the leader of a band of thieves is that correct?" The hair on the back of Ezra's head sprang to attention and he felt his blood rush upward to his brain and he felt as if he may lose his balance. He took several deep breaths which helped to relax him for he sure did not want to intimidate his friends in any way. Only seconds had passed but he felt as though it had been an hour. Thanks for the sessions he had gone through with Schmuel and Barabbas which taught the Patriots how to react to such questions. Ezra laughed, "Ha, ha, ha, I do not know who may have told you such a story but I am not a leader of any band of anybody." He was very convincing as he crossed his legs making sure not to cross his arms. "Oh come now Ezra we have it by a very reliable source that you have been part of or a leader of a gang of robbers; tell me the truth!" Daminion now was shouting for his patience was wearing thin even in this early part of this interrogation. He knew his temper had boiled much too quickly but it was done and he would not hold back he would continue the pressure! "I will give you one more chance to clear yourself by telling me the truth or I will begin a series of tortures that will extract whatever I want from you." Still Ezra clung to his statements with a tenacity that would make Barabbas proud yet he knew if it came down to torture he was not sure what he might do. Then and there he made himself a promise to hold out as long as possible with the thought that he would take his own life if possible rather than be a stool pigeon. The questioning went on for two hours, they having stripped him of his clothing, while four guards took turns flogging Ezra's body with fresh hewn wet olive branches and still Ezra gave no indication of breaking although his perspiration and blood was beginning to cake upon his body for they had removed him to the dungeon and the movement of the guards stirred up just enough dust so it hung in the air like a pall than when the branches met with a dry spot on his body the bleeding began anew and the rivulets of blood and sweat rolled down his body. After fifteen minutes of this torture Ezra could not take it anymore and he steeled his mind forcing himself to see his grandmothers face, the person whom he loved dearly. Forcing his eyes shut he willed the face of the great lady to come to mind. Yes as he passed out and dropped to his knees his countenance altered and a wide grin came across his face for there in his mind's eye stood the beautiful black haired petite lady smiling back at him. Although his hands were chained to the ceiling of the dungeon, the blood from his wrists mingling with perspiration and dirt spilling down from his shoulders he breathed a great sigh as his own grin met that of his precious Sitty (grandmother).

Daminion glanced in the direction of Ezra's stare as the chief torturer saying, "What does this thief see, perhaps he sees the end of his days," and he let out a rude and raucous laugh, "Ha, ha, ha you will soon tell me what I want to know just as all criminal's do sooner or later." "Leave him," came the harsh shout of Daminion, "give him time to renew his strength then we will begin anew and this time there will be no stopping for beware enemy of the state when I return you will wish you were dead." And they left the dankness of the cell with only the flickering of the lamps throwing their shadows across the dark wall of the dungeon. Soon Ezra awoke his body shrieking with pain. He tried to stand but his muscles would not allow such a shock. His thoughts sprang across his brain, "What can I do now, I must not give in I must muster more strength and try to think of a way out of this. Oh I do hate myself for my drinking now for that was my downfall. I must try to get a message to Barabbas." He knew not how long he had dangled in chains from the dungeon ceilings but a soft gentle voice awakened him, "It will soon begin again and I doubt you will live long for they will begin the next session by pulling out your fingernails one at a time." Ezra looked into the smiling face of a very young boy whose blond locks hid his right eye and Ezra caught the happy glint in this young man's eye. The youngster had sneaked back into the dungeon to talk to him and Ezra could hear the love and caring in his voice. "Please tell them what they want to know, I cannot be here to watch because I watched as they did the same thing to my uncle then they caught me and now they pay me to bring water to the guards when asked, but I took this job hoping to help another for I could not help my uncle." Ezra thinking quickly whispered, "You are a good person and someone who I am proud to know; listen to me, I can make you a wealthy young man, if you will seek out a man I know, he will pay highly for the information regarding me. His name is Schmuel and you will find him somewhere in the vicinity of Jerusalem or Genneseret although you may never see him continue your search near the forest then when you find him tell him all you know of my circumstances this day and I assure you he will reward you beyond your wildest dreams. Please carry my story for I know, tell Schmuel Mahjkish, I will not live long. Once more, he will reward you richly for this information." The young man gave drink to Ezra then scurried off and out of the dungeon never to return, he knew he would not be missed for his only job in this jail was to replenish water to the guards and now he felt a sense of great accomplishment for he had injected himself into another's life struggle knowing his efforts would make a difference. Thinking back he frowned then looked toward the heavens he smiled crossing himself saying one word, "Thanks," looking toward the heavens.

Ezra still smiling watched the youngster scamper off the pain so great he could not imagine the inference by

Daminion that he would not be able to withstand the next series of pain and he did not want to think of the unimaginable pain that would come with the pulling out of his nails, in fact the thought of it regurgitated him. Ezra began swinging himself back and forth not knowing what that might do for him although it did hurt for the chains cut into his hands as his swinging continued. He was doing his best to continue the pain exerting as much pressure as he could yet he knew not what might occur. He tried looking up to the ceiling of the dungeon where the chain was attached and noticed the spike holding the chain to his right wrist moving slightly as he swung. Seeing this he swung harder which made his wrists bleed more profusely and yes, yes the spike looked as if it was beginning to break loose which made him shift his weight as fast as possible as the joy and the pain came simultaneously. "What will I do if it does break loose?" Speaking out loud and listening intently he thought he heard a voice and raising his head to look around he saw nobody thinking, "I must be becoming majnoon (crazy)." Now he was sure he heard a voice softly but yet loud enough to hear, "I am He who Schmuel spoke to you of, the same who turned the water to wine and fed the multitude near the banks of the river. Know you will suffer no more." Ezra smiled not knowing why but he knew the voice was telling him true and a soft cloud of assurance and love fell over him and he saw his Sitty standing in front of him smiling down at him her eyes sparkling. As he looked up he saw the spike in the ceiling slowly break loose then the ceiling followed lowering itself upon him and he smiled as he fell into a deep sleep.

****

Nabeel Shookrallah ran as fast as his twelve year old legs could carry him and as he ran out the west gate of the city he dropped a coin on the counter and grabbed a hunk of cheese and a large pear from one of the sellers stands. Nabeel was unaware he had been followed by another lad about his same age. If he had noticed he would have seen several young, very poor children akin to himself taken into service by Simon Antropidous as spies. They were to keep their eyes and ears open to report anything that seemed out of the ordinary. The promises of food and money Lord Simon offered seldom came but these youngsters were starved and would offer their own skin for food and shelter for what they knew of the unordinary was zero. The young man following Nabeel saw him take the cheese and fruit and flitted down to that same seller and grabbed food also waving at the grocer signifying he was with Nabeel. The grocer smiled knowing the plight of the youngsters; for if he had been closer he would have told them to take more.

He had no idea why he followed Nabeel but the hungry youngster tailed him out the gates of the city and into the countryside. Nabeel really did not know where to continue his search for this Schmuel for he had questioned many people and yet none knew who this Schmuel was, but a promise made would be a promise kept. Arriving at a spot near the forest where the prisoner suggested he look, and as chance would have it, he saw a very large man with a ready smile coming toward him and he was hoping he would finally make a good contact, for all the others he had stopped knew nothing of the man he sought although there were times when a couple of people had mused but for a moment, then decided they did not know him. He stopped in front of the man, "Sir I hope you can help me," he blurted his conversation quickly for he was tired of this speech, "I am looking for a Schmuel Mahjkish perhaps you know this man I must find him for I have a very important message for him." The Giant could not believe his ears, "What did you say the man's name is I might know somebody who knows him?" Barabbas settled down on his haunches to speak to this lad. "Sir, his name is Schmuel and I need to speak to him!" Barabbas asked, "What message do you have for this man; perhaps I can help you." The boy said nothing and repeated the fact that he was looking for Schmuel but would say nothing more. Barabbas thought he would try another approach, "Tell me why you are looking for this Schmuel or I will wallop you hard." Still the boy would not say a thing and turned to run away but of course he was not fast enough for Barabbas saying, "Come with me," as he scooped up the young man he slipped a hood over him noticing another child who was perhaps following.

As Barabbas let Nabeel down on the cave floor he removed the hood; the youngster whispered, *"wow!"* his eyes wide a huge grin broke across his face, mouth wide open, the table laden with fruits, breads and jibbon (cheese) seemed to beckon him. "Sit down young lad and make yourself at home, eat as much as you like while we await the arrival of this man you are seeking."

The abundance of food distracted the boy, eyes darting from one dish to another yet he dug in stuffing his earth laden lips with figs then bread then cheese and back to the fruit then more cheese. The food was being forced through the cavernous hole in his face so fast he couldn't swallow with the speed that necessitated his chewing as bits of food fell to the floor where a large dog was grateful for the leavings. The Patriots watched in pleasant awe nodding their approval for their leaders had taught them to share, they smiled as they watched this youngster put away more food than his little tummy could hold. Concerned that he could gorge himself Barabbas said, "Alright my young friend that is enough for you we don't want you to become ill." He moved the food away from the youngster saying, "Come with me now lie down upon this pallet and get some shut eye, we will locate Schumer soon." Knowing Schumel was due in from the northern headquarters he would await his partner's arrival outside the forest. As he came out of the forest area he caught a glance of the young man he had seen earlier; ah yes another gaunt young one who needed a home. Saying aloud, "I will walk a distance now and await the arrival of my second in command for he should be arriving very soon." He glanced back for he heard somebody following him and here was the two who felt as if Giant was something like a father to them. Ayoub and Majheed had to walk quite fast in order to keep up with the man's long strides. Ayoub's voice still as shrill as it ever was, "Don't walk so fast big man we want to greet Schmuel with you." They followed the well worn path which they had taken for years a hundred yards as the path took a ninety degree turn around a small building. Majheed ran to get ahead of Barabbas as he rounded the building and they heard a smaaacck and they saw Majeed, who had run into a youngster and was lying on top of him. "Aha," shouted Barabbas, "this is the young man I looked for when I found Nabeel and took him in, Majheed don't be so hard on young people, ha, ha." A knot was growing on Majeed's forehead and the young man under him was gasping for breath. Barabbas reached down picking both them up.

Majheed was able to stand on his own but Barabbas cradled the alien youngster, "Come men let's get this young man into a shelter for he is out cold and looks as if he might need something to eat." As they turned to return to the hideaway they heard the familiar voice of Schmuel shout after them, "Hello my General is that any way to conscript new members to our cause, I hope everybody is O K?" Barabbas shouted back, "Welcome home Schmuel

I hope your travels have brought good things to our cause, sorry but I must hurry for this young man needs my attention immediately!"

Schmuel followed them into the cave as Barabbas attended to the young man Ayoub brought cold water making poultice for his and the youngsters head. Soon the young stranger awoke and rose from his pallet he spied the food his eyes grew telegraphing the deprivation in his body. "You look fine now young man come, eat be comfortable." the youngsters eyes flitted from Ayoub then to Schmuel and Barabbas questioning the fallibility of the offer for many times in similar situations food had been dangled before him as a prize then when his answers were wrong the prize had been withdrawn. The Giants eyes sparkled and he motioned for the youngster to dig in. Without hesitation he dove into the food with both hands flying. Acting the guardian Ayoub grasped the youngsters hand softly, "Slowly, slowly no rush eat all you can but I will watch to see that you do not gorge." The youngster stopped, thinking he had done something wrong. He cautiously smiled then slowly began to really enjoy his fare. They all watched as a feeling of warmth engulfed them pleased with the orphans honesty. Soon he leaned back smiling, "This is the first time I have ever been given food and never this much I am sorry for eating so much." His true feelings overwhelmed he began sobbing tears streamed down his face mingling with the remainder of dust on him. He sobbed trying to speak, "sssooo, gasp, sooor gasp, sooorr, gasp", while the gasping kept his little head bouncing up and down as one would when sobbing so tremendously.

Barabbas' heart went out to the youngster and he picked him up holding him tightly to keep him from sobbing, "Please don't cry young man you are with friends and none will harm you, relax, you need some sleep." The kind words quieted the young man. Finally when he could he tried to explain in between sobs, "I do not think you will like me when I tell you what I have done, oh, oh, oh I must tell you I followed Nabeel here and then went to the Roman guard telling them I saw you. They have been looking for people like you and I was told the Magistrate would make me rich for helping to find you."

He broke down and again began sobbing for he had never experienced such respect and it would be his wish to reverse his actions of the last hour. Then Nabeel sprang from his position on the floor of the cave, "Yes, yes, for I witnessed your friend Ezra's last minutes," as he turned to Schmuel explaining, "I was to find you and warn you, as he told me, he would be forced to tell where your hideaway was for I pleaded with him to tell for their next move would be to pull his fingernails out." They shivered thinking what horrendous and indescribable pain this would produce. Suddenly warnings from outside the cave could be heard from far away echoing closer and closer.

Schmuel and Barabbas jumped simultaneously toward the opening in the cave Barabbas speaking first. "O K men everybody on the rope and the stone," half of them pulled on the stone while the rest got behind the huge eight foot boulder. Barabbas kicked the large rock used to break the large boulder and they began pulling and pushing and suddenly the huge boulder rolled into place hiding the opening. Soon they could hear commands being shouted in Roman at first in the distance then the voice grew closer to their cave, "All right men somewhere near here is the hideout of the so called Patriots; look for an old building in the forest or maybe a large clearing deep inside. There will be great rewards for finding the location." Then another voice, "Captain I hope the information from that young scallywag is right he said he saw them come directly into the forest. Perhaps there is a cave in the side of this hill I will take my men and circle the hill to look for an opening." Then scurrying, shouting and running could be heard as Schmuel held his finger over his lips then opening both hands and in a sweeping motion to each side which told the men to lay quiet

****

Morning found the new youngster within the arms of Schmuel lying on the cave floor where they settled the eve before staying quiet while the Roman guards searched the area. Barabbas stirred then stood with his finger upon his lips warning them again in case the Romans had left a guard near the area. Barabbas nodding to Fouad made motion to the top of the cave and Fouad slowly climbed to the trap door using hand holds which had been cut into the side of the walls of the cave, to the escape route they had devised in case it were ever needed.

There above his head was a two foot square cage like door Haleem had fashioned with small branches of trees laced together with vines and just enough dirt to allow grass to grow over the top. Slowly raising the cap peering in all directions sure no guard had been left, he crawled out staying on his stomach to the top of the hill. On his head a tiara of limbs and greenery. Peering over the side of the hill toward the city he slowly spun until he had searched the full 360 degree and when he was positive there were no spies stationed near he signaled a thumbs up denoting an all clear then shook his hand with his index finger showing, that meant O K for the first go round but now he would check again. Repeating his previous actions once again he was now assured everything was clear.

Climbing back into the cave, "I saw nothing at all except I could tell some of the limbs had been chopped off but other than that they seem to have found nothing." Then from in front of the cave opening they heard the unmistakable sound of the heavy animal skin shoe afixed with heavy wooden souls warned them Roman guards were ouside of the cave.

The Patriots were in the process of rolling the huge boulder back in place when one of the men held up his hand. They held their positions until they could verify it was a soldier for they could not see out. Barabbas, Captain Schmuel and Jameel had anticipated this might happen and had drawn up a plan. Now was the time for a game of fox and hounds.

Two men would climb up through the escape gate then the first would ease himsself over the top of the hill and down onto the ground. The second would circle until he was seen by the enemy then he would fein surprise, taking off running at top speed toward the deep forest knowing the Romans would follow. After that another two would follow close behind and head for the deep were all deep forest. The fox would then feign exhaustion, turn and face the Soldier.

So as the plan worked Jameel was the first one down from the top of the hill and as he rounded the turn and saw the Roman soldiers he spun and at his top speed ran toward the jungle area. Surprised and delighted two Romans sprang after Jameel, "Stop in the name of the Roman Magistrate," Jameel just laughed as Big Tanoush, almost seven foot tall, and the other huge boulder of a man, Kodaan, a Eunuch, followed just close enough to watch but not so close the soldier would know they were behind him. After circling within the deepest part of the forest then slowing down little by little allowing his buds to catch up then stopped, panting hard almost dropping to the ground Jameel leaned over grasping his knees with each hand and gasping for breath wheezed, "I give up," gasp, "I cannot run any further what is it you want of me, gasp?" "I arrest you in the name of the Roman Magistrate, ha, ha, ha, we will receive a reward for this!" Pulling leather restraints from his tunic they began tying the wrists of Jameel, being engrossed in this function they did not hear the two mammoths behind him. The Patriots took the guards in tow; first masking their eyes then binding them hands and feet. Jameel using his dagger cut a large hanging vine which they strapped onto the leather binds of the men's wrists then Kodaan pulled the opposite end of the vine raising the soldiers slowly into the air. "We have not covered your mouth which will allow you to scream for help, so it should not be long until they find you." Then just loud enough for the soldier to hear him Kodaan, in his deep resounding voice said, "Now let's get back to Yemen before they find him, lets first go east then we will cut south that should throw them off."

For the first time in their existence the Patriots had a great deal to worry about. Barabbas decided they would move back to their location in the north. Once again half of them took the northeast route and the rest the northwest trail. Inside the cave they rolled the boulder back in place so from the outside during the warmer months the vines would cover it then in the colder months the boulder was so large it fully covered the opening. Within an hour the sun slowly eased itself behind the Western Mountains and the cave was spotless again. Barabbas stood saying, "We will follow our usual plan and moving out group by group. Now three at a time up and out slowly then join your group leader at the designated spot. Travel slowly pay your way and *do not steal nor take anything free, pay for everything you eat and drink. Do not make yourselves conspicuous, watch to see you are not followed. If any problems arise your leader whoever he be either myself or Schumel, will make necessary decisions or changes. BE ON YOUR WATCH!* We will meet just south of Nazareth at the usual location, begin!"

TOO CAUTIOUS?
SURPRISE, SURPRISE!

Three days later Barabbas' group suspecting they might have been followed, split into two groups. Theirs was the inland route to Gennesaret and as they approached the oasis just south of Nazareth all of them heaved sighs of relief for it looked as though they were not followed after all. Barabbas' and his men sat down in a small clearing atop a small mesa where they could overlook any approaching caravans or riders. "Aha, we have come a long way, soon we will be joined by our brother Patriots and three of you can move into Nazareth for additional food and water for what we have left will not substantiate our needs."

Barabbas' eyes were closing as he rested his head against a rock grown over with greenery, "All of you get some rest they will be here soon enough."

Soon except for the two sentries Judah & Kallial they were dozing. Now that two runners had circled one southeast the other southwest returned to report no followers. Nagiatee Jamoun a Captain of the Roman Guard sent to follow the Patriots was pleased as he watched Kallial and Judah return to their camp and watching from afar could tell by their relaxed attitude had reported none following them.

The Great Magistrate Simon had found Nagiatee in the African Corps, this man was the ultimate in trappers cold hearted never giving up until his quarry had been found. Nagiatee followed them from the densest part of the forest and slowly trailed them staying inside the cover of the trees then waited not far from the Patriots until the yellow and red rays of the sun had turned to deep gray in the west at which time their leader one Nagiatee Jamoun sent four of his best men to take care of Barabbas' sentries whispering, "You Jaman with Narooth will take the north and you Dubnoon and Daergh will take the south sentry. Do not kill but only stifle them so they cannot give a warning only then signal when you have accomplished this."

As Nagaitee and his band waited the four slowly circled the clearing then waited until they saw the others. What they did not see was Barabbas' second unit who had fortuitously watched as Nagaitee and his band had slowly crept upon Barabbas' group. Jameel signaled two of his smallest men to the north and two to the south motioning them to take care of the two attackers while the balance of unit two circled around the remaining attackers to make sure they would not play a part of any misdemeanor upon the Patriots.

Just at the moment Jaman, Naroot, Duboon and Daergh raised their cudgels Samir, Sameel, Fouad and Judah, of Barabbas' second unit struck their blows upon their enemies. Each of them caught their foe settling them quietly to the ground. Jaman put his fingers over his lips making the sound of a night bird; waiting six seconds he made the sound again and out of the darkness came the attack force headed for the clearing. Suddenly their enemies faced burning lanterns and turned to go back but now they were facing unit two.

Jameels group did not move they just stood there smiling. Then Jameel stepped forward, "Well now it looks as though the hunted has become the hunter. Gentlemen let us give our guests a rousing welcome for I believe they would like to *hang around* for a while!" He turned as Barabbas and the remainder of the group walked up applauding the Patriots. "Jameel, my Lieutenant, what are your plans for your guests will you have them for dinner or what is your pleasure?" Laughing loudly and grabbing the hands of his men they danced around singing.

"I will show you my General what I have in store for these gents; you see I am going to hang them." At that the aliens gasped and most of them turned white as the sands of the Big Sea. Then Jameel began laughing and his men joined in for they knew his plans. "Come bring them into our humble abode, encircle them and we will have some fun. Come Kodaan bring your cooking crock for we have a surprise for you." "Most of the guard had never seen a Nubian dressed in such a fine headress and of course it was surprising to see a black man with nothing but wrappings around his middle. Never had they seen a human being this large their eyes grew ever larger as he entered the clearing licking his lips and smiling an ankle bracelt with gaily colered feathers hanging. He walked over to the fattest of the group feeling his body all over and squeezing the fat parts of the man and in a deep bass voice and thick African accent, "Um Yum dis one luke best ha ha," as he squeezed harder on the man's middle, "feel fat maybe taste good, lots fat," turning to Jameel, "hold him I get big cauldron." He rolled his hands together in delight and giggling, "he, he, he."

    The Patriots could hardly hold their laughter for watching these would be assassins whose color went from normal to powder white. Two of the men fainted crumpling to the ground with a thud while the fat boy Kodaan had caressed was trembling and the pores of his body must have grown for perspiration was almost flowing from his body his clothes were rapidly soaked as he shouted. "Oh Zeus please save me from this catastrophe and I will build a giant statue to you that can be seen for miles. Nagiatee I thought you told me when I joined we would be the strongest gang in the land and you would make us rich, please save me." Barabbas laughing, "I must tell you fat boy Nagiatee has lost his enthusiasm for he is lying in a heap next to me." The Patriots were having a ball at the expense of their attackers. Barabbas motioned Jameel to follow him into the darkness and when they were out of hearing of the rest he said quietly, "Now lets have some fun have the Nubian come and pick up the fat one and take him out of the clearing. I will tell Majheed to wait for Kodaan outside the clearing and when he takes the boy out, Majheed will take care of the rest, we will have great fun!"

Those other guards, inside the clearing, had settled down awaiting the next move, relieved that it was not them to be the next dinner for this big black man; yet they were not prepared for what was about to happen. Kodaan peered around the large opening and when all had seen his shinning black face he strolled in licking his chops and drooling. He walked directly up to the young obese lad raising him under his arm and walked out, the young man screaming and pleading for his life. "Please, please don't eat me I know I will be tough and I am not as sweet as I look." When the lad was picked up his face was almost beet red and all those eyes watching grew huge as his face went from red to chalky white consuming the boy's entire countenance. He continued pleading until they could not make out what he was saying for his voice had been muffled. The Patriots knew the voice of Majheed but the others could not know what they heard was not their own man.

Kodaans' voice loudly, "Aha soon the water will boil but I think I will put you in so you can become accustomed and it will make you more tender become accustomed to the heat you will not notice it as you pass out." Then the screaming voice of Majeed, "Oh no please oh my oh please help me Zeus I pray to you help, help help, help, help, help," until the voice could not be heard anymore. It became deathly quiet for about three minutes which seemed an eternity then the voice of Kodaan broke, "Phew, phew, not taste good!" They could hear him spitting, "I find better tasting one, I go look." The Nubian came back into the clearing walking around the strangers reaching down and caressing them one at a time then finally saying, "Phooey none ripe enough," acting disgusted he left.

Before the Patriots left their guests by themselves, Barabbas, wearing a mask along with the Nubian Kodaan said to Schmuel, "Oh I almost forgot did you tell them of the giant bats inhabiting this area?" Barabbas said loudly, "Should we tell them, oh I guess we should because if they are bitten their screams will direct the rest of the bat population toward that noise." Then turning toward the captives who were listening intently Barabbas said, "I should tell you only shout and make noises for attention during the day for if you make any noises during the night the huge bats inside this clearing will eat you alive." Barabbas had caught two huge bats earlier and tying them together so that when one saw them from a distance it looked as if it were one humongous bat the wingspan being almost eight feet wide. Jameel had tied a piece of cane to span both bats then hung it from a tree with a very thin black thread not to be seen and Barabbas nodded toward the high tree and Jameel pulled on the cord which allowed the bat to swirl down toward those on the ground. Mahjeed gave a blood curdling and very noisy hiss to correspond with the descending bat. Jameel let the bat drop with a swoosh within inches of one of the captives as it brushed his ear. Screaming a spine tingling shout that rang across the clearing frightening his comrades, "Oh, oh, ohhhhhh my ear is gone he took my ear off *and ,and ,and."* the man's voice trailed off as he plummeted to the ground his face buried in the soft grass.

    The Patriots laughter was being stifled yet they were rolling on the ground holding their mouths shut tightly for fear of giving the ruse away. Narrowing his eyes Barabbas loudly whispered, "They are called Tiger bats and only eat during the day and follow the noises to their prey, so remember do not shout or talk in the daylight only at night." Barabbas and his men bound them hand and foot then tied them to vines and pulled them high into the trees that when the soldiers traipsed through the area during the day they were not seen and of course were not heard for if they shouted they might be eaten by the Tiger bats.

****

    Later the Roman Magistrate of Nazareth was inundated with reports of strange noises coming from the

Two Men Named Jesus

forest near the oasis, horrible eerie sounds as that of ghosts, spirits, ogres and more. This was the most intense pressure ever put upon this office and the Office manager brought in two additional scribes to handle the overflow and the Captain of the Palace Guard was called to help. More soldiers were sent to the area to search finding nothing after three nights and four days could find nothing then finally his men having been missing for three nights and four days and as he stood face to face with his General neither of them knowing their next move. They sat their faces a study in pure puzzlement when General Icknobells said, "Take the entire cadre of 60 men and search for the bodies must be found even if they are dead."

If it had not been for a brave young boy of fourteen nothing but bones would have been eventually found of them. This was the third day and a young man and his dog entered the area that none others would enter for trepidation had set in for miles around. The news spread speedily with the crowds growing hourly yet the perimeter around the search maintained itself for none would come closer for fear of the unknown. There was stationed only three guards at that perimeter though none were needed. A gasp came from the crowd as they watched young Aspathian Nobrieaty and his dog yabraht (rolled grape leaves) walk slowly past the guards and they could only watch with awe. Aspathian's ego and bravery were boosted by those watching him, yet he slowed as he neared the entrance of the forest and the Roman guards knew he would not enter the forbidden area. Then a grin pressed itself upon Aspathian's countenance as he gained another inch of ego. The unusual thing about this crowd was they were extremely quiet; now, if they had been, as most crowds, noisy, the prisoners hanging in their upside down prison would have heard them and that would have saved them, but, with their backs to the forest they did not see this brave youngster with his dog enter the dark forest while the crowd awaited with anxious anticipation. The longer it took the further away the multitude retreated for they knew not what might take place. It was so very silent that any noise within miles could be heard.

They waited and waited and waited until *suddenly* it seemed the ground shook and the trees began to bend in the wind for shouting could be heard from inside the green cave. Words could not be made out for there was so very much noise that grew louder and louder and when the multitude heard it they also began shouting. Some began running in the opposite direction but the most resolute of them remained their eyes open in fear and misapprehension yet retreating very slowly still keeping their eyes on the opening of the forest.

Meanwhile inside the forest Aspathian and his dog slowly, very slowly moved toward an area of the undergrowth that looked to be a brighter spot where the sun was shining down. As he slowly approached that area and entered he must have jumped three feet off the ground for all ten of those enemies of the Patriots saw him at the same instant and they began screaming their heads off which startled him so completely he rose in the air and landed on his bottom looking up at the men all screaming like a bunch of banshees. The Roman guards with their lances and swords drawn charged the area as fast as possible. As they entered the clearing they saw Aspathian pointing into the air and looking up they saw one of the most unusual sight their eyes had ever witnessed. All they could hear was ten voices shouting variances "Get us down from here, yallah (hurry) we are running out of blood soon we will perish! Hurry!"

This would be a lesson for these thieves who attempted to get the best of the "King of Thieves" and they would now carry the tale of the fearless Patriots throughout the world, although none would know what had happened in that forest for those enemies of the Patriots would never divulge their indiscretions for they messed up big time and allowed themselves to become the attacked. And so their notoriety grew and the stories, true or imagined, flourished as the months stumbled over themselves and the tales turned into legend fueled by those imagining themselves as pupils of this fearless group.

****

S. Eugene Cohlmia

Barabbas, Schmuel, Ayoub, and Majheed were sitting at the east gate of Jerusalem basking in the sun one morning in May partaking of their favorite breakfast and surrounded by a milling crowd, Majheed punched Barabbas, "Listen, listen to what this guy to your left is saying." They all leaned closer toward that table behind theirs craning to hear the conversation. "I tell you it was the wildest melee I have ever witnessed in my life." The man speaking then turned to his right saying, "Tell them Falfal, tell them what we saw was it not a fight or what." He did not give his partner time to tell his part for he continued the fable. "I swear Barabbas was at least eight feet tall as the soldiers charged him running down the hill with their spears and swords, there were twenty soldiers," The other man piped up, "At least," as the first teller not missing a beat persistently continued, "and you will not believe what that giant of a man did; as three of the soldiers charged down the hill their spears locked in an attack position, Barabbas grabbed the spears, the soldiers holding on to the weapons, and using the spears as a handle swung the three in the air and when he released his hold upon the spears the three Romans sailed through the air for at least fifty yards," inhaling as quickly as possible he gasped, "then when the other soldiers saw this they fled; I tell you I have never seen anything like it," gasp, gasp, "and that Barabbas with fair skin and that almost blond hair looked like a giant Adonis, oh you should have been there it was a sight to behold, him with that beautiful smile of his." The other gent wanted his few minutes in the spot light also, "Yea, well how about those other Patriots they were not afraid of anything they strolled around the gate eating and drinking the sellers provided them with anything they wanted, and, and, and I heard that he gave a farmer forty shekels for no reason at all." Perhaps the story of another hooded man stealing from the rich and giving to the poor had its histrionics here in this historical City. The tales propagated it seemed as the legend of Barabbas and his Patriots grew.

****

On his own without the knowledge of Barabbas, Schmuel had schooled three friends sending one each month to the headquarters of the Magistrate asking for a job. It had taken almost three months for one of them to land the job. During the training sessions of Litellia, Manchunia and Fellinia, Schmuel made sure the three of them were alone for this was to be a secretive mission. They would continue making inquiries attempting to be hired in the Magistrates office. After some time nothing was working so Schmuel told Manchunia to apply and if they said no he was to tell them he would work for nothing for a while and if they agreed after two weeks they would hire him. The controller of that office agreed and so now Manchunia was employed by their nemeses Simon Antropidous.

The Legend Grows - Riches Parallel

After a trip to Genneseret to clear out the headquarters and sell off all the treasures of the last two months the group returned. For a year the assembly of the City of Tiberius worked to reach an agreement with Circus, Circus, of Rome to perform at their civil anniversary. Now with the agreement signed came a large troop of Jugglers, Magicians, Acrobats and other acts along with the reigning Champion Chariot driver, the Champion of the Horse races and fifty of the best, fastest and experienced fighters who would stage mock battles. There would be displays of trained animals as well. This would be a time of reverie for those fans would come from all over the Provence and it would be something to behold for some the only chance ever to see anything as amazing as what they were about to witness.

Once more the Patriots were warned of their responsibilities; know your group only, do not speak to other Patriots not in your group. In the event they accidently ran into each other they were to ignore one another as if they were aliens. Some took boats across the Sea of Galilee, others around the Sea and others travelled the eighteen mille hugging the coastline to Taricheae then southeast to Tiberius. Schmuel's last instructions were, "If you are arrested recall your oath of secrecy. Remember Ezra gave his life to keep us free, he lives yet within us as his reminder to remain diligent. He rose speaking with them and Barabbas noticed for the first time the gray hairs on Schmuel's head and he reflected thinking, *"I know it has taken time for those colors to come into his hair but why am I just now noticing it?"* Ayoub and Mahjeed nodded their heads knowing what Giant was thinking. Schmuel, The Old Man, as they were now want to call him continued his instructions. "You have all been given "the seed" and have sworn to use, as a last resort, in the event you are captured and cannot face the interrogation or punishment that will follow." Some of the men felt into their tunics to make sure they had the packet of drugs that would put them to sleep making their interrogators assume they were dead. It was a drug brought from Madagascar by a Dundoony Machadoom who came to be one of their members.

The day a new intrant from Madagascar was sworn into the Patriots was to be a great milestone. Machadoom slowly took stock of them noting that all the directions and decisions seemed to come from Schmuel and

Barabbas together. After six months he approached Schmuel. "Sir may I speak to you on what I believe is a very important matter?" Schmuel answered, "Come follow me into my offices tell me what it is that seems to be bothering you." Machadoom sat and wasted no time. "Each time we are to go on a raid or a new assignment you remind us of our vows, yes?" Schmuel nodded assent, "Why yes Dundoony and I will continue to do so!" "Oh yes Sir Captain but I believe I have information as to an item that would help us all," pausing he rose reaching into his cache and taking out a leather bag. "Here Sir is a mixture of plants used as a drug when chewed then swallowed will make one pass out and give the impression that one is dead and upon inspection none can argue the point. After some one to two hours, depending on the person, one will awake anew as if nothing has transpired; it is a remarkable thing for I have actually tried it." Schmuel was of course impressed and after several trials with the drug he was convinced and so each member was given a dose to be utilized *only* as a last resort.

****

The opening day of Circus Circus dawned to find huge crowds moving upon the City of Tiberius. It was a sea of humanity flowing into the area from all directions for if one stood on the highest hill where Herod Antipas, founder of this city, built sculptor after sculptor of himself that future generations might praise him, one could imagine that sea moving toward the City yet never ending.

A remarkable city; Herod built it on the same design of Hellenistic and Roman City's whereupon the streets crossed each other at right angles, a most unusual plan for cities in in this The Syrian Peninsula, and those new to this City were quite amazed.

The beautiful Stadium on the seashore also built by Herod Antipas would hold only a portion of this mass of humanity speedily building to a crescendo as the horns, lyres and viols slowly but aggressively advancing upon the ears of the mass developing its own tempo when suddenly it seemed as if the lyres and viols were directed to fade and accept the boom, boom, boom of its base drum having developed its own set of do at a musical production. The Patriots were extremely pleased for a gathering of this magnitude where each group or body of people seemed to move in no certain direction as though a whirlpool had been divided into countless other pools and it made no difference which direction one moved you were always with and against the flow. With one constantly pushing and bumping ones way through this sea the Patriots were taking advantage of their good luck. As always the poor were passed up by the thieves for they would concentrate on the well dressed and the upper class easily noted yet at the same time those in need might find a surprise when they reached home or into their tunics for that too was an important part of the King of Thieves instruction. "We must help those in need take from those wealthy who can well afford it and give to those who have less." Those same recipients might find themselves stopped, pulled aside and given certain gifts with a well intended lecture. "Do not expect these gifts again; now make good use of these and learn to earn what you receive." That direction was given the Patriots by their "Old Man," Schmuel.

Moving through the crowd Tanoush' group made up of himself, Haleem, Jonathon, Jaman and Narooth working slowly through the crowd as Barabbas, Schmuel, Ayoub and Jameel being group leaders mingled throughout the crowd outside and inside the stadium watching for Simon Antropidous' personal Ascharri (soldiers or police) answering directly to him.

One could well recognize those ascharri for they wore Simons crest upon each sleeve of their outer garment that all would recognize their allegiance which was another ego builder for, The Great Magistrate, this being his own description of himself. As they moved through the ever expanding crowd Jameel, one of the most adept at this trade like his brother thieves all having been well trained by the two Greeks, Cleothus and Corythus experts at this game, was moving slowly through the crowd behind a well dressed man whom he assumed was a merchant. Jameel continued following this man thinking in his mind he had found a real mark. He glances around for any of his men for he wants to do the bump and run. The first thief bumps hard into the mark and immediately the second thief picks his pocket. Together they confuse the mark for he only feels one person bumping into him. Following this well dressed gent who has a mantle of blue with small gold disc's sewn into the hem of the garment flowing behind him as he walks. He glances up and sees, yes it is; great it is Haleem. Haleem, noting the glow on Jameel's face and seeing who he is following, perceives his buddies next move nods toward Jameel meaning, "I've got the message." Within ten seconds Haleem is approaching the mark walking in the opposite direction. The gentleman is smiling for he is enjoying the roar of the crowd and the mass of people.

Suddenly Haleem bumps the gent's left side so hard he loses balance and falling (what luck) Jameel reaches out catching the man before he hits the ground. Jameel could not ask for a better situation for as he helps the man by steadying him he helps himself to the marks valuables; that being a large bag from inside the wealthy mans tunic. The Gentleman sputters saying, "Thank you, thank you young man I possibly would have harmed myself if you had not been so kind as to catch me." Then reaching into his tunic, "Here my good man, allow me to reward you for your kindness," pulling another leather bag and reaching inside it bringing out a Gold Daric (worth 20 Sheckel's) and a Silver Drachma handing them to Jameel who genuflected saying, "Sir I thank you for your generosity but it is really not necessary for it was my pleasure to assist you." Just then another Gentleman, dressed in the same manner as the first approached them. "Kallensia, my friend, are you all right, I saw you fall fortunately this youngster caught you, you should reward him." "Oh my dear friend I *have* rewarded *and* thanked him." Turning toward Jameel then saying, "May I know your name young man?" For a moment Jameel was flustered for he had his mind on the bag he had just stolen from this man and knew he should flee but before Jameel could answer Haleem ran up saying, "Come Cresantius we must go for we are late and we told your mother we would meet her at the city building." Not waiting for any more conversation he grabbed the arm of Jameel and raced toward the outer section of the arena bumping his way through the crowd when they heard a shout and looking back Jameel saw the mark screaming, "Police, police I have been robbed, I have been robbed." They ran toward the opening when they saw three guards dressed in the colors of the Magistrate attempting to get through the crowd to the mark. When they saw the guards they slowed for they did not want to bring notice upon themselves. They locked arms and pretending to be drunk slowly walked toward their goal laughing. As they approached the guards they made a ninety degree turn and began moving somewhat faster. Their scam worked and the guards paid them no heed as Jameel and

Two Men Named Jesus

Haleem walked out of the arena heaving great sighs of relief. "That was a close call my friend you made a nice haul but we left the codger with his other bag, come let's see the take." "No, no Haleem you know the rules, never open or study your take until you are completely in the clear." "Yes my friend I am sorry but I am sure that is one of the greatest hauls you have ever made for that man had to be a Senator or a high up mucky muck, don't you think?" Having reached the outer limits of the crowd Jameel sat down on a boulder near the walkway saying, "I am sure it is one of the best takes ever when we get home we will see." Turning toward the arena again Haleem asks, "Should we go back now, I don't think we will be suspect in that crowd, see I have this huge mustache which I will put under my nose and you can use that ugly mop you carry on top of your head with your patch over your eye; I think we will be safe, OK lets go." "Listen to me Haleem have you forgotten your training, do you not recall the rule, we are not to return to that venue?" Haleem shrugged his shoulders, "Wow what picking's we're missing." "Not to worry we will return tomorrow for much more."

The following morning Barabbas speaking to his men, "Yesterday was very lucrative although it seems Jameel and Haleem became separated, when they finally connected they were both busy with a Mark it seems. They had no third and the situation became fairly tense for the mark found too quickly he had been robbed but for the crowd they may they have been caught! It seems our dear friend, the Magistrate, may have flooded the city with his own men along with the regular Roman guards." He paused, took a long sip on his coffee cup saying, "We will begin this day and every day we are here to work in threes. I hope there is no need to explain so take turns at being the lookout while your brother Patriots work the crowd. Keep a sharp eye out for the Magistrates men for they are not easy to spot until you see the crest on their shoulders. That's it men now go and have a successful outing, once more be *very, very careful*."

****

Working Circus Circus was going smooth, and the Patriots had collected many items of extreme value, until the fourth day. This morning's instructions were being recited by Schmuel, "Men, we are on our last day working Circus where I feel we may have spent too much time consequently I want to put you on your best watch, be aware of all the happenings around you, as you select a mark make sure that person is alone and if not separate the two. As always do not work more than two at a time unless you are able to flip-flop them. Go to work but if you become tired take a break and relax."

****

They arrived at or near the arena in groups of threes and paid no attention their fellow Patriots.

Two Men Named Jesus

    Samir, Yantouny and Narouth separated and began walking through the mass of people staying at a sure distance where they could watch one another. Samir signaled his partners by raising his hand high into the air and pointing toward a very well dressed man slowly strolling through the vendors. Samir following the gentleman almost attached himself to that man. Samir strolled at the same pace as the gent and when the mark moved Samir moved with him. When Samir was sure Yanatoun and Narouth were ready Samir began a conversation with the gentleman, "Oh what a great find," he said out loud and sure enough the gentleman looked to see what he may have missed. Samir was holding up a beautiful and most unusual large silver coffee server having a spout and handle of gold. Holding it up Samir was giving it the once over very slowly turning it over and over. "I believe this is one of the most unusual breet (carafe) I have ever seen," holding it up and calling for the merchant of the booth, "Sir, tell me about this breet?" The merchant hoping for a quick sale, stepped up saying, "It seems you have found one of the most precious coffee servers I have ever seen, a real treasure that has come to me from the country of Rus and is extremely valuable." By now Samir had the attention of the mark and soon would take him as he listened to the dissertation yet not hearing a word.

    "Thank you for the information, I will return with my wife and make you an offer." "I will be here but do not think you are going to bargain me out of this item." Still with the breet in his hand Samir turned somewhat putting him nearer the mark who asked, "May I see that Sir I am interested in such treasures and it will soon be our wedding anniversary and it would be an ideal gift for wife of many years." As he said this Yanatoun slightly bumped the mark into the counter keeping his head down so as not to be seen and when the gent raised looking toward the crowd on his right Narouth crashed into the gent from the opposite side. This was Samir' chance to convince the mark he was a helper as he grabbed the man around the waist holding him up Samir picked the man's treasures from inside his tunic and as he straightened he flipped the bag to Yanatoun. As Yanatoun was rushing away three men with large mantels with cloak attached turned to block his way. Throwing off their cowls they captured Yanatoun with only a small struggle. Yanatoun had not had a chance to pass off the bag taken from the gentleman so he relaxed and would take his punishment. As they bound his wrists he saw six men of the same ilk take Samir and Narouth into custody. As the crowd fell back allowing the police an aisle to remove the three they began hollering unintelligibly which sounded like, "Mauhubnee, mauhubnee, mauhubnee, mauhubnee!" Which meant absolutely nothing to anybody other than the Patriots, and to them it simply meant, "Trouble, your Patriot brother needs help." Of course upon hearing this resounding across the mass of people only the Patiots who understand the meaning. They all ceased their actions falling back to their lair immediately.

"So now they have beaten us at our own game," Stated Schmuel, "they set a trap and we fell for it all the way!" Barabbas, "Yes it is done now, we were not expecting this so I sent Jameel and Kallial to follow the Roman guards to find where they will house the captives, when they return we will work out a plan to get them released," sighing loudly! Catching the eye of Barabbas, Schmuel tossed his head toward the cave opening and walked outside. Soon Barabbas strolled out following Schmuel into the forest to a spot behind a huge shrub where they could see out but could not be seen. "Do you have any idea how we will free them?" "No but let's not forget they know we'll attempt a try." They quieted when they heard voices approaching. Looking out they saw Jameel & Kallial and waved them over that they could speak to them before going inside to the crowd.

"Where have they taken them," asked Barabbas. Jameel glanced at Kallial smiling then said, "You won't believe this but that Magistrate is very cunning," looking at Kallial for support and he nodding yes. "As they left the arena a Cadre of guards approached accompanied by Banfortia the Magistrates Captain of the guard and took our brothers in tow. We fell back so as not to be noticed then followed, dropping off from time to time. They took the three to a building housing the Magistrate, which is near

Herod's jail, so we waited to see which dungeon they would put them in." Kallial took over from there saying, "Just as I was about to turn the corner of the building I heard voices, I jumped behind a large shrub and as I did they brought the three of them out with hoods over their heads and we followed. Each of them had a guard leading him and as we left our hiding place Simon Antropidous hollered at them from the back door whispering something to one of the guards, when he went inside we followed the guards."

Jameel stepped in, "We followed them as they wound their way up one street and down another I suppose to confuse. After thirty minutes they came to that old deserted house that backs up to the hills at the east end of the city. They circled the house until they were sure nobody was watching and took them inside. We waited ten minutes then peeked inside our guys were strapped to a large post in the middle of the room and hobbled so I assumed that is where they would remain." "Yea we thought this might be a diversion and they would move them again, but I guess not from the way they were bound," added Kallial. Back inside the cave Barabbas turned to them stating, "Any suggestions men?" Madool stood saying, "My group believes we can attack and rescue them, we feel our group can do the job ourselves. His group hooted agreement. Never one to discourage his men Barabbas answered, "That may be a plan which I believe we can hold until we hear others?" Then, "Commanders will now meet in his office.

****

Schmuel had pre arranged a meeting place with Denoppolus his spy who by now had been in employment of the Magistrate for several months and with his pleasant personality, blue eyes and ready smile beaming from a Greek countenance with blond hair arranged neatly upon his head, fair complexion, he was becoming a favorite of Simon Antropidous. Schmuel met the Greek where none would suspect, in the deepest part of the city where it was dank, dark and most of the time exuded a most nauseating odor for here in the bowels of the City a totally lower class of thieves, robbers and any who remained outside the law resided and most were not want to bathe. With no inlet for water the stench were that of stagnant sewer and the Roman guards dreaded being assigned the weekly inspection. When they did enter it was with a large Cadre heavily armed.

Wearing cowls over their heads which would hide most of their faces Schmuel asked, "What have you for me." "Nothing much my Lord, the Magistrate keeps much to himself and has only a few confidants." "You mean you have not heard of the capture of our three men?" asked Schmuel, surprised and shocked the spy answered, "No, no I did not know of it for you see when anything of great importance happens or is about to take place I along with the other non official employees are ordered to retire to our rooms." "Then we must make you much more valuable to Simon and possibly you will glean information we can utilize, now go, and hang the flag when you have information." The flag Schmuel referred to was hung in a huge oak tree near the forest when Deanoppolus had a message he would hand a red flag one which resembled the leaves of the oak indicating a message.

"Deanoppolus," the Magistrate shouted out his office door, "Come, I have an assignment for you." The young Greek stood at the door waiting to be summoned inside, Simon was so pleased to see the influence he had on his employees he turned toward his Captain jerked his head toward the entrance. A broad smile broke across his countenance the pressure of his ego awaiting a signal to burst forth from his brain. "See Captain how docile this one has become, he is one of my best followers and one can see the love he pours out to me. "Come Deandroppoulos, come in, I have an assignment for you." Simon Antropidus' Captain Postonio, and an Ethiopian was standing near the desk as Simon began, "This is an important mission and you will be under scrutiny the next few weeks so if you are alert and pass the inspection it will mean an increase in your salary." Wow," thought the Greek! Captain Postonio nodded to the Greek to follow him out. Your job is to take a message to my men. Are you familiar with the hill of the big rock on the east end of the City?" He asked. "Yes Captain I know the hill. "Good, make sure you are not followed; when you leave here do not go directly to the house but take an indirect route. When you get there go to the back of the house and rap four times on the door, wait a few seconds then rap twice and wait, if you hear nothing leave and return here but if your last knock is answered by two raps instantly followed by two more then you will wait until the door is opened to deliver this basket of food and provisions. Tell the guards we will move the prisoners soon return immediately again using a surreptitious way back to this office." Do you understand?" Deandropolous smiled, "Yes Sir." Thinking, "Oh man will Schmuel will be happy," still to himself, "Don't get cocky fella' you might trip so watch your step you have many people depending on you." Following his orders he passed through the east gate then out toward the hill of the big rock. Checking again as he passed through the east gate he was bumped by an old hermit. He could tell he was a hermit by the body odor and the sack cloth he wore. As the old fellow bumped him he whispered, "You are being followed by one of the Magistrates own men, I am a Patriot, now push me away and curse at me." Deandropolous acting as if he would regurgitate pushed Truedious aside roughly shouting, "Get out of here you old hermit, no I have no alms for you get away." As he said this people around them laughed. Now thinking "thanks Schmuel I should have known you would send someone to watch."

    He waited a short time after he made his last knock on the door and as he was turning to leave he heard the rapping answer. The door opened and a voice said, "Come in fast." The provisions were yanked off his back unceremoniously almost throwing him to the dirt floor. When his eyes became accustomed to the dark of the house he saw there in the corner tied hand and foot to the wall of the house and to the rafters in the ceiling, "Any message?" Deandropolous relayed the message and left.

****

Schmuel took his morning walk past the oak tree. Sure enough there was a red amid the green leaves. flag which was red. That night Schmuel donned his sack cloth for his meeting with his Roman worker.

Now knowing their three men were for sure kept in the old house at the base of Rock Hill they needed a plan. Barabbas threw out this idea, "We will take twenty men to the old house and walking near the house we will pretend we are partying and raise a racket that will wake him up." Jodan, Judah, Haleem will climb up the hill taking large rock with you then at a signal throw them on the roof and windows of the house making it sound as if the hill is falling. Meanwhile Trogad's group conceal themselves near the door that is the only door. The rest of us will begin shouting very loudly. The guards will react by coming outside to investigate as they exit Jameels group will take them hostage tie them up leaving them inside the old house. We gather our men and return to the den." He paused looking around at his men asking, "Any questions," he paused then, " we must be fast and make no mistakes, be ready?"

Everything went as planned. The three patriots climbed the hill and when they were in position they threw down ropes and those below tied on gunny sacks loaded with rocks. When Jodan, Judah and Haleem were ready each with two large bags of armament they signaled. Their eyes on Schmuel, his arm elevated in the air and dusk settling upon them he waited a few seconds then dropped his hand. The rocks slammed down upon the old house breaking some of the tiles and making a horrific noise while the hooting and shouting of the rest of the Patriots sounded as if the army of Constantine was attacking. The door sprung open three guards running out tripping on the rope Jameel had stretched in front of the door and they spilled all over eating dust. Before they could rise they were hooded so they could not see their attackers then bound hand and foot. When the door opened Schmuel and Barabbas, preceded by Majheed, carrying a flaming club, charged into the house ready to greet their brother Patriots. Majheed held the light up high and there in the corner were the three buddies bound and wrapped in sackcloth. Barabbas pulled the first one up, "We are here my brothers to take you back," Barabbas' voice trailed off as he pulled back the shroud over the man's head. A surprised shout came from the Giant, "Majheed bring the light these are not our men." Schmuels bewildered voice rang out obviously confused,

"Nor is this young man one of ours, aghhh, aghhh Simon Antropidous has duped us again that snake, I believed we made sure our men were"........suddenly his voice trailed off and he shouted, ***"Go, go, go, go, go, go we have been tricked we must scatter, you all know the drill do not stop for anything!"*** Barabbas dropped the prisoner whom he had been holding who crumpled to the floor of the house still bound, Barabba shouting, "Be careful watch every avenue of escape!" Barabbas gathered Majheed in his arms, the suddenness broke Majheed's grip on the flaming log splattering fire over the floor of the house. Seeing this several of the Patriots gathered the three prisoners pulling them and the guards outside away from the burning house. Yes they had been suckered in for the first time. "This Magistrate is as sneaky as the snake he resembles." Barabbas shouted seeing his Patriots scattering in all directions.

****

It was deep night as Barabbas, Schmuel, Ayoub and Jameel stood just outside their cave. Jameel said, "Thanks all of our men have returned none are missing, I can't believe we were as lax as that; how did it happen, we saw them take the three into that house?" "Yes," said Schmuel, "but we did not go back to check and we did not place any of our men there to watch the house, I will take the blame for that, the fault is mine, oh hell!" Barabbas pulled Schmuel to his chest saying, "No no Samir (substitute name for Samuel.) if there is blame it is mine and mine alone for I am the leader of these good men; set up a meeting with our spy in The Magistrates office!

****

The meeting with Deandropolous took place inside the forest just outside the city of Jerusalem. "Ok Deandropolous give us what you can; have you heard anything that can help us." Barabbas suggested. Schmuel now spoke up, "Think of anything that may help, something you may have overheard pertaining to our boys, perhaps you heard something in passing, a small snippet of information." Deandropolous thought deeply his head bowed to the ground with his eyes shut thinking back over the days he had been in the Magistrates office. It was deeply quiet for several minutes seemingly he had fallen asleep, then suddenly his head popped up as if it were on a spring. "Yes I think I heard something, it may not be anything but a week ago they were discussing the arrest of three men and the Captain of the guard saying their new dungeon should be ready soon and they can transfer some of the prisoners, but it meant nothing to me until now." Barabbas quietly answered, "This could be something of course for we know we are like a small spear in Simon A's craw and he would do anything to capture us, and now before I forget send a runner north to warn our brothers in Gennesaret. Looking at Schmuel still deep in thought, Schmuel grabbed the lead in the conversation, "Deandropolous can you give us any information as to the location of this new jail?" The informant shook his head pausing, thinking, then, "I will do my best to find out more but now I must return for they keep track of how much time we are away." Schmuel opened his mouth but Deandropolous held up his hand saying, "Not to worry my Captain for I checked before I came and as always I wormed my way here, I will contact you as soon as I have any information."

****

Two runners were sent north to Gennesaret warning them of the situation in Jerusalem. Schmuel explained, "Tell them to curtail their operations in that area *completely*. Make sure he understands the situation we are in here, I suggest they move the operation, temporary albeit, to Damascus or better yet the smaller town of Abila which is in the Roman district of Abilene, tell him to ferret as much information as possible as to the relationship between that Governor, Tetrarch Lysanias, and his counterpart Simon Antropidas." Barabbas listening, spoke up, "I have given this some thought; I want you to tell Braheem to plant an additional spy in Lysanias' offices," he paused mulling this over, "select a couple of his most outgoing pleasant personalities who can make friends with somebody within the Magistrates office he should let us know when it has been done.

****

Two Men Named Jesus

A few weeks of idleness began to catch up with the Patriots in the Jerusalem district. Arguments broke out daily on extremely trivial matters between the closest of buddies. An afternoon of relaxation saw two of Jameel's aides playing a game of Shatranj almost come to blows as the game progressed. It seemed that Manjour, playing black, had captured one of the Kings Aides belonging to the white team of Caprichion. These two had played this game for years and were the best players of Shatranj among the Patriots. They always laughed and cajoled each other as their game progressed but up to this date had never had as much as a spat no matter who won for over the years they were as evenly matched as two players could be. Upon the capture of his Bishop Caprichion flew into a rage, "Manjour that last move was illegal, I was getting myself a drink and you moved vertically with that horse, I declare a foul and insist you forfeit now!" As he sprang from his chair his face boiling beet red he took a stance primed for a fight. Hearing the commotion which was somewhat unusual Schmuel inserted himself between the two whereupon at that instant Caprichion swung a right toward his best friend Manjour. The blow caught the taller Schmuel on his shoulder almost knocking him to the floor. Jameel dove catching his Captain before he hit the floor and as he pulled Schmuel up turned to Caprichion saying, "I cannot believe your actions, what is happening to you, we all must relax and enjoy this time off, no, no I should have seen this coming for as active as our men are they cannot bind themselves to inactivity for long. Here is what we will do. For the time being we will attempt to relocate our headquarters. I will discuss this with our General Barabbas and will soon make a decision." He sighed heavily continuing, "Meanwhile I challenge you all to begin a search for a new location, moving out of the Judea area toward the north in the district of Samaria. I will not wait for Barabbas' verification of this order I take the onus for I do not know when our leader will return."

Luckily it was only a week until Braheem became a member of the Magistrates office in Caesaria Phillippi. It so happened as Braheem cased the area walking around the building seemingly admiring it he was met by an old friend a chum he ran around with as a youngster. Favarh recognized Braheem immediately, "Braheem Hawany what are you doing here, I can't believe my eyes it is really you? The last time I saw you we were only twelve, remember when my family moved from Bethel to Jericho?" Braheem stood there for several seconds deep in thought for he did not recognize his friend, then he broke into a smile, "Wow Favarh it has been a long time I remember now oh yes what good memories ha, ha, ha. I also recall when we evened the playing field with our nemesis that great big bully. He was about to hit me and I thought you got scared and would not play along, when all of a sudden you came running up behind him jumping to the ground on all fours, gasp, and when I saw you I jammed him in the stomach and ran for cover. I did turn around to see him hit the ground it sounded like a melon, ha, ha, ha, ha," both laughing so hard they fell to the ground their arms locked together. Soon the laughing subsided and Braheem said, "Let's go sit at the gate where we can talk and get some arrack to drink." "Great, great I have just gotten off work for the day. This is going to be a great time, huh?" "You bet," replied Braheem. There is nothing like a friend to bring one down to earth and that is what took place inside the east gate of Caseria Phillippi. They talked of home and family and so much more. "Tell me Braheem what are you doing in Phillippi?" Braheem hesitated for he had not planned on this and was not sure what he should say, so he threw out a test line. Having been schooled by Schmuel, "I hate to tell you this but I am wanted by the Romans in several provinces but I am not sure if," and he laughed, "if uh this is one of them." A smile broke out on Favarh face and he volunteered nothing for he wanted to surprise his buddy, "This is your lucky day my friend, I am in the envious position of being employed by the Magistrate Lysanias and I am able to delve and find out any information you need." Just then the owner of the café smiling asked them to leave, "I have remained open almost an extra hour for I saw the two of you enjoying yourselves." They thanked him and left. Meandering around the city in no particular direction, or at least Braheem thought so, they came to a doorway deep within the city where the streets and the homes were neat and trim. Favarh stopped, put his hand on Braheems shoulder turning him toward the gate of a beautiful courtyard. "Braheem welcome to my home, come in for now this is also your home and I insist without any argument you will live here as long as you like." Braheem opened his mouth to say something but Favarh shook his head saying, "If you are thinking to refuse my offer I will not listen for the only way this will not happen is if you are married and have your own abode someplace." Braheem laughed near tearing up, "No my friend I am not married but I cannot thank you enough for such an hospitable offer; now let me tell you the truth, you will understand soon why I hesitated before and why I did not fulfill my trust in you, wow, I am so glad we found each other." Favarh' face became sober, "Tell me everything, what are you wanted for, did you kill somebody, what dastardly deed are you accused of, none the less I will work to get you cleared of whatever it is, you see I have been schooled in Roman law, now tell me the truth." Of course Braheem thought long and hard finally convinced in his mind everything was copacetic and Favarh was to be trusted, "Do you remember when we were kids and told each other secrets, and do you recall how we sealed our trust for each other?" "Oh yes I recall." Braheem held out his right hand and Favarh took his hand in his left then turning as far around as they could bumped their backs together then they turned back around facing each other, bowed their heads each touching at the others forehead. They then broke that position laughing so hard they fell to the ground.

Braheem finished telling his story to Favarh for now he could tell the truth and not worry that it could harm him or the Patriots. The tale finished as they sat down to eat a scrumptious looking meal the servants placed before them. Small talk continued until Favarh who had been deep in thought for a couple of seconds said, "Braheem I want to be a part of your work, so this will be a meeting place for you, Barabbas and Schmuel as well as any others named by Barabbas, now it is almost morning but we will sleep now," pointing out the window, "for as you see Mister Sun seems to be rushing toward his position in the heavens."

The following morning after a hearty breakfast, "Favarh will you go with me to see Barabbas for nothing is done without his approval and it will allow you to get to know each other?" Favarh smiled for he felt at ease with Braheem and what a pleasure to have this old friend near. "Of course Braheem when would you like to go for I have the rest of today?" "If you will give me time for I must locate my General and talk to him; is it O K if I bring him back here?" "Of course, do not forget what I said earlier, this is your home too and I shall await the meeting."

****

Braheem walked through the beautiful courtyard with its mixture of fruit trees flowering shrubs with flora to brighten the eye of the beholder and stepped out into the street, whose bricks, warming to the sun as it arose, were already accepting a variety of shod feet. Braheem stopped in order to confirm his direction then headed toward the outer part of Phillippi. By the time he reached the next row of homes he stopped, his brow furrowed for his thoughts were buried deep. He turned looking back over the way he had just traversed, his face a picture of uneasiness. Slowly he made his way back toward the home of Favarh, unaccustomed but yet speaking to himself out loud, yet under his breath. "I may have just set up a trap for myself along with my entire crew." The gate to Favarh' home was only thirty feet from him when he stopped looking around, there directly in front of him was a café just opening. Although there were tables on the walkway he went inside looking to find a table from which he could watch the gate of Favarh' home, "Good this is ideal." He took a seat at the rear of the café as the owner smiling, approached totake his order. "Maahrrhaba ah'lain ya zallama shoo bit hib?" (Good day Sir what would you like?) The man offered him another table inviting him to move. Braheem smiled, "Lut (no shookron Ume,[uncle, a form of respect] "May I have coffee and talamy (bread)?" "Awhah,"(yes). Sipping the rich black coffee he watched the gate of Favarhs home, he watched through lunch time and was still there at mid-afternoon with no movement in our out of the house. Thinking "I guess I can trust him and he will never know I suspected him of being an enemy, but then I must protect the position of The Patriots."

"How could this be, what a break for us and what a pleasant surprise for you Braheem." It is hard to believe that we will have a headquarters here in Phillippi, I am overwhelmed with Favarh's hospitality, I hope we find a place for the crew soon for the guys are becoming impatient and fidgety." One could tell Barabbas was extremely pleased with their new situation. They were in Favarh's favorite café having lunch when Schmuel and three of his men entered Schmuel signaling to Barabbas for privacy. "I have found a most ideal location; I will take you there when you are ready, by the way I believe we should give Braheem more responsibility for he has made himself an integral part of the Patriots." Barabbas shrugged, "That is up to Captain if that be your wish, now let us all go inspect our new headquarters." Braheem was surprised, "Are you saying our Captain has discovered a new hideaway for us?" Just then Schmuel entered, "Hello Braheem I hope everything is going well with you?" "Oh yes Schmuel and by shear accident I ran into a friend whom I knew as a young boy." Braheem related the story to Schmuel and as the story progressed the Captains mouth gaped open. When Braheem had finished Schmuel said, "Unbelievable, things like that happen only in dreams or stories, wow what a great occurrence. Is everybody ready to view our new location, then, follow me or one of the other guides I have designated?" As always when necessity demanded it and when they were all going to the same location they followed in groups of four, five or less and each group followed the designated guide.

They stopped at the foot of the mountain watching a flow of pilgrims that never lessened moving slowly up the steps carved into the mountainside to a huge plateau and looking further one could not miss a cascading waterfall dropping seventy feet into a collection pond two hundred fifty feet long and eighty feet wide the mist from the water emitting a cooling. The mountain protected its own for on three sides of the pond rose walls that looked to reach to heaven itself where those same pilgrims could walk along the edge of the waters and drink of it. This was the headwaters of the Jordan River which had been flowing for as long as anybody could recall. Although it was a tourist attraction ninety nine percent of these people came to see the famous falls and the purest water any had ever seen or drunk. Here was serenity in its original and magnificent form for as the crowd grew the level of voices seemed to remain the same and one felt a quietness and pleasantness unsurpassed which none ever questioned. "After you have seen our new headquarters we can go up the mountain and see what the attraction is." Schmuel said as they walked in the shadow of a dense row of huge trees behind which were thickets hiding whatever was behind the tree line. The tree line meandered up a large hill beginning an arc along the line of trees hiding something. Ayoub asked, "Hey Schmuel have you lost your way we've been walking now for twenty minutes?" "Yea," spoke up his best buddy Majeed, "I think he's lost, what do you guys think?" Just then Schmuel stopped and looking in both directions he reached inside one of the thickets pulling it back as it opened much like a door. "Wow Schmuel how did you do that." As they looked they saw the roots of the thickets, resembling thick worms and although still in the ground the roots weaved their way into the body of the huge bush and allowed it to be pulled forward hence the doorway. Schmuel said, "Quickly enter fast to allow all of us entry immediately then we will move the bush back into place." They were all speechless. Again Schmuel spoke, "Now turn and look toward the top of this hill behind us and anybody tell me what you see." Barabbas and the Patriots, which by now had dwindled to forty for Barabbas had allowed some older gents and others with families who wanted to return with them so to retire.

They strained their eyes for they thought there was something special they were to see. Limping toward the front of the crowd Majheed said, "Schmuel it is a beautiful place, love the way the trail winds up toward the top of the hill and the beautiful cedars on both sides and look flowers growing so profusely between them, but I don't see anything in particular what are we looking for."

Schmuel laughed, "I wanted you all to see whatever you would; now follow me and I will take you to our new home." He began his assent with all of them following him. Barabbas fell in beside Schmuel saying, "I don't see anything that appears to be a house or barn or anything resembling them," laughing he pushed Schmuel' arm and began laughing as well, the merriment rang through the Patriots for it seemed to have become infectious. They slowly climbed the hill which revealed itself as a picturesque mesa where huge old oak trees resembling lords of the forest with some of their branches reaching into the sky toward the warmth of the summer sun awaiting a wind while other branches reached their long arms out on all sides as to form an umbrella from the sun. On the leading edge of the mesa, looking back toward the Mountains of Lebanon olive trees stood and looking out over the vista saw that this, the opposite side of their hill sloped so steeply that it would take many hours and perhaps several days to climb to the top but the beauty of the growth of plant life and the trees was phenomenal. Haleem standing at the very edge of the mesa commented, "Look how the trees and plants grow, they are reaching to the sky and it looks as though they will fall off the side of the mountain." Out of the side of this small mountain sprouted every kind of tree found in that part of the world. Cedars grew profusely and one could see olive, dogwood, maple, oak and many other species. Standing on the precipice looking down yet holding fast to Barabbas

Majheed said, "I think this is the most beautiful scene I have ever had the pleasure to see." Brabbas nodded his head in ascent, "Yes my little one I must agree with you but I see no cave or any dwelling to fend off the winds, rains and snow this place would invite." Turning to Schmuel he said, "O K Captain we are all here and I am becoming apprehensive let us not play more games show us our shelter." Schmuel smiled walking away from them motioning them to follow; they neared an area of large bushes much like the ones they had seen at the entrance of this property. "Gather round gents, Ayoub take hold of that bush nearest you and pull on it." Ayoub reached down pulling the huge bush toward him and it, like the previous one swung open to reveal a large ant hill as big as a small room. There as they looked they saw an entrance into the ground which the ant hill seemed to hug for its protection. "Look inside men you will see a ladder that will allow you to enter your new home."

As the men were climbing down into the opening Barabbas stood watching them; Majheed with Ayoub at his side, Schmuel on the opposite side of the opening. Barbbas spoke, "I must say Schmuel never have I met anyone as resourceful, you never cease to amaze me coming up with surprises for our enemies, finding not only a place to lay our heads but one that will be cool in the summer and warm in the winter. O K my young charges take your turn getting down the ladder." All knew he was hinting for those below to help the two into their new living quarters. Barabbas was the last to climb down the ten steps to the floor of the cave. As he ambled the length and breadth of the new abode he shook his head. Majheed said, "This is the biggest place we've ever lived it looks as if it would accommodate so many more people." "Yes," answered Schmuel "Take your time for it will take you an hour to inspect the entire cavern for it has three levels and you will notice odd utensils and other things that tells us this place has been lived in many times prior." Barabbas, "What did the seller think when the Wealthy Shiek from Yemen offered to buy the mountain, I am curious." Schmuel answered, "They could not believe it for it has been on the market for many years and they wanted to ask me many questions but my interpreter," pausing he laughed, "Jameel told him that his master was old and as it was many mille to Yemen they must start right away and besides that my false beard and hair was becoming hot and itchy and we both wanted to move on so we could get out of those disguises." "So," Barabbas said, "you told me you made a great bargain and now that I see your purchase I must agree, by the way do you think he knew of this cave?" "I don't believe he did for as you know I fell upon it accidentally and during the legalities I asked several questions as to what he had used the land for and he told me he grew grapes for wine and sold the fruits from the orchard but he did say that he had not been on the grounds for some time for his overseer took care of it and he pointed to the gent accompanying him so I questioned him as to what was atop the mountain and he told me it was too dense with trees and one could not grow anything there." Barabbas said, "I never dreamed the amount of money you spent would be something as unusual as this beautiful place, once again Schmuel you out bested yourself." He began clapping and the entire company joined in. Smiling broadly showing teeth Schmuel resembled a child who was about to tell them all a great secret. "What is it Schmuel what are you hiding you look like my sister when we were children for she was always hiding something from the family," Majheed queried. "Yes my Captain tell us what are you hiding from us, you are smiling like a cat that just caught the bird?" Barabbas smiling then laughing for he like the others were enjoying this game. Schmuel still smiling that know it all smile, "Follow me gentlemen I do have a great surprise for you." He turned walking to the back of the cave turned to the left continued walking until he came to another turn to the right. After another forty feet they came to a blank wall and stopped. Curious Barabbas said, "O K ashirrhty (my friend) what now? Here we are at a wall so what do you plan on showing us now?" Schmuel pointed to a three foot square niche in the wall. It looked like a depression, the top some 36 inches from the opening then sloped forward and down to about twelve inches from the opening. Barabbas stepped forward examining the grotto very closely with Ayoub, Majeed, Haleem, Judah as the rest passed by taking their time inspecting it to their own satisfaction. "Look closely my friends study, study now what do you think you are looking at?" Now they were all becoming impatient with Schmuel began hissing and booing him of course playfully. "My General," Schmuel spoke to Barabbas, "Come forward place your hand into the grotto," Barabbas did as he was asked, "now search for a handle or something resembling one, you will not see it but you will feel it." Barabbas reached into the grotto his hand pushing through the sand on the bottom of the opening then stopped looking up with perception in his eyes, "Aha I feel something, wait, yes it is the feel of haft what do I do now?" Not realizing it Barabbas turned the haft and the bottom of the grotto opened up revealing a ramp of sorts reaching the ground some forty feet down. "What a find," Barabbas said, "wow a back door, this cave is the most ideal we have ever had. I love it although I hope we never have to use it, but if we do…" he trailed off. They knew they could not gain access to the den from the back so they wove a rope from dried hemp then digging a rut from the top of the slide to the bottom and covering it over with the bountiful sand always forming inside the ramp.

****

The Patriots had been in their new home atop the mesa for three weeks and were well ensconced. Three day's gave them time to settle into their new home as each of the two man teams claimed their space on one of the three levels of this magnificent grotto each of them arranging their belongings to fit ones own personal needs. "Now that we have the time let's go around to the fore part of this mountain where that mass of people were congregating." Schumel said, "Do not forget travel in no more than five in a group, meet back here as the sun goes down, you have a free day enjoy it." Group by group they made their way up the ladder, down the mountain to their goal. The crowds were still large and the lines approaching the steps up to the mesa reached back to a line of trees some fifty yards. They arrived at the top of the mesa and were amazed at the magnificent water fall. Braheem said, "Look it seems the flow of the water falls to its destination but take a look at the pond and see how serene it is." As they looked they mumbled their agreements for it was quite unusual to see the cascading water of a fall landing hard into its own pool making only small splashes upon the back of the mother water. They strolled around some kneeling to take a drink and some just looking around, for it was an awesome sight to behold the three walls and from here they looked like tall stalagmite fingers reaching to gain access of the heavens. The mass of people were enjoying their time not loud as most crowds but a constant hum rising and falling in concurrence.

Suddenly the crowd silenced for those on the lea side of the mesa began looking up toward a small like stage with steps leading up to the area that looked like a dais. Ayoub whispered loudly, "Look Barabbas it is that beautiful man we saw in Cana, you remember at that wedding where he waved his hand over those jars of water and the servants drew wine from those same jars, and we saw him again in uh, uh where was it?" Barabbas said, "Bethsaida," "oh yes Bethsaida where that humongous crowd was and he fed thousands of people with a couple of loaves of bread and five fishes, wow, remember?" "Yes little one," Barabbas answered softly, "I remember and I still feel a quiet presence when I look at him, now let us listen to him."

The man called Jesus easily wakled up three steps until he stood on a broad area where he could speak to the crowd. He spoke to the crowd for several minutes until a lawyer asked Him a question, **"Teacher which is the greatest commandment in the law?"** *Jesus said to him, "You shall love the Lord your God with all your heart, with all your soul, and with all your mind.' This is the first and great commandment. And the second is like it, "You shall love your neighbor as yourself. On these two commandments hang all the Law of the Prophets."* (Orthodox Study Bible – Mark 12: 36 – 40.)

Then those in the crowd who had questions came closer to Him as He fielded their questions. Barabbas nodded his head toward the steps and they slowly and quietly went back to their den. The small groups were unbelievably quiet as they talked about their feelings while they had listened to Jesus speak. "I really feel good in fact better than ever and I feel a great calm and," Ayoub paused glancing around at his fellow Patriots, "yes, yes as well as all of you, what a great speaker He really impressed me!"

****

Barabbas called them together in the large room below the entrance, "It is time for us to make ourselves familiar with Phillippi and its surrounding's not to begin our business yet for we will let you know when we begin again, so now go." They scattered to the four winds slowly, not allowing themselves to stand out in a crowd.

HOPE AND A NEW ERA

    Still wondering where they were Yanatouny, Samir and Narouth accepted the slop supposedly called food from the jailer who slid the trays under the opening just large enough to accept these trays. The jailer's Captain standing near waiting for them to get their food, "So you will not tell us where your leader is and where his lair is. Ha, Ha, Ha I suppose you think we believe you when you do not speak. Soon we will understand the signs you make to each other for our Magistrate will figure it all out. Meanwhile eat, eat for soon I will return to begin our questioning again. Oh yes, let me see your backs," and he motioned for them to raise their dirty tunics; they turned raising the sack cloth they were clothed in, "three weeks now and you must like the torture for I count at least thirty lashes on each of your backs, will you be ready for more this afternoon?"

    The three looked as if they did not know what the Captain was saying with questioning looks and furrowed brows. Ten minutes after the guards left the three captives still had said nothing. The advantage of this dark dank dungeon cell was the fact that it was very dark and the further back into the cell the darker it was. They eased themselves into the far back corner. Samir put his hand over his lips, listened, then when he was satisfied there was none near he whispered, "We must attempt to find someone who can get a message to the Patriots, we have been here three weeks and I don't think they know where we are." Narouth whispered "There must be somebody we can recruit!" Yanatoun shushed them for he heard somebody approaching. The supplier of the guards walked by the cell and the light shown upon him they almost jumped out of their skins. Yanatoun sprang for the front of the cell but Narouth grabbed him holding him back. Yanatoun whispered, "What are you doing did you not see who that was, it's Parithea who left the Patriots a few months ago for he has a wife and three children." Narouth held on to him saying, "Not now not yet perhaps we will have another chance before they come back to render torture." Samir nodded his head and they settled down on boards that sufficed as their beds.

They must have dosed for it was quiet in the dungeon. The scraping of sandals on the hard floor of the dungeon woke them. Looking up they saw Parithea slowly moving toward their cell. They had not noticed it before but their old friend was limping almost dragging his left foot behind. Walking up to the cell his hand raised above his eyes to sharpen his gaze he peered into the darkness whispering, "I recognize you my friends and I will get word to Barabbas immediately." Samir eased himself slowly forward in order to see if anybody was near or following Parithea for this could be a ruse. "Thank you Parithea but who will you send?" Samir stood studying the jailer's eyes for signs of betrayal. Parithea was not nervous nor fidgety which told Samir he was comfortable. "What are you doing here Parithea I never dreamed you were a guard." "No no Samir I am supply only my job is to make sure the guards have food and drink several times a day. You see I move up and down from the fifth dungeon up to the first supplying the guards. When I left you I came directly to my home here in Caserea Phillippi but there are few jobs available. I looked for several weeks taking on many odd jobs until one day my cousin told me he was moving near the Plain of Sharon to Dora where his In-laws' live. He turned in his resignation and the Captain of the Guard told him it was up to him to find a replacement. So he chose me, a grateful relative, I keep my mouth shut which they like and I say nothing unless asked for that is the way the Captain of the Guard wants it." He waved and went on about his business.

Not yet sure of this good fortune Samir thinks to himself what would Schmuel do? His Captains words echoed in his minds ear, "Haste brings mistakes, think things out thoroughly and in the end you will find the truth if you will but have the presence of mind to think clearly." Soon the noise level picked up and they knew the Captain was returning to begin the questioning of them again. Once more they would steel themselves for the sting of the whip which they knew would come soon and if Parithea was near Samir would watch to see if there was kinship or any semblance of friendship between Parithea and the guards.

The noise of the cell door opening aroused them and a voice from above shouting down to this level, "Captain, the Magistrate has sent me to order you back to his quarters!" "What is his concern, did he give you a message for me?" The voice from above shouted back, "No sir my Captain I am but to tell you it is urgent." Gruffly the Captain shouted, "Tell my Lord I am on my way," turning to the guards accompanying him, "Lock the cell and come with me it looks as though I must wait another day for my fun, but," turning toward the cell he shouts, "do not think you have been neglected you thieves I will return and when I do I will make up for this and add a few more lashes!" As he turned laughing, proud of himself he ran headlong into Parithea scattering the tray of food into the air and onto the walls of the dungeon. "Will you never learn lowly servant stay out of my way; now run back and replenish what you have lost and, and clean this mess NOW!" as he stormed off mumbling and blaming the supply for his own blunder.

Parithea wasted no time now for it was his quitting time. Returning to the supply house he turned in his apron and tray and left immediately. He did not know where the den of the Patriots was but he would scour Phillippi hoping to catch site of a Patriot he would recognize. He walked from the east gate through the shops moving slowly methodically searching the faces as he went. He walked the half mile to the west gate through those shops then out toward the residence areas of the city. From there he moved on to the south gate of the city and he noticed the sun was beginning to make its way to the earth to hide once again in the west. Seeing an old friend who was manning his vegetable shop he stopped to visit with him. "Sit down Parithea you look worn has your work at the jail overloaded you," Laughing as they shook hands. "No Hassan I have been looking for an old friend who may be in our city." "Tell me his name and if I see any strangers I will ask if he knows you." Hassan said. "If only I knew a name I would give it to you that you might help make my search easier." "Well then here," handing Parithea a cold drink saying, "Sit and drink this for I must begin folding up my belongings and loading them to return home, wont you come with me I am sure Sarah will have prepared ample for this evening meal." Parithea answered, "You know I must get home to Amelia and the children for they will wonder where I have been, thank you for your hospitality Hassan." They waved at each other as he walked out the south gate of the city. Somewhat dejected and with his head down not watching where his feet led him he slammed into a giant of a man whose voice said, "Well old fellow do you not see where you are going, is it your age that makes you not see or are you blind?" Parithea dared not look up for he knew the sound of Barabbas' voice, oh how fortunate can one man be and with no hesitation he threw his arms around the big man saying, "I have searched this half day long for one of your ilk and was about to give up when I bumped into you, you big oaf," As his arms locked around Barabbas' middle. "Who is this that has attaches his self to me?" he asked as he pushed Parithea from him. "Let's have a look at," his voice trailed off and he just stood looking down at Parithea. Suddenly his mood changed and he pretended not to know the man saying, "Hey old man do you think you know me who the heck are you I am just going for a leisurely walk along the forests edge."

His long strides took him away fast for he did not want to be seen with Parithea in public never knowing what might take place or who would recognize him. Parithea knew exactly what to do now as he turned in the opposite direction walking casually away. When he was comfortably away from the area where he saw his old boss he turned walking toward the forest his eyes searching through the dusk of evening. As he walked slowly near the underbrush his eyes straining now for the sun was beginning to hide itself in the western earth he was suddenly jerked into the underbrush the limbs, like fingers of the bushes and trees scored his skin. "You old reprobate it is so good to see you what are you doing here, is this where you live what is happening?" Parithea gasped, "Let me down Barabbas and I will tell you. I am so fortunate to find you for I have news for you." "Yes yes my friend what is it?" Parithea answered, "I am sure you have been looking for three of your men right, well I know where they are." Barabbas sat down on a large boulder while Parithea related the information regarding the three. "What a total coincidence I cannot believe they are here for they were arrested in Jerusalem a month ago when Circus Circus was there yet we followed them to an old abandoned house but failed in our attempt. That Simon Antropidus is a real sneak he sent them here to his counterpart the Magistrate of Galilee, who would ever thought, no wonder we could not get a line on them." Barabbas seemed deep in thought then, "Parithea I want you to go about your business at the dungeon with no more thought of us." "But," Parithea began and putting his hand over the man's mouth Barabbas said, "No no I do not want your employer to find out we are friends and I will not ask you to help us free the boys." Again Parithea began, "But my dear friend I must offer myself in some way!" "No Parithea that is an order we will have nothing to do with you in this instance, for it may jeopardize your family and the life you have here, remember, this is an order and you recall your vows, you are still under my command." Parithea smiled hugged the Giant saying, "It would be a pleasure to see all my buddies but I understand I too could endanger the Patriots, yes, yes I understand I do not want to know how or when you will make your move," he then turned as he walked away saying, "Bless you all."

****

"Jameel" Barabbas speaking to the Patriots, "you will be responsible for the climax of this operation and it will be upon you and your group to carry this out without a hitch." He looked at Jameel who acknowledged his charge. "Yes my General I will carry out your orders just as you laid them out to me and we have rehearsed our assignment once but will run through each move again and again until we are convinced there is nothing to block our plan." There was a quiet within the cave for an unusually curious thing was taking place, Barabbas' face was a work in contemplation. "Listen carefully each group will be assigned a position and a particular assist to insure a safe and rapid release of our men. Jodan yours will be the initial movement that will, properly presented, capture their attention and move their interest outside the dungeon." Barabbas exchanged places with Schmuel who took over from there. "Judith the next move will be yours and your men must gain the interest of the crowd which by now should be extensive." Judith nodded his assent for he knew nothing more was needed. "The remainder of you will meld yourselves among the travelers and shoppers at the East gate of the City. We chose that gate for it is always the busiest entrance and on weekends it is conglomerate of the world for travelers from Syria in the North and all of Asia descend upon this City. You will know when to begin your move. Gather your groups, those of you who have active parts practice to perfection. Those of you remaining practice your actions to insure our ultimate goal." He waved them away each to his own group.

****

The following Sabboth (Sabbath or Saturday) found the Patriots moving toward the East Gate of Caesaria Phillippi. Schmuel watched from a hill facing the gate as his men gathered in groups. They waited until the final group signaled their readiness. Schmuel was readily seen from all points he stood and stretched his arms upward as if he had just awakened. Watching from below and recognizing his signal, Jodans group came marching out of the oasis toward the gate their musical instruments demanding attention and the crowds gathered around as they marched toward the gate. Behind them came Magnes the Magician pulling colored ribbons from the ears of a donkey and a monkey and as he pulled those ribbons out of the animal's ears and mouths they changed colors which captivated the crowd who voiced their approval by much shouting and applauding. Behind the Magician came tumblers Corythus and Cleothus jumping and tumbling over each other and lifting each other over their heads by only one hand then pulling epees and pretending to sword fight as they danced lunging at each springing over each other while keeping time to the music. Each thrust of the swords brought gasps, then applause from the throng which continued to grow until there was little space. Then came the lion tamers each with a lion or a tiger on a leash giving the Kings of the Jungle just enough room to almost reach the crowd who bound back seeking refuge and yet laughing and hooting their enjoyment. They paraded near the jail and dungeon where they slowed for there was a large space outside the gate of the prison which itself was almost sixty feet square with four guards stationed across the opening. More and more guards gathered at the exit of the jail as the music became louder and louder and the blending crescendo of the music and crowd swept together so the sound moved even to the lowest part of the dungeon bringing up those sentries to gape and applaud as they stood enjoying the entertainment which left less than a handful of sentinels in the lower bowels of the prison.

****

So it would give them ample time to do their thing one hour prior to the signal Jameels group had slowly made their way to the rear entrance of the dungeon. Jameel approached this entrance which he had found a week before having received information that it was seldom used and known to very few. Jameel and Tanoush the strongest of the Patriots stopped, gazing at this rusted steel gate. Tanoush was a huge person of almost seven feet tall with a mild personality unless riled than he was a force to be reckoned with at which time his normally light skin took on a maroon cast, his blond hair seeming to duplicate that same color. Tanoush leaned down looking over the large rusty padlock squeezing its fingers over the staple. He pulled on the lock testing it to see how much pressure it would take to break. After several pulls and twists he turned to Jameel, "Boss this padlock cannot be broken but perhaps we can force this small steel rod into the key slot hoping to slip the slides into place." Some fifteen minutes later they were still trying to open the padlock when one of the group said, "I think I can help Jameel." Stepping from the rear of the group a small gray haired man stepped forward taking a small vial from his tunic. "This is olive oil which may loosen the rust and give us a better chance at releasing the tumblers. During my childhood my uncle was a jailer and he used oil to clean rust from the hinges and locks of the jail." He poured oil over the padlock then turned it upside down then dropped it to allow the oil to permeate through the lock. "Give it a moment to soak in." He told Tanoush.

They stood back and waited a few moments then the old man, Scamolian, pulled on the padlock and they all could tell it was much less tight. Tanoush inserted the small steel pick then a thinner one working it around slowly. After several eagerly anticipated minutes

Tanoush took one of the oak cudgels out of his bag to begin hammering on the lock. Before he could do so Scamolian voiced, "Aha." And when they looked the lock fell gently open. Jameel turned signaling toward the shadows of the buildings standing close and from that area came four of Jameels men carrying bags and dragging dry limbs. They hurriedly rushed inside with their loads while Jameel placed the lock over the staple so that it looked as if it was still closed. While two of them placed themselves in advantageous positions where they would be able to observe anyone approaching, the other six took the steps to the bottom which was the fifth level and quietly placed green broken limbs and dried leaves in several piles. Meanwhile Jameel and Scamolian slithered off toward the cells. They passed each cell peering inside until there was only two left and were becoming apprehensive. They looked at each other with questioning looks. Scamolian heaved a huge sigh and as he turned to the next cell and peered in he could see no movement. "This seems to be an empty cell yet it has a padlock on it." Samir strained his eyes against the darkness narrowing his lids to get a closer look.

Suddenly something sprang from the depths of the cell toward them frightening them. As they stood a face was nearing them then another and an additional one. From inside the darkness of the cell came a whisper, "Jameel it is you, wow I can't believe my eyes, is it really you, how did you find us, we don't even know where we are?" As Jameel and Scamolian' eyes attempted to pierce the dark broke it slowly broke away to reveal the faces of Samir, Genendo and Fareed. Samir grasped his hands together and raised them in the air as a victory salute mouthing "Huzzah."

While this was taking place, the remainder of Jameel's men rose to the third level where they duplicated their previous actions stacking their materials which would await ignition from the man standing by. At the cell of the prisoners Tanoush took a huge cudgel wrapped in sack cloth from one of the men and raising it in the air with all his strength and a noisy whoosh pounded it down upon the rusty padlock several times. Realizing that would not work he pulled a pry bar from his waist and pushed it into the staple holding the lock. He then inserted a second pry bar into the opposite side and began twisting the two bars as hard as he could. The sound of squealing metal broke the silence but the noise did not carry for it was absorbed by the sound of the music and the crowd from above. Again with brute strength Tanoush pried again and the lock screamed in its pain but did not open. When they looked closely they could see the curvature of the lock was twisted. With that encouragement and two more sets of hands on each side of the pry bars and at a signal they pressed with all their might against the stubborn metal as it cried out to the darkness then suddenly broke in a wail. Tanoush twisted the lock off, pulled the gate open and the prisoners were free. There were short welcome hugs then they froze waiting.

Awaiting another signal Tanoush reinserted the lock into its hasp making it appear as though it had never been opened. A minute later which seemed like an hour the music became louder and louder; this was their signal. Jameel stamped the floor with his a bat and soon smoke was pouring from the two levels of the dungeon and the two who lit the fires were moving fast up the stairs toward the rear of the prison. They all sprang for the stairs up the steps two and three at a time. Jameel's group arrived at the rear gate first and stood waiting until the two from level five and three came charging up then Tanoush reopened the gate while they all filed out repositioning the padlock into its staple. The smoke was billowing, roaring speedily up from the bowels of the dungeon challenging the light of day and the thick smoke darkening each area as it crawled up, up toward the parapet of the first floor then hurriedly making its way through the openings. The dense black smoke engulfed the guards standing in the doorway looking out the barred windows of the prison and caught by surprise they were disoriented for fingers of the smoke wrapped themselves around them cutting off the air supply choking, gasping and coughing running helter-skelter bouncing off the walls of the buildings.

The Captain of the Guard standing outside the gate saw what was happening and shouted, "Here, here come to me," and he ran toward the water trough, "dip your napkins in the water and cover your eyes follow me," he shouted then, "Open the gates, hurry open the gates," shouting to the Sergeant of the guard inside the gates. The gates opened and they roared into the prison. Now realizing the smoke coming up from below demanded, "Get below and find the fire, check each cell." Soon several of the guards arriving on the third level found the burning green limbs located in a place where they would spread their evil dark smoke against stone walls which would not burn. They shouted to their Captain they had found the source while another group having arrived at the lowest level also shouted that they had found another source. The Captain, incensed, shouted, "Check all the cells on all the levels see what is taking place, if this was done by any prisoner that means there is an open cell. I pity the poor guard whose position finds missing prisoners."

The Sergeant hoping to put himself in a good light with his Captain said, "Perhaps this was an inside job my Captain, should we question the guards?" Irritated yet more the Captain shouted, "No, no keep your ideas to yourself Sergeant I will let you know when and what to think!" The Captain was not looking forward to explaining this situation to the Magistrate. Each cell was checked beginning with the first level down to the fifth where the three Patriots were, or should have been. "You Charge Guards, check each cell make sure the prisoners are alive and we have no casualties when you have ended your inspection report to me." Each level had its own

Charge Guard ranked just below Sergeant and they began their search. Holding a lantern high so the light would shine into the cells each area was checked. When they came to level five, cell five they peered inside and could see the sack cloths covering the three prisoner's who were shivering under those dirty rags, or at least they imagined the three could be seen; before they lit the fire, prior to their departure from the dungeon, Jameel puffed up the three sack cloths against the wall than stuffed straw in them making them look like the three men were huddled inside. Seeing this Tanoush stifled a laugh imagining what could come of this farce.

****

Back in their lair the Patriots were throwing a party to welcome their three buddies' home. There were no scheduled speeches only good food, drink and camaraderie to welcome them back. As they were eating Samir stood raising his glass, "Thanks to our Commander and Schmuel our brilliant uh, uh, how bout Executive Administrator, a new title befitting him." "Huzzah huzzah huzzah, chorused the Patriots, for they truly respected both their leaders!" "We are so glad to be home, and such a great ruse played upon the prison guards, I wonder if they have noticed we are gone." Braheem shouted out, "Of course they know you are gone for I am sure they kept close watch over you." "No, no," Samir sprang to action, "they seldom came into our cell but to interrogate and beat us, but we will know for there will be such an uproar when that Captain finds out we are gone and all his men will suffer for I have never seen such a temper in all my life and he will nonetheless lay blame on any other than himself. Having witnessed his temper and his screams of anguish when he is crossed I truly empathize with his employees especially those closest in rank to him." He then laughed out loud. "Ha ha yes but then he must face the Magistrate Tetrarch Lysanias who as we know strives to be as intolerable, revolting and disgusting as his counterpart Simon Antropidus Magistrate Tetrarch of Jerusalem.

****

As dusk began its decent into the western sky and wisps of smoke still stretching their ugly fingers into the night sky the Captain of the guard stood at ground level looking into the dungeon. He was so proud of his new bright red cape and plumed helmet Captain Youseff Mandindo's voice carried like a lions roar upon vultures wings over the parapet spinning down and around circling into the depths of the dungeon frightening his men jarring them from their doldrums. "Hear this," he shouted, "each level will now count prisoners, not from outside the cells but you will enter each cell, count and mark them with the purple ink of the Phoenicians' only then it will not wear off, *now get to it and report to my office with your count when finished!*"

The four guards on level five heaving great sighs and looking up to see if their Captain was watching, moved out to the closest cells. These were the darkest cells in the entire dungeon and this floor welcomed the worst or most wanted prisoners. The four guards began with the furthest cell from the center of the stairway and worked their way back across the open area that looked up to the first level then back to the north side of the dungeon to end their search with the darkest dankest cell built far back into the earth. The four of them came to that cell where they expected to find the three Patriots. Peering into the blackness they could see the three of them huddled together under their sack cloth blanket, or so their minds told them. The chief guard on this floor unlocked the steel door not noticing it opened with little effort for Tanoush had clicked it almost shut. As the chief guard opened the door it screeched in disapproval and he shouted, "All right you thieves come out now." He stood waiting for the sack cloth to come off and the three of them stand. No action under the cloth made the guards anxious, they knew not why, then one of them punched the cloth with his spear and it fell to the floor empty, fish hudden (nobody there)! They stood looking around the cell punching swords and spears under the pallets, raising their lamps high so they could see well. The chief guard's face wilted and then faded of all color as the other three stood looking at him jaws agape. He motioned them out of the cell and slowly walked to the opening, guardedly looking up in the event their Captain or Seargent happened to be looking down upon them. Hurriedly he motioned them toward him, standing on the first step going up the back way of the dungeon, he whispered, "I don't know about you guys but I'm going to make my way up to the top of this prison and leave by the back way before we are caught for we will be blamed for the escape of those prisoners and I know our Magistrate will make an example of us and I will not wait to be murdered." At that he took off his slippers and ran up the steps as fast as his legs would carry him his three guards hurriedly followed him almost tripping up the stairs. As the chief guard rose to the top floor he glanced back toward the voices he heard then began working on the padlock hanging on its staple. He touched it and it fell off for Tanoush had left it broken. The four guards wasted no time in making their getaway although the chief slowed them down lowering his head headed for the animal gate of the city for very few used this gate for the stench from the dung and the chance that one might step into a soft mushy stinkpot was too much for those other than animal handlers. That was the last anybody ever saw of those four men and they were swallowed up by the oncoming night.

****

An uproar in this capital city of Jerusalem for the Tetrarch Lysanias was furiously angry making himself a

Two Men Named Jesus

laughing stock. This was reminiscent of the Magistrate Tetrarch Herod and his infamous, angry temper preaching to the multitude and because of his anger and blasphemy was eaten by worms in the face of a huge assembly of the Sanhedrin and a throng of laymen.

The large battalion of Roman soldiers, officers on horseback followed by the brigade of foot soldiers stood at attention awaiting their Tetrarch while the laypeople of the city stood by watching this exhibition yet fearful for they also knew not to demonstrate; they too like the soldiers remaining quiet, so very quiet insuring against Lysanias' wrath. Lysanias dressed in all his glorious garb sprang out of the great pillared headquarters reminiscent of the great buildings of Roma, his face a depiction of demons, not red but waned of all color contorted into that of an ogre, wrinkled, twisted into repulsiveness which made those in the street surrounding the headquarters of the Magistrate as he jumped into his chariot recoil at the sight of this man's face. Yes his anger caromed him into a false and unknown character shouting at his driver, "Move, go, hasten," he screamed at his driver yet looking out toward the officers on horses for he meant it for them as well, "Move, move, move we must find the hiding place of Barabbas and his so called Patriots. When I capture their leader that will quiet them, you have your orders now break into your Regiments and your assignments; group one search north, group two west, three south and four east, let not a town, city nor countryside go unexplored and remember the first capture of any Patriot will bring you enough money to make you a very wealthy person, but if you capture Barabbas or any of his Captains you will receive a pot of gold and silver enough and bring you riches forever!"

****

Only Barabbas and Schmuel knew that Braheem was now employed by the City of Caseria and his boyhood friend Favarh worked inside the Tetrarch' office and small bits of information being sent to the leaders of the Patriots aided them in their plans that would soon take place. Braheem and Favarh were not to come near the Patriots for one never knew when Roman spies might discover their secret.

****

Barabbas and his men watched from vantage points near and around the City of Caseria Phillippi assigning ten men to follow group one on their march north. If it became aware that the northern platoon was coming close to their den it would be necessary then to send a runner to Barabbas and Schmuel and those inside the bunker knowing if the front was not readily accessible the back would be. Assured the den was safe from the soldiers Barabbas signaled the remaining men to follow. They came to a small area of dense trees and undergrowth where he stopped saying, "Relax we are going to give the Tetrarch something more to infuriate him. Schmuel and I have developed a plan that will show the dungeon to be somewhat unprotected, now listen closely. Barabbas detailed his plan while they all listened smiling knowing that this would again exasperate as well as exacerbate Tetrarch Lysanias.

****

A LESSON UNAPRECIATED

They waited two hours until the stars had been painted by dark clouds and the black descended upon everything making it impossible to see further than a few yards into the ebon obscurity of the night. Thirty Patriots in groups of three began making their way again to the rear of the dungeon waiting for Tanoush to once again do his magic with the padlock. Once it was open Corythus and Cleothus with the help of Jameel, Patripiose, Samir and Jodan stole their way into the five levels of the dungeon each of them discovering the resting place of the guards on each level. A soft call of a night bird, which would not be unusual for the dungeons were full of bats and night birds signaled them to drip the elixir Corythus and his brother had brought from their homeland upon the lips of the guards. They only had to wait a few seconds for as the guards automatically licked their lips they passed out immediately. Now they moved quickly finding the keys on the chief guard opened each cell where there were prisoners and led them up from the four levels and out the back door of the jail allowing only three or four at a time and being accompanied by some of the Patriots. When the mission was finalized Jameel faced the released prisoners speaking, "Wherever your home is you should not go there now nor ever again for you will endanger your families. Search for a new home and never allow your face to be seen in this territory again, that is all of Israel and Syria for you may rest assured this Tetrarch will hunt you down and make minced meat of you. May I suggest the huge country of Rus to the north where none of these people will venture, for there they are not welcome?" Samir almost shouting, "What are you waiting for, go, go, go!" They needed no additional encouragement as they scurried off in many different directions.

****

The Magistrates office again was in upheaval and the ranting, cursing, shouting coming from that office was being heard several blocks away and once again the populace remained far off for they wanted no part of this senseless, inane, mad fanatic. Nothing had come of the Romans search for the Patriots although they did come close but there was no realization of the proximity to the prey they hunted. Little did Lysanias know those of his army who had taken the northern reconnaissance had circled the small mountain in which the Patriots were ensconced and some of them had an inclination to move up the hill to investigate but the old farmer; not resembling Jameel at all although it was he, incognito also, Majheed who loved acting, flitting from one line of vines to another singing something but what who knew; the old farmer bent over tending his grape vines rose slowly holding his hands on his back his beard thick and his old hat topped his head keeping the sun from his skull, told them, "Welcome soldiers you are much too early for the old wine for I have sold it all and the new wine must await its turn in the barrels, yes, yes, it must be aged." The Magistrates Platoon Sergeant asked, "Is that your home there atop the hill old man, who do you live with do you not have help or do you operate this farm alone? "My wife and son are assisted at times by a cousin or two but we do well although it is only a small operation."

****

Lysanias called his Captains in one by one cursing at them throwing fruit, fruit bowls, smoking bowls and anything not attached to the floor or walls. Screaming at the top of his lungs, "What kind of fools are you men to allow a lowly thief such as Barabbas and his band of cutthroats best us, do you realize we are the laughing stock of the land, have you, Carmedias, fired or killed all those guards who were on duty that night?" Carmedias a man of his own and having more courage than was wise at this point answered, "My Lord I believe I told you those men were some of my best but they were drugged and, like before, the rear gate was forced open. I was not here for I was with you on our search for Barabbas and his band of thieves." Lysanias' eyes grew large as he bound to his feet shouting, "You are being insubordinate you ungrateful wretch perhaps I will strip you of your Captains bars and lower your rank to a lowly guard again." He stood then his eyes narrowing to a slit attempting to impose his will upon this his Chief Captain of the Dungeon. Carmedias stood his ground not shrinking from the staring eyes of this his Tetrarch. They both stood glaring at each other when after a few seconds the Chief guard said, "Do what you will with me my Lord but I have given you the best years of my life and have been a loyal and obedient soldier!"

The Tetrarch' face changed suddenly and he shouted, "Everybody out, get out all of you, not you Carmedias I will have a private word with you!" The huge room cleared expeditiously and the two of them left standing facing each other neither backing down both sets of eyes glowing at the other. Now the cat eyes of the Lysinias met those clear honest eyes of his Chief whom he had known now these four years and who had taken much more abuse piled on him year after year. Which now it had reached its zenith and Carmedias try as he might could not contain himself as he thought, "It is now or never he may have my life but it is time I faced up to this monster." Then aloud he began, "Lysinias I speak to you today as never before and I say to you, face the possibility that you may have now met your match in life," Lysinias listening but not wanting to hear what Carmedias was saying, the Tetrarch' nostrils flaring his breathing fast his heart pounding but the words he would say stuck in his throat then he heard, "and I say with compunction," the magistrate held his hand up facing Carmedias but the man would speak his peace or die trying, so not ceasing he continued on, his own hand held high against the voice of his superior, "you must admit, Barabbas has matched you double for each of your discrepancies and he may not be a superior General but he has blocked you each step of the way. So now my Lord accept that fact or shrink into your own little world that eventually will tighten around you and consume you; let go of this thing that threatens your very life and allow your brain, that has worked so well for you all these years to reinvent itself and proceed from this point; that is all I have to say!"

Lysinias stood there his mouth agape slowly he shut the opening in his face and a peace came over him. He smiled; his countenance became alien to that of a moment before, from the horrendous ogre he resembled just a short time ago the words of his old friend Carmedias like a sword struck hard into the man's ego, yes the smile was real as he took Carmedias in his grasp saying, "Never have I been spoken to in such a forthright manner, and I might say the most honest I've witnessed, you with your unmitigated frankness have brought me down where I belong. I am now more relaxed than I have been since being appointed to this position by the Emperor, all these years I have feared for my inadequacies and now you have made me realize I am simply a man whose ego has mired himself in the mud of false reasoning." He stopped, pushed Carmedias away from him and for the first time in years smiled saying simply, "Thank you old friend I have forgotten you have helped me gain this position and now I owe you my renewed life, thanks."

No more was said as he turned and shouted with a much more reserved and less raucous voice, "Come in, come in all of you and witness your newly remade Tetrarch, yes come, see and I will welcome you all into my offices with renewed fervor." They hesitated for they saw a new man whom they had never seen before for their Tetrarch was actually smiling his hands outstretched earnestly welcoming them back into his life. This day the life of Lysinias and those around him would change making the life of his subjects easier and he would promote Carmedias to his Senior Centurion for now he saw the wealth of knowledge this man possessed. Later his hatred for the Patriots hitherto roiled inside him and would become as a cancer for this would be his main goal.

****

Schmuel and Barabbas discussed the new face of the Tetrarch. "Although he may have changed and bettered himself to his men we must not allow that to lessen our resolve and we must strengthen ourselves and never drop our caution." Schmuel said, Barabbas nodding assent. "It may be time for us to use Braheem or Favarh for I thought not to enlist them until it was absolutely necessary." Barabbas continued, "I am happy neither of them was working that day for the Magistrate would have had their heads as well." Schmuel was thinking and said, "We are scheduled to meet at Favarh' home in a week I anticipate picking up information helping us in the coming days." Each of them made their way to Favarh' home in the wealthy section of town. Schmuel dressed as a wealthy merchant from Syria; one would know this by the length of his tunic which came to his knees, while Barabbas, because of his height and looks donned a pair of trousers, something alien to this part of the world, but not in Rus where he would be noted from, as well as a cap with a high stiff point and carrying a woven wool cloak over his arm. If one knew Barabbas they knew he was extremely uncomfortable in these ostentatious clothing. They were brought to this wealthy mans gate by an enclosed charioteer which pulled up to the large gate. The driver of the four wheeled charioteer jumped down from his perch setting a box like step near the carriage allowing the passengers to step down away from any puddles of water or mud. They were welcomed into the house by the Master Eunuch then ushered into the gardens where Favrah welcomed them onto plush chairs.

The meeting would take place prior to which they were served a sumptuous buffet befitting a king. There were all types of fruits some of which they had never seen, such as a small fuzzy green fruit resembling a huge olive, a yellow acidulous fruit called pineapple, although

Two Men Named Jesus

it did not resemble any apple they had ever seen and much more. They exchanged pleasantries, and visited regarding almost nothing until their appetites were sated. As the servants removed the plates and returned with coffee and deserts they began. Braheem turning to his friend Favrah, "I have little to report although I know there is something afoot for the Council General's office where I work is in a tizzy trying to get the Treasury to increase the monetary output. I suspect this may mean that the Magistrate will ask the Emperor to increase his budget perhaps to allow him to increase his security force, then turning to Favrah adds, "Can you shed any light toward the information I have put forth?" "Yes in fact I know something is taking place for our auditor has been summoned into Lysinias' office several times this past week for meetings that extended almost an hour, but your guess is as good as mine and it is only a guess and I must apologize for these turns began just twenty four hours ago." Braheem thought for a moment than said, "As well as in my office the action on this seemed to begin yesterday. I will keep my eyes and ears open and hope to get back to you when and if I have anything." Favrah nodded, "Yes I will do the same." They sat back then thinking if there was anything other than that on the agenda finally Barabbas nodded toward Schmuel who said, "Alright gents leave as you came one or two at a time and it would be best if you took an alternate route back to wherever you go from here."

****

Sure enough confirmation came a few days later Lysanias called for a boost in nomisma (Greek for money, or nomismata Roman,) to cover the cost of a full battalion under his command. As the Patriots received the news they were told this would be secretive and not for the common man to know or hear about. Thanks for their spies in the Magistrates office.

A few days later an emissary accompanied by a most adequate entourage dispatched by Caesar arrived to meet with the Tetrarch of Caseria Phillippi. The Tetrarch had a lavish meal prepared for this man who was ushered into the office of Tetrarch Lysanias who bowed and scraped to show his allegiance but yet never mentioned a word regarding the increase in his budget. The Emissary had very little to say until his appetite was satisfied and this was considerable for the man was rotund in his 50 some years his grey hair neatly trimmed with the shaven face of Rome then he smiled asking, "Now Tetrarch tell me exactly why you should have this new amount for your treasury for I must be fully convinced this is a certain investment our Caesar would sanction." Lysanias answered, "Yes Consul I will verify this for you." Tetrarch Lysanias then explicated the history of the Patriots making sure he made his narrative interesting enough to the Consul and unashamedly he added a few of his own imaginative tales.

In his own mind he needed the nomisma and was sure his new Battalion would counter his new move against his arch enemy. This had not changed regardless of the feeling he had for his people now his passion and zest for the capture and downfall of the Patriots was yet as strong as it was before, and it was now becoming an obsession and his main objective. Lysinias ended this deception with, "My dear Consul provide me with this stipend and I will give Caesar Barabbas' head on a staff and run his so called Patriots to ground whereupon they must disengage their thievery and disband what they call the Army of the Patriots." And Lysinias continued with this tirade not having gone unnoticed by Caesar' Consul. He would let the Magistrate sermonize while he enjoyed the repast set before him and in his mind the Emissary laughed as the Tetrarch was engulfed in his fantasy. When finally the Egoist reached the end of his obligatory (or so in his mind) tale the Consul knowing Lysinias would be jolted out of his chair he said, "Well Tetrarch, you will get your desired monies it will be in your treasury within forty eight hours." And he smiled for yes what he had anticipated took place Lysinias virtually fell out of his chair as Consul walked to the door cleaning his hands of the crumbs of his delicious and yummy repast waving to his entourage to bring his carriage and with another wave of his hand casually dismissed himself from Lysinaias with nary another word. As they rode away a celebration slowly swelled among those staff members of the Magistrate and he himself watched as the carriage drove away and although absurd, stuck his tongue out and brayed like an ass, it was something to see!

****

This day Magistrate Lysinias was quietly ecstatic for one of his spies had brought verified news of a foray by the Patriots upon the south gate of the City, it being the next largest entrance and of course found plausible for such a move. He sent for Carmedias, his newly appointed Senior Centurion. "Carmedias I have information the Patriots will descend upon the south gate next Sabah for as you know that will be the celebration of Equinox and a time for the wealthy as well as their servants and employees to participate together along with the Laity." Carmedias nodded, "Yes my Lord and they will come from miles around to celebrate this twice a year happening and," Lysinias interrupted smiling broadly, "And you and your men will be ready." Nodding his head as if he had a new thought, "Your men will be clad as civilians," Carmedias gasped for this was something new for the Roman Guard were proud of their position and wore their military out front for all to see, "and will mingle with the crowd spending dinars on their families and enjoying themselves eating and drinking of the wine." Pausing he waited for Carmedias to grasp this new idea and when he was sure his Centurion understood he continued, "Your men must keep their eyes peeled upon

Two Men Named Jesus

the crowd and especially the wealthy for as you know they are Barabbas' main target. This trap will be laid and we will make arrest after arrest for here is what we will do. Make your arrests quietly with no commotion and we will slowly take them into custody a few at a time, I am giving you a full platoon of men who will mingle with the crowd not knowing they are officers." They shook hands smiling happily for this would be one of the years crowning accomplishments and Lysinias could hear the words of his Caesar proclaiming him the years outstanding Tetrarch.

Now in his mind's eye, dreaming, he could almost hear the words of the Emperor as he bestowed another title commending Lysinias' great work. Carmedias watched noting the ethereal look in Lysinias' eyes knowing a dream was passing through him but questioned it not.

****

The Patriots began this Vernal Equinox early with a breakfast of their favorite meal consisting of fresh talamee and camash, (two inch thick round bread & pita) jibon, (white goats cheese) all available fruits and of course the rich thick Turkish sweet coffee to top it off. When they had finished Barabbas gave them their day's assignments. Designating them by groups, "Jameel your group will take the east gate of the city beginning an hour before noon, the gathering of the crowds will begin to grow, working the crowds for not more than three hours or if there is a suspicion you have been discovered immediately cease your operation and leave. Kallial you will take your group to the north gate where the largest crowds will surely assemble. Work this area not more than three hours unless a problem may arise. All of you work slowly and in pairs only taking partial amounts from your marks. Remember if you venture stealing too much from one source you will be more likely to be noticed." As usual Schmuel finished, "Return slowly to our den watching that you are not followed but if you suspect you are being followed signal help and crisscross back to confuse. Do not overextend yourselves for penalties will be strict! Now go!"

****

The District of Abilene would be celebrating this Equinox festival with all the spectacles of a small circus sans Chariot Races. There would be sideshows to tweak ones imagination such as Emingus' spinning table with vertical rods stuck into the top spaced ½ inch apart and numbered. One purchased three 1 inch wood rings for a quarter of a dinar then tosses the rings so they would drop over one of the rods. Each rod was numbered and the number referenced on the screen behind the toss game showing what one won if two of one's ring's landed on the same rod. There was a wheel of fortune where one could buy a number spin the wheel so as to land on ones favorite number. And the games went on and on. There were many magicians to arrest ones imaginations, knife throwers, strong men who would wrestle any challenger and if one stayed a full round with the strong man their prize would be a dinar, two full rounds would win one three dinar and if any lasted five full rounds with the strong man he would win one solidus of gold. Carmedias and his Tetrarch were walking casually near the south gate of Philippi dressed as Laity pretending to converse with one another and those around them. "Well my friend how does it feel the weight of a Generals epaulet on your shoulder, I recall when the Emperor promoted me to my present position I did not know how I felt for the first few weeks then it slowly sunk in and I officially became the Tetrarch of Abilene. You must know in your own heart you are deserving of this promotion." Lysinias stopped talking his eyes seeking out something beyond and behind Carmedias. Carmedias slowly turned to see what held Lysinias' attention. He saw two wealthy gentlemen fondling and studying silver and gold utensils and directly behind them a possible thief with his eyes in the air but his hand easing the gentelmens valuables from their tunics. Carmedias nodded toward the thief and suddenly there were three guards dressed as laymen nabbed the thief and another, surely an accomplice who was relieving another gent of his bag of coin. They bound the two thieves' hands behind their backs and hustled them off toward dungeons. "Continue picking these men off and soon we will have the prison full, tell your men to keep them cuffed and in one location we will interrogate them personally." Of course crowds such as this inevitably invited thieves for this was a time of easy pickings and as the day closed upon the mid afternoon there had been no arrests within the last hour. The Lieutenant of the guard left the prison to find his General that he might make a report. "Sir, we have detained some thirty thieves but none of them seem to be the caliber of the Patriots and they do not seem to be overly concerned in the fact they have been incarcerated. They are all repeat offenders although minors and we have had them as guests some many times before."

Upon hearing this, the Tetrarch and his General, went to the prison to investigate hoping they surely had some of the Patriots under arrest. After two hours of interrogating each of the prisoners it was definitely determined these were not the thieves of Barabbas although several of them voiced their pleasure in the fact they were considered as such for to be a part of that august group was their ultimate desire. As Tetrarch Lysinias stood inside the prison looking over the captives once again his nostrils flared as a crimson tide seemed to envelope his being then his breathing became like an animal painting his countenance in that darkest of red colors. "Once again that man has bested us. "Do you recall from whom we received this information call them in and question them thoroughly perhaps we can get a line on the Giants direction. Oh I cannot believe this I am sure we have missed an opportunity to capture him, send runners to each gate, seek as much information as possible find what occurrences have taken place or if they have arrested anybody." After thinking a new idea jumped into his head and he shouted, "Oh no we have left the other three gates near unprotected with less than a squad at each gate; we have walked into his trap once more!" He shouted, "We begin first thing tomorrow to scour the countryside and Oh yes I will offer rewards for the capture of any Patriot, release these others for they are petty thieves and can do little harm; release them at the same time frightening them to the point where they will either move from this area or seek a trade!"

****

Looking down from a small hill near the south gate Braheem, Sharif and Min had watched the proceedings. "I cannot tell who the enforcers are but they are dressed as lay people and I am sure we will be able to spot them as they make arrests." Sharif snickered, "The Roman sergeant I picked last week to tell my story was very eager to hear it." Min suggested, "The way you were dressed in those dirty sack cloth's and the dirt in your beard and hair would have made me sick to see you if I had not known you." He laughed out loud. Sharif continued, "I told him I had a bit of juicy information for him that the Magistrate should reward him for then I held out my hand to receive any stipend he may have given me." He laughed, "Ha ha he slapped my hand and told me if he deemed the information worthwhile I would get a reward so," he could not hold back the laughter, "ha ha, ha, then I expounded on Schmuel' story and soon had him in my pocket, ha, ha, ha he threw me one dinar and ran for the Magistrates office that's when I knew I had him!" Braheem said, "Whatever you do Min don't let yourself be seen in that guise you used for they will seek that guy out!" They laughed enjoying their ploy. The three of them settled down to watch the goings on as Braheem counted the numbers they took into custody for he would report to Schmuel later. At home they separated the loot into their respective piles and Schmuel with his helpers, Majheed and Ayoub put figures on each piece or group. Schmuel looked up from his accounting saying, "It seems we will be able to give twenty-five families enough to put food on their tables for at least six months. They all smiled and nodded by giving one another congrats.

****

The day after the unfortunate blunder (call it what you may) the Magistrate Lysinias gathered together his new Senior Centurion along with four men promoted from the ranks to Sergeants by Carmedias who now spoke to them before they went into The Magistrates headquarters. "Gentlemen, for your own best interest during this meeting do not voice your opinion if it would conflict with the Tetrarch's. Smile and nod your heads, answer any questions short and to the point. I doubt if he will ask you your opinions for he expects his orders to be carried out to a T, are we all in agreement?" They smiled and nodded in agreement. The meeting was short, sweet and to the point for the Tetrarch presented them with a plan to reward anybody presenting any information leading to the arrest of any Patriot. "The reward will come from this office and will be superior to the minor monies of denarii, avitus or solidos, and more than most citizens will ever see at one time; so the reward will be given upon verification. And it will be three daric which will feed the average family a minimum of six months."

He stood back as if admiring himself in a mirror his chin rose and his head bobbed several times as if congratulating himself then he peered at his guard audience perplexed as if to say, why are they not applauding my gracious move? Carmedias watching this ostentatious drama a smile broke his face as he whispered to himself, "He has changed some of his attributes *although he has not changed his ego attitude*, whoops we'd be forewarned to acknowledge this man for he is a *great man in his own mind!* Carmedias stood applauding loudly, the newly elevated men, having understood the earlier warning as regarding their Tetrarch, stood and followed suit! The applause broke out as if spontaneously the Centurion and their Captains motioning the correct action, the Tetrarch, pretending surprise, genuflected only slightly toward his guard several times then stood at attention grinning slowly and with great dramatic prowess raised his napkin to his eye dabbing an imaginary tear.

The Officers signaled the troops to continue the applause and from the rear a few hoots which encouraged a broader smile and a billowing of the chest standing there resembling an effigy of a departed Roman God. By this time their hands turning red and smarting happily ceased their applause instantly. Acknowledging what in his mind was adoration Lysinias again wiped another imaginary tear then motioned for them to sit down. Their leader waved as he walked out the door motioning for Carmedias to take over the dais. Carmedias gazed out over the faces of his three hundred men, "Captains and Lieutenants remain the balance of the guard will resign to your quarters and prepare for an extended deployment." As he saluted the guard slapped their right hand over their chest loudly returning the salute then filed out noiselessly in masse. When the last man had left the small arena Carmedias proceeded to give them their orders. "Each squad of seventy-five men will have an area to search," his Aide de Campo Toufeek rolled out a large map of Israel placing it upon an easel for them to see, "as you see the there are ten provinces; each Commander will be assigned two. Idumea in the Southwest including the province of Nabatea in the Southeast to the Northern tip of Lake Ashpaltitus and all the area from the shore of the Great Sea west to the border and to the Southern tip of

Two Men Named Jesus

Israel, this will be Area A and assigned to Captain Abnarah. Area B is the Province of Samaria on the western shore of the Big Sea on a line line from Appolonia east across to Trans Jordan and the Province of Decapolis and will be Commander Toumeeth' assignment." Pointing his baton to the map and touching the City of Dora, "Commander Abjuhrr you see the line I draw from that coastal City in the Province of Galilee West to the Tetrarchy of Philip and North including the Province of Abilene in Syria. You will select your own city in those areas to headquarter in. The Captains and their Lieutenants surrounding him awaiting what would be their direct orders. "Gentlemen you are dismissed please attend your units and report to me when you have finalized your ready positions." They all snapped a salute to Carmedias who brought his right hand over his chest in response.

****

CAT & MOUSE - A GAME?

Reminiscing as they strolled along the small stream that flowed from Mt. Herman in close proximity to Phillippi, enjoying the slight cool breeze caressing them, Barabbas, Schmuel, Mahjeed and Ayoub still four friends of the original Patriots, with Jameel accompanying them, "Although almost ten years ago we had no idea nor thought we would grow into an organization such as we have now," looking at Barabbas Schmuel continued, and that we be headed up by such a kindhearted and just man." Barabbas' face sobered and if one looked close a tear could be seen welling up within his eye, he answered, "I am nothing without your brain Schmuel along with the settling nature of Majheed and Ayoub for all of you have kept me grounded, we have never killed anybody and I add it is my wish we never do. Yes, I believe we truly have a great organization although we have from time to time had to ferret out a few who would never grow with our cause for their direction was not ours. We must remember our lieutenant Jameel," acknowledging him with a nod. Ayoub as always walked holding the garment of his brother-like Barabbas saying, "Look how clear the water is, did you know it flows from the Mountain and to think these streams from the Mount of Lebanon as well have fed Lakes Hulea, Gallilee and the Dead Sea for thousands of years. I remember my Grand Father told me it flows on south below the Lake of Asphaltitus (Dead Sea) then returning to the Mountain range in the south." As they strolled Majheed nudged his big brother saying, "Hey Giant look ahead see that guy walking along the path he's wearing a red faded, soiled tunic, watch him closely for I saw him pick the pocket of the Gentleman just ahead of him." "Oh yea I've got him in my sight, the gent he stole from looks to be a person of modicum means, oh yes see the lady with him let's move up and surround the thief and his mark then we will close in on them and guide the three of them to a place where we can talk to them."

Barabbas walked ahead moving in front of the Gentleman and his wife then slowed for them to pass him but remained on the left of them. Meanwhile Schmuel moved to the right of them and the other three took up the rear closing the circle. Barabbas moved into the gentleman's space walking at his left elbow and as he closed in the gent looked questioning this big person's move. At the same time on the right Schmuel closed on the right of the Lady touching his elbow to hers saying loud enough for her husband to hear him as well, "Do not be alarmed for we are about to save you from a thief who is walking directly behind you." At the same time at the rear of the thief Jameel, Ayoub and Majheed closed their sphere to surround the three of them. The thief attempted to stop but the rear guard pushed him along. The Gentleman turned his eyes toward the thief scowling at him. The wrists of the thief were suddenly clasped by the giant being now at his side and as he looked up his face quickly became ashen his lips dry the terror flooding over him his legs wanting to fold. As the thief settled Jameel reached under his arms holding him up saying, "Stay with us now fool, don't make any wrong moves and you will live to see another day."

A group of seven people were walking toward the sparse beginning of the forest near the well used path but as they closed the distance to the more dense area they walked inside a clearing and settled to the ground. His eyes glaring at the thief Barabbas growled, "Now young thief hand back the treasure you took from this gentleman and," leaning down Barabbas jammed his face into that of the thief, "I promise not to take your life." Almost before Barabbas finished his sentence the man's hand came out of his faded tunic handing over a large leather bag. Barabbas nodded toward the Gentleman and he took his bag. He opened it to inspect and verify that nothing had been removed then when he was sure, "Thank you my friend for this is all we own in the world other than a small home on the edge of Caeseria where we grow vegetables which we sell for a small income. I invite you and your friend to my house that I may show you my gratitude for what you have done." Schmuel answered, "No my friend you owe us nothing we witnessed this young man picking your pocket and knew what we should do now go and we will come by one day to see you." "Please do for we are grateful to you." With that he took the arm of his wife and walked away smiling.

    The young thief kept his head down knowing he would be better off not saying a thing. Barabbas turned back to the thief, "Young man surely you know having witnessed your thievery we could turn you over to the Roman guard and perhaps receive a reward." Backing away Barabbas made room for Schmuel, "What name are you known by young thief?" Without hesitation the young man answered, "Sir I am called Abeille and I come from a small town not far from here called Cadasa and have had no luck finding a job but I am a good carpenter, three weeks ago I made friends with a man about my age, his name Bajhurr, and he taught me the art of pick pocketing. I only do it for, uh, uh you know, so I have enough to eat." In order to establish some surprise Schmuel said quickly, "I'll bet you are one of those thieves in that ruthless organization so called Patriots." The young man was looking into a very sour face standing directly in front of him. For a moment he thought *"Wow they think I am one of those Patriots, I only wish I were but it's better I don't fib!"* "Speak up you little thief or I will be forced to take you to the authorities." The young man raised his eyes from the ground and looked into the solemn face of his interrogator. "No Sir I am not and I do not know any of those people but if I did I would not tell you for they helped my own family last year!" Schmuel smiled facetiously thinking, "this guy is a plant; I think he has been told to worm his way into the Patriots; wonder if he knew who we might be; probably not a coincidence." Then asked Abeille "How do you know it was the Patriots that furnished your family with something to eat they probably did it blowing their own horn bragging about it." Schmuel laid this groundwork giving the kid a chance to side with that accusation but he did not budge from his viewpoint. "No we were told not to say who the food was from by the man who brought it and he said he was only the uh, uh I think he said bringer or something like that," then, "oh yea he said deliverer." They all sat down on the grass now not saying anything for now it was up to their leaders to decide what to do with this young man. Barabbas told the youngster, "O K you can go now if you tell me where you live I may want to see you again." "I live behind you deep inside this forest where I won't be found." Schmuel spoke up immediately, "Do you and your friend find it comfortable in there?" Uh, uh, uh oh yes it is quite nice for there is a nice clearing where we sleep." He laughed nervously. Schmuel ended it with, "Alright young man you can go now. Schmuel turned away from the young lad his finger on his lips to let the Patriots know not to say anything.

Back at the cave they reviewed the information taken from the young thief and each of them gave their opinion of the meeting with the young man then when all but Schmuel had been heard he spoke. "I was hoping one of you had noticed two things about this kid." They all looked at him with wonderment. Barabbas spoke, "O K my Captain so we are not as observant as you tell us what you saw." Schmuel chuckled, "Did you not notice his sandals were new and they were not eastern made they are war sandals issued to Roman Warriors and guards only if you had looked closer you would see that the soles were much thicker. Then the design on the hem of his tunic was a design used only on those of the same group they are hemmed in leather to keep from wearing. Majeed, "Tell us what you are saying Schmuel what do you mean his sandals and his tunic?" "Yes my brother his sandals were made in Rome and the tunics worn in Roman circles are the only ones with leather design on the hem. In other words gents I think that kid was a spy and an imposter was sent to seek us out hoping to join us. Oh yes and one other thing; recall when I asked him if he and his buddy lived in that clearing he hesitated and fumbled for an answer." Turning to Barabbas, "We must have a meeting Barabbas, now!"

He walked back to the enclosed area in the far rear of the cave where the two of them held their private meetings. Barabbas sat, "Well Schmuel what do you suggest?" "Here is what we should do, when and if this young man contacts us again we waver by not saying much allow him to lay his plan out for I am sure it will be a trap of some kind. I believe he will show his eagerness to join us and we will throw all kinds of snags in his path seeming not to be interested. We will continue this then when he lest expects it we will offer to induct him into the organization. I will come up with some drawn out plan, nothing that resembles our true process, but some unusual questions urging his assurance of culpability." Barabbas smiled, "It seems you have everything under control as usual Schmuel fill me in when I return; it is time I visit the southern operation. Barabbas turned shouting up the hall to Jameel, "Jameel ready yourself for the trip south for we will leave when you are ready." Down the shaft came Jameel's voice, "I am ready when you are my General for I have anticipated this would be the day I have packed my satchel with all the necessaries." Then, "Goodbye Schmuel my Captain, stay well and keep these guys in tow, ha, ha, ha." Came back the voice of Schmuel, "Be careful my friend.

****

Later as Schmuel, Aboud and Majheed were shopping the three of them were inspecting fruit when Aboud whispered, "Don't look up, but that young man Abeille has been following us since we entered the souk." Schmuel turned the opposite direction to the bread makers to purchase a load of camaash. "Shopkeeper please give me those three stacks of bread and these four stacks of talamee and I will also have that pot of sweet talamee." As he stood he glanced toward the point where Abeille was seen and yes there he was not looking at them although Schmuel knew what his aim was. They loaded their three bushels of fruit and bread into their carriage leading the donkey toward their hideaway. "Abeille is following us; do not let him know we are aware of the tail. We will enter the forest taking the old trail into the densest part then hide and surprise him." When they were in position they waited for Abeille to come upon them. He had not seen them take the turn although he knew they must turn soon. When he was upon them they leapt out of the forest surprising him laughing as if this was a game. "Aha Abeille, surprise," Ayoub shouted surprise and fear clearly marked the young man's face, "Wow you guys scared the heck out of me and I just wanted to check in with you." Schmuel and his buddies pretending it was a game laughed in order to relax Abeille. He immediately stated, "Well guys if you will have me I would love to join your group." Schmuel looked at his buddies saying, "What group are we a part of guys, do you know?" Both Ayoub and Majheed looked at him with reservation. Abeille laughed nervously, "Come on you guys I know you are Patriots and I want to join."

****

Lysanias standing in his chariot proudly watched as the units marched out to their new assignments. "Captains when you are established in your particular areas inform your men of the rewards offered for an arrest of *any Patriot*. I will not give you that information but your Captains are aware of my intentions and will relate to you as they see fit."

Watching the movement of the troops on the north hill above the large Placa was Kallial, Majheed and Ayoub. Watching from the other side were Samir, Genendo and Fareed and they nodded to one another in understanding of the rewards program. Samir said, "We must find to what extent Lysanias is extending himself on these rewards." The six of them were to observe and later make their report to their Captain Schmuel. Other reports would come when the D unit was situated in the area near Caesaria Phillippi which was one of the wealthiest areas in the District of Palestine.

The Patriots renewed their activity in the Palestine area. Barabbas' gave them a new directive. "From this day none will operate on one's own; you will operate in groups of three only. I believe utilizing more than three would be dangerous. In operating with three this is how it should go down. Spot your mark and study his movements for a time. When you are positive the mark is not a plant and is affluent enough to scam then you will use the bump and pick. It is always easier to pick in a crowd. As always we do not take all ones assets. By the way we must begin looking for more caravans or large companies such as the Ghalaloumia Company who made our growth possible, I am sure those of you who were with us at the time recall. On second thought I suggest our Captain select several of you to search the area for large distributing companies where we can possibly plant a spy."

Abeille was allowed to join the Patriots in the Jerusalem District but not in their usual hideout. A large area again deep inside the forest area was trampled down with food supplies loaded in the trees attempting to make this resemble an area that had been utilized for some time. Prior To Abeille' initiation Schmuel instructed the Patriots *not* to answer *any questions asked by Abeille.* And now the initiation began. "Do you swear to uphold the rules and laws of this organization under penalty of loss of life?" Abeill answered immediately, "Yes." Schmuel would not utilize any of the questions normally used. "Do you swear never to talk to *anybody of your association with this Organization?"* Answer, "I do." Schmuel continued inventing new vows to offer this suspected spy. When the questioning was over, some thirty minutes later, the entrant was blindfolded and escorted deep into the darkest part of the forest where he was given huge peeled and deseeded grapes being told these were the eyes of tigers and he must eat two of them.

Abeill turned the grapes over and over in his hand his psyche concocting repulsive images of a tiger claw emanating from those eyes he must ingest which would undoubtedly shred his stomach rearranging his internal system to a nameless phantom no longer the clear figure born to his mother. He leaned forward his mouth a huge chasm as inside his esophagus lengthy fingers devoid of moisture scraped the walls as his entire body wretched. The man's face contorted into a multi colored mask wrinkling itself into an ugly picture not resembling the young face his mother knew. The Patriots watched from various vantage points, many in tall trees others inside the dense undergrowth yet others lying on the ground in the deep grass. Schmuel glared at them with a smile on his face for he knew they were enjoying this so called initiation doing their best to hold the laughter. Corythus and Cleothus who had been chewing on grass and roots came close to the initiate their mouths open wide and breathing hard into the man's face. The rank odor emanating from those orifices acted upon Abeill once again to urge the dry upheaval of his interior. His mind reintroduced those irritating fingers inside him as once again his mouth stretched itself open and he felt as if those same inside's would soon be torn out of him. Fear wracked Abiell throughout his normally two hundred pound body now like a pasta noodle eased itself to the ground in a feint. There would have been much more to this initiation process but Schmuel decided the Patriots had enough happiness and relaxation for this day and he knew it would be sometime before this young man would gain his composure and as it turned out Abiell slept for four hours thereafter.

Schmuel sent word to Barabbas detailing his plan to expose the spy Abiell and at the same time called a meeting of the entire crew, inside their newly found clearing deep in the forest for he wanted to make sure there were no questions as he wanted his plans proceeding without a hitch. "Next weekend there will be a huge gathering at Qumran Khirbet, the City of Salt, as it is known. They are celebrating the rebuilding of several of the buildings. I understand it will be huge. We will have a crowd to work in excess of three hundred or more which will increase our coffers considerably. All the regular rules apply." He turned toward Tanoush and Haleem saying, "Tanoush I am assigning our newest member Abiell to your group, you have done a remarkable job of training him and you say he is capable to operate on his own." Tanoush nodded smiling, "Oh yes my Captain he is ready for what we have in store for him." As he winked at them for during the training Abille was not allowed out of Haleems sight.

There was only one man that questioned that statement but only for a moment for then he remembered that his Captain must have some covert action in mind. This gent had been gone over night and had not been foretold of the newest actions. He turned to his leader

Jonathan signaling for a private conversation. As they met in the rear of the cave Jonathan whispered, "I did not know you had returned," then admonishing him, "why did you not come to me for possible new orders, you realize your actions could have spoiled Schmuel' new orders. I will not fill you in just make sure you follow my lead this weekend." The Patriot nodded apologizing, "I'm sorry Jonathan I was weary upon my return and failed to seek you out." Jonathan nodded acknowledging the young man's regret.

"What a great day for a celebration and would you look at the food over there, wow I've never seen so much great food in all my life. Oh my they have my favorite yaabraat ahryesh (rolled grape leaves) and look mallfoof (cabbage rolls) as well boy am I gonna enjoy this day, come on Ayoub," Majeeed shouted, "Let's fill our stomach." Schmuel laughed at them, "Ha ha ha you guys are going to eat too much, hope you don't get sick!" Fouad followed them saying, "Hey guys wait for me I love that stuff too, and I can't wait to get my teeth into the fatayah and sphyha (meat pies) wow am I going to be in seventh heaven, wow, wow!" As they rushed toward the food pavilion they could not help but spot a rotund gentleman around fifty years old with salt and pepper hair and a ready smile and was gorging himself with food in both hands and a servant holding a large silver plate stacked with all types of foodstuffs. Ayoub bounded toward the gent and bumped into him and when he turned to see what was happening Fouad picked his pocket so easy while Majheed bumped into the servant turning him around where he could not witness anything that was taking place then picked his pocket as well and unloading the tray of food into his own leather packet. "Oh my Sir, I apologize for bumping into you please forgive me."

The old man more interested in the food he was pushing into the hole in his face smiled and garbled something none could understand as bits of food attached roiled together with saliva swirled over his lips and down his chin as if it were a hot lava flow and those watching turned away in disgust although this plump *seemingly* famished human (?) seemed to be in paradise unaware of the world around him; this fat boy worshiped his only pastime, *eating!* Now Majeed, Ayoub and Fouad had done their job and melted into the crowd as they slowly, each using a separate way left the gates of the city. Tanoush, Haleem and Abiell had watched as this show had taken place. Tanoush pushed Abiell forward toward the crowd, "Did you see how professional that was done, now it is your turn, go mingle among them, spot your marks and relieve them of their wealth. We will meet you at the hideout when you are finished; remember if you see any of us do not speak just ignore us."

Abiell moved toward the large gate of the city overflowing with humanity. He thought to himself, "It looks as if I am in the game and they have fallen for my story I am sure they are watching me so I must make a stab at robbing somebody as soon as possible." Seeing a tall skinny man of some height dark of complexion and very little hair and accompanied with two Eunuchs one on each of his arms, "Aha he thought there is my first mark and this guy looks like one of the wealthiest persons I have ever seen". The path was ramped and Abiell was on the upper part of it as he bounded down the path to charge into this fine example of the Elite dressed in such finery reserved for those of that ilk. Abiell slammed into the gentleman so hard it spun them both around allowing Abiell to reach into the man's tunic and pull out one of the largest money bags he had ever seen. In one fell swoop the bag was seized and transferred into Abiell' own tunic. The gentleman was thrown toward the ground with such force allowing Abiell to make his escape. Each servant automatically grasped an arm of their master curbing his fall. The two Eunuchs straightened up their eyes glaring toward Abiell as he raced away. A shout was heard a few yards from the three just attacked, "After that man he has rammed into the Chancellor." Another voice from the other side of the square from the Captain of the Roman Guard, "Four stator's to the man who apprehends him." From all side of the quarter came shouting picked up by guards stationed at fifty feet intervals their voices circling the Placa from the north end and returning to the starting point. "Hold your ground!" Keep your eyes peeled!" "Find the young man in the red tunic!" Once again fear gripped Abiell for he realized none of the guards knew his position in the Magistrates office, they did not know he was a spy working in the camp of the enemy. His legs were moving so fast he wondered how is body could keep up with itself. "What a silly thought." He shouted as he ran toward the forest hoping to find the clearing of the hideaway soon. Finally reaching the clearing where he was sure the camp was located he stopped dead in his tracks his eyes growing in uncertainty for there was no indication that this was a lived in clearing. His mind was playing tricks on him he closed his eyes for a few seconds then slowly opening them expecting to see some of the stools and packets that had been scattered around by the Patriots. Shouting, "I must be going crazy." Looking behind him turning in a circle hoping to see something to affirm him for he knew this was the correct location. Seeing naught that might help his sanity he sank to the ground again washed out wondering if he were really going batty. The pressure made him weary his mind saying, "relax," as he crashed to the floor of the clearing seemingly deprived of rest; then darkness engulfed his entire being crushing his will to move.

Back at the Placa in Qumran Khirbet Captain Abnarah shouted to his men, "Close ranks, encircle the Plaza and hold any thieving suspects! Squeeze the crowd into one mass and allow them to leave at the point of my station." He stood with his ten key Roman guards surrounding a ten foot gap. Speaking to the crowd, who by now had been instructed to remain calm and quiet, "Come through slowly as we inspect each of you and answer only the questions you are asked, *do not offer any opinions, keep your thoughts to yourself* no one will be charged or harmed unless found guilty." Then the crowd, with the Patriots dispersed throughout them, slowly crept by the station of guards answering the questions until finally the mass was no more. Schmuel smiled to himself as he was released and looking back he saw there was only a handful of that large crowd left to make its way out of the contained area.

Once again maintaining caution as his companion Schmuel's great insight had blocked another attempt by the Roman Magistrate to apprehend the Patriots. Foiled again Lysinias stood shaking his head in disbelief mumbling incoherently while nearby Carmedias, the Magistrates Captain, steeling himself for the explosion that eventually would rear its ugly head into a crescendo spewing weighty demands on all those around turning a sunny day into clouds of anxiety; Carmedias sighed heavily shrugged then slightly turned his head his eyes conveying a tale of exasperation to his officers and men whom knowing what was about to occur a look of clouded resignation flowed over them. The anticipated storm did not descend upon them as they expected for Lysinias thinking back to the scolding received from his Captain at his prior outburst he hesitatingly gulped down his pride. He would now demonstrate his magnanimity by presenting a newly invented Magistrate to his people. This thought brought him to his senses for he was after all (in his own mind) the controller of his destiny. "Men," he began, his face offering nothing less than a totally happy smile, "you are dismissed," turning to Carmedias, "stay we will talk."

As the men filed out to their various stations Lysinias sat offering his Captain a seat. Not a word was spoken for some time for Lysinias was deep in thought and Carmedias could only watch and imagine what was going through his Superiors mind. "It seems another plan backfired on us. This necessitates a new approach we must begin at our highest level that is our own interior perhaps we have a moll within our organization?" The thought reminded him of his own mole Magianas which brought a frown, "Where do you suppose Magianas is, we did not apprehend him and yet he has not shown himself. Was it not your orders for him to report back?" Carmedias answered, "He was ordered to report when he had viable information; he should be returning within the next day with the location of the thieves headquarters."

Captain Carmedias instigated the investigation quietly and covertly thus none would know save him what was taking place. It would be an easy thing to find a mole within the organization for there were only three others allowed within the inner offices of the Magistrate. Carmedias set traps of all kinds hoping to ensnare the spy, for little doubt was given by Lysinias, "There must be someone," as he related to his best friend Simon Antropidous, "for we are mated at every turn, oh that I had your numbers Simon then I could ferret them out." Simon's chest swelled and his height grew for, much like his counterpart he too owned an enormous ego and as all were, legends in their own minds thusly growing their images several fold. "Thank you Lysinias but we continually monitor our offices and maintain tabs upon our key employees." Lysinias smiled thinking, "Yes Simon we all know how thorough your office is, yes you have the finest of everything; go away and leave me alone."

****

Awake in the clearing his brain reconnecting to his nervous system Magianas found himself a different person than when he awoke that morning. His brain began its finest function in several years. He had been duped and he was not about to be bested by the likes of those common thieves. First he must think back attempting to outline where he had failed, "What mistakes did I make, how did they realize I was a spy, or did they, yes I am sure, and how did I present myself that they would have made me so easily?" All these and many other questions floated inside his brain as he sat clearing his head. Orally he said, "I will find their hideout making myself a wealthy man for the Magistrate will enhance my coffers when I give him that information." Magianas's first move was to find a set of old clothes, this was no problem for scattered outside the animal gate of Jerusalem among the large boulders standing there and over the ground one could find discarded raggedy clothing perhaps where those of slight means cast them off and changed into more acceptable garments gained from who knew where. Searching at night he found just what he wanted, garb not altogether the most desirable but at least they had lain in the sand long enough to have cleared some of the stench emanating from them. He took what would become an element of his new found identity to his home then waited 'til the darkest hours of the morning donning the stench laden garb then slowly climbed the ladder to the roof of his abode. Raising the trap door slowly holding the old leather handle so the door could not slam down he raised his head out the door making sure nobody was on the roof and none were atop the adjoining homes he was glad for this time of year for it was too cool for sleeping outdoor that is if one had a home. Magianas found his way in the darkness of the night through the alleyways where he lived toward the west then reaching the cattle gate easing out so none would see him. He made his way up the small hill and stopped half way up where he dropped to his knees, closing his eyes he splashed dirt on his head and face then with his sleeve wiping his face so the earth would penetrate the pores of his skin. He would stay out this night in a niche of the hill he had discovered earlier in the week camouflaging it with limbs and brush to hide and warm himself. He settled into the niche pulling a heavy large sack cloth over his body. "Well," he mused as he settled in, "this is not so bad after all I hope I can become accustomed to the stink of my clothing." He laughed then coughed as the odor reeked its way into his nostrils automatically turning his head to escape the smell, which did not help and as weary as he was he knew he would toss an turn before sleep invaded him, yet his mind had no time at all to think of other things for he was into the black tunnel of sleep as his head hit the soft brush of his pillow.

****

The merchant Gallus frowned at the poor old cripple as he walked toward the souk where Gallus & Co was setting up his market for the day. Gallus had made the best deal he had ever made with the Magistrates office for the largest site in the souk. As they worked Amianas turned to Gallus, "My Lord here comes that stinking old cripple again I ran him off yesterday, he sat near the fresh vegetables and fruit his body reeking with that foulness and when customers saw him it must have revolted them so our sales were off terribly. Shall I send him off again?" Gallus was feeling generous this morning, "No, no Amianas go to him before he reaches us and give him a few fruits then ask him to keep his distance and you will give him two meals each day, but he must remain far enough away from us that he will not be considered a problem." Amianas looked questionably at his patron Gallus saying, "I hope so Sir, I hope so; I will do as you say." Amianas looked up to see the old guy standing in front of him leaning on his crutch and presenting a most horrendous grin a mouthful of rotten broken teeth. "I am going to feed you each day but you must promise to keep your distance from this market; if not I will be forced to call a Roman guard and move you out of this area, do you understand?" "Yeth, yeth," the old man lisped sending forth a blast of air from that orifice reeking of a mixture of the most distinctively putrid stench Amianas had ever experienced, "Please step away, move back to that boulder near the large cedar I," his voice hesitant, "will send your, whew, whew, provisions to you. Do not come closer and each day I will send food to you, alright?" As he pushed the old beggar away he watched as the old man retreated to the boulder and sat down his sullied face streaked with lines of dust yet shaking his head in agreement. Amianas could not force himself to deliver the foodstuffs to the beggar so he turned to an assistant, "Come, here take that beggar these fruits and cheese and make sure you feed him three times a day, *BUT, whatever you do, do not allow him to approach our Masters market area, do you understand!*" Not shouting but almost so harshly spoken the servant was taken aback, "Yes Amianas I understand!" Each day the beggar sat at his boulder as if it were a dinner table awaiting his sustenance. Upon finishing his meal, which came to him twice a day, he would then walk off simply strolling in various directions humming a not to certain tune then be lost to sight until time for his next meal. The cripple beggar became a fixture near the souk although none neared his area in fact just the opposite all circumvented his boulder so after several weeks a new path had been formed representing a barrier the stench *never, never decreased its* dreadful output. This day the old beggar limped slowly toward the dense tree line holding his crutch under his left arm and dragging his left foot. As he headed deeper into the overgrowth a strange thing occurred. He pulled his crutch from under his arm carrying it in his hand and suddenly his left foot supported his lean exceptionally. When he was sure there was nobody watching, he became less of a cripple. He sat down near a small stream took off his skull cap and from under his tunic pulling out a clean rag he dipped it into the water and wiped his face and looking down into the clear water he gave a deep sigh of relief then leaned back against a boulder relaxing. Thinking out loud Magianas said, "I am tired of searching for those guys, it has been three weeks and I haven't found a clue as to their hideout but I will keep looking and when I do it will be my time for I will be a wealthy man, ha, ha, ha, ha!" his laughter resounding across the clearing bouncing off the dense tree line and back at him louder yet. Surprised he almost jumped out of his dirty clothes. "And I'm getting tired of all those roots and garlic I eat, oh how I wish I could find them."

Day after day Magianas searched. He had gone deep into the jungle of trees finally coming out through the shrubs below the mountain searching its sides with his eyes. The formation and slope of the mountain was such that only about a half mille could be traversed for after that on both sides it rose so sharply a mountain goat would have a terrible time gaining access. He knew there must be someplace else he had not looked for; suddenly he stopped thinking saying, "I'll bet they have a house someplace here in the city so I will begin looking at extremely large houses which will be in the suburbs, yes I will, but not until the morrow." He laid his head down and soon was fast asleep.

The crowd was the heaviest Gallus and Amianas could recall; happy they were for the market was turning over product at an amazing rate. The most generous Gallus smiled as he watched a young girl and boy, obviously twins, holding hands while walking in and out of the aisles of foodstuffs. The children's clothing old and faded yet clean and Gallus could see the desire for some of the fancy figs they stood there studying. A smiling loving gentleman behind them said, "Let's go children we must leave now if we are to arrive at your Aunt Genevieve's house on time, come now." Gallus moved closer to the three reached the carton of figs saying to the man, "Sir it looks as though I have scores of these figs as well as apples and rather than discard them to the pig's would you honor me and take them home with you?" Then without hesitation he pushed the bag and cartons into the man's hand and before the Gent could answer, "Thank you sir for helping me I hope I haven't overburdened you, have a great day and God Bless!" This was the way of Gallus the merchant. As he turned he could see the cripple beggar leave his position at the boulder turn and move toward the area of arid sand and tall ant hills. He mused, "What will happen to that old beggar what in the Lords name is planned for him, why would anybody want to enter that forsaken area where nothing grows and where the sand maintains its heat, tsk, tsk, tsk."

Magianas stopped at the entrance to the arid gardens entering and crawling behind a six foot ant hill. "I think I will sleep here tonight for I am weary of that forest I will settle behind this hill where it is warm and sleep tonight and I will be near the souk that when I wake my food will be waiting for me. I am happy Gallus is so charitable." As he said this he snuggled down into the warm sand for a night's sleep.

The sun was expanding as its rays burned off the clouds racing to gain the highest peak in the morning sky. Magianas stirred from his sleep slowly opening his eyes recalling now where he had spent this night. He held his breath for a second for he heard voices nearby. He identified the voices as those known to him but could not put a name to them until one said, "Come on Ayoub pick up your feet for we must hurry back with the goat's cheese and fruit." "Yes yes I know Majheed give me a hand with the pull cart, I am glad the souk is close by, it will not take us long to fill our order, oh I almost forgot did you check the coffee, do we have plenty?" "Do not worry your head Ayoub I have it under control." Magianas gasped out loud when he realized the two voices belonged to Schmuel' two young friends. He poked his head around the ant hill as the two were passing nearby. "Aha," he thought, "they came from inside the sand area but where exactly there surely is no place to hide in this desolate area?" He would await their return then follow them hoping this was the clue he finally needed. His mind raced ahead and pictures of wealth and pleasure crowded his mind until he felt he would swoon. He sat back down to wait for Ayoub and Majheed to return. Thirty minutes later Magianas heard the voices of Ayoub and Majheed once again, having not been ready for this he knew they would be much too close to poke his head out to see them. He waited until their voices slowly diminished then rose and walked around the tall ant hill and out into the hot sand. He could not see them but he could hear their voices ahead of him although he could not make out what they were saying. He sprang from ant hill to ant hill attempting to keep hidden from their view in the event they looked back. The voices moderated once again for some fifteen seconds then ended abruptly. Magianas sprang from his hiding place knowing if they discovered him all would be lost. He assumed his eyes were deceiving him it must be the dazzling heat from Old Sol for he saw neither Majheed nor Ayoub. Instantly he closed his eyes massaging them hopping when he opened them again he would discover them. No such luck and once again he circled the ant hills one by one jumping from one to another. As the hot sand seeped into his sandals uncomfortably warming his feet he ran for the shade of the large oak trees at the edge of the desert. Settling under the cool of the trees he looked back studying the strange looking area of ant hills being caressed by Old Sol generating a slight haze that danced across the top of the sand almost indistinguishable making it difficult to focus the eyes. He stood like a statue both hands shading his eyes squinting his gaze slowly moving his head from left to right then back again across the near horizon. Frustrated now being annoyed that he lost them, "They were there then suddenly they were gone with no trace not even a discernible track." Then thinking he might be wrong, "Perhaps that was not them, hum, oh heck what am I thinking of course it was them but how on this earth did they vanish into thin air, I hope I'm not going nuts?" He closed his eyes and settled to the cool grass at his feet where he relaxed for some moments then got up and moved toward the opening of the tree line facing the south souk, for a moment confused for he entered from the east souk, "No matter he thought I will go home and rest."

Jameel entered the cave with seven rabbits he had just trapped, "Here you go cooks something besides lamb and kid to eat and how about some cabbage to go with them." "Thanks Jameel how many do you think these will feed, if you want to eat rabbit you'd best catch seven more, and I will cook them using my recipe," taunted Majheed laughing. Jameel smiled asking, "Is Schmuel back in his room I need to talk to him?" Ayoub pointed toward the rear of the cave. "Schmuel my Captain," Jameel said peeking his head in, "I discovered something we perhaps should talk about," not waiting for a reply, "I have been in the sand trapping rabbits around the ant hills and discovered foot tracks not coming from our pathways but out of the forest then back across the sand coming out under the trees to the south opening, should I post a lookout to watch the area?" "Hum, Jameel I will leave it up to you but keep me posted for up to now we have been fortunate keeping ourselves under cover." "I shall Schmuel, thanks for your input." Leaving the inner rooms of Schmuel and Barabbas Jameel motioned for Samir to follow him. Stopping at the door of the cave he peered through the peep hole checking the exit. He stepped outside Samir followed they stopped a few feet from the entrance. "Come Samir take a look at these sandal prints here near this large ant hill, see aren't those sandal steps?" Samir knelt in order to get a better look at the foot prints then he stood following the prints through the sand to the tree line stopping and looking down at the grass. "Do you see any indication of any foot prints here Samir, I sure don't but of course the grass is very thick?" "I don't think it is going to matter for I assume you want me to set up a surveillance team; do you think it should be twenty four hours a day and how long should we maintain our watch?" "I prefer you to begin immediately and continue the observation for how long it may take for we do not know for sure if our concern is real or not." "All right Jameel I will use Genendo, Fareed and Sensonian if you agree." Samir waited for Jameel to answer him for he was retracing his steps back to the ant hill where the footsteps were first found. "That sounds like a good plan Samir keep me posted for you know our Captain will want to know any results." At that they went back inside the cave Jameel deep in thought musing what might come of this find he turned raised his head closing his eyes deep in thought. Those sandals may be the heavy kind we were advised of before?

Night found Genendo high inside one of the large oaks at the edge of the small desert and Sensonian backed up against one of the tall ant hills wrapped in sack cloth from head to toe the coarse weave allowing him to see perfectly well. A thin fish line stretched from the tree down to Sensonian for each would be on watch for two hour intervals with a second line fed into the cave with a rock hanging on it, if pulled hard enough the rock would hit a small metal plate awakening whomever was in charge. The first watch would be the responsibility of Genendo whereupon he would yank the fish line hoping to awaken Sensonian at which time the latter would take the watch, and so it went throughout the first night. At their meeting to lay out the watch Samir said, "Let's hope this is nothing to worry about but as you all know we have been trained to ever prepare ourselves for any initiative. You two will be replaced by Narooth and Jaman tomorrow and they will spell you the following day, depending on how long this investigation remains important, I will add two more men the fifth day." The first two nights there was nothing, no movement within their vision. The first two nights a bright yellow moon dressed the desert in its best finery. The third night Genendo was awakened by a yank on the line; slowly opening his eyes fixed upon the opening of the cave and turning his head slowly he saw something move in the shadow of the oak tree, he froze looking through the sack cloth. It was a somewhat cloudy night which was ideal for a sneak attack although they did not know what to expect. Genendo looked up into the oak for any added direction, nothing forthcoming he turned his eyes back to the form at the edge of the clearing. It was good he did for the person began his slow trek across the sands still warm from the day's Sun. As it was sometime after midnight they did not know what to expect although they were prepared to anticipate a squad of men to follow the first spy.

The man was moving slowly at intervals moving a few feet stopping then moving again until he was within eight feet of Genendo, now behind the ant hill waiting for something to happen. The sneak settled down near the ant hill away from Genendo issuing a sigh which told the Patriot he was settling in. He glanced up toward the oak and saw Sensonian give a yank on the fish line connected to the cave and noticed the line was yanked from inside telling him they understood and were watching. Magianas was the fortunate one this night for he settled down and soon was fast asleep. Genendo waited for a signal to move and after an hour, knowing the stranger was asleep, was given a signal to move back inside the cave via the summit entrance. He waited another twenty minutes or so then made his way to his rear then west toward hideaway climbing to the top and entering there. Magianas had outfoxed them this time only pretended to be in a deep sleep. He could feel the movement of Genendo although there was very little noise except that of slight scraping of sand under his sandals. Magianas waited patiently for almost an hour then slowly made his way back out the entrance to the forest not making any foot prints in the sand thinking, "I have done it oh yes I have found the Patriots home and now I will find my place in history for I will become a wealthy man for this information; now I will go home to sleep then tomorrow I will see the Magistrate, "yahoo", he shouted, "yahoo, I can hardly wait for the sun to rise, yahoo," and he looked back making sure he was several blocks away from the forest and back into the city. Back inside their shelter they reported to Jameel who then took the information to Schmuel. "It was just some cripple looking for someplace to spend the night." Jameel laughed, "He didn't see Genendo for he settled behind him near an ant hill and fell fast asleep we waited long enough to make sure."

LOSE THE BATTLE - WAR BEGINS

Ayoub and Majeed's sleeping quarters were in the rear of the cave very near the ladder, the exit out an the top of the hill. Barabbas had built a four foot high wall around the kitchen facilities and the sleeping area of the two. Barabbas was like a father to these two youngsters, as he called them although they were both near twenty one now. The respect the Patriots had for these two was unusual and they all treated them as Barabbas and Schmuel with great respect.

It was near the early morning when Majheed awoke to the sound of Ayoub' soft groans of pain. He looked over at Ayoub who was still asleep yet moaning, seemingly in pain as his body squirmed and twisted. Majheed leaned down with his lips to Ayoub' ear, "Ayoub my brother are you alright?" Majeed' hand shook the younger ones shoulder adding, "Wake up Ayoub what is wrong?" Ayoubs eyes opened, "I have a queasy stomach Majeed I ate something that is churning in my innards oh, oh, oh." "Come Ayoub get up, come with me we will climb the ladder so as not to bother the others I'm sure you will feel better with fresh air in your lungs." Majheed climbed the ladder slowly reaching back to take the hand of Ayoub for his club foot did not fit the rungs of the ladder well. Majheed eased the trap door open to the outside peeking over the top of the hill. This was usual no matter what time of day or night; it was an order from Barabbas; never go out without checking first! They eased out of the cave Majheed helping Ayoub, "Lie down my brother take several deep breaths, you will feel better soon I will be here just relax." Majheed raised himself from the roof of the hill then hastily dropped down holding his index finger over his lips then motioning Ayoub to stay low. Ayoub raised himself slowly to look over the edge of the hill squinting his eyes for the darkness was ebbing slowly but the sun was not yet in charge of this day. Ayoub could see several forms moving slowly toward the ant hills, he whispered, "What is going on, who might they be, we had better get back down the ladder and warn the others."

The sickness vanished instantly with that they almost slid down the ladder. Majheed put his hand over Schmuel's mouth then shaking him awake. Looking up Schmuel saw the concern in Majeeds face. Knowing something was wrong he whispered, "What Majheed, what is going on?" Majeed's anxious voice whispered, "Schmuel there are men crawling toward the cave from the west toward the ant hills."

Meanwhile Ayoub had rushed to Jameel waking

him explaining the problem. Between them they woke the others as quickly as possible. Soon they were all standing around the center of the cave awaiting orders from Schmuel. "Jameel, take Ayoub and Majheed with you and flee now. Hide Ayoub and Majheed with Ankarnina at her farm then go as fast as you can to Barabbas in the north. All of you follow them and as many as possible make your way to any of the prearranged hideouts or to your family if they are near." Jameel grabbed Schmuel' arm, "Schmuel you must go now for you cannot be taken." Without waiting for any answer from his Captain, "Tanoush, Haleem, Kallial and Fouad you will accompany our Captain away from harm," turning to Schmuel, "Say not a word for Samir and I are taking charge as you are to save yourself," he shouted, "GO, GO, GO!" Samir shouted, "I will take care of Majheed and Ayoub, I will deposit them with my Aunt Ankarina then as we have planned I will find my way to Ca," he slapped his hand over his mouth, "the north."

Schmuel' four escorts literally carried him to the ladder and out into the night. Jameel' voice could be heard from the roof of the hill encouraging others to go while he guided them out of the cave.

****

The sun was almost up and suddenly the noise of the Roman Guard could be heard. *"Grab them as fast as you can, there run catch those two. You, fast, fast close the net close the east end, hurry, hurry now we will soon have them all! Look there go three of them catch them hurry, faster."* Soon the Roman guard, two hundred strong captured twenty eight Patriots including Jameel who had made sure Schmuel, Ayoub and Majheed had gotten away.

****

Schmuel sighed thinking, "at least Samir got away too. They counted twenty eight prisoners, thanks they didn't get us all; some place out there is the balance and they will soon be with Barabbas who *will* have a plan." Samir, Majheed and Ayoub scrambled down the side of the hill the voices of the Roman guard shouting and banging their lances and swords against anything they could to make noise. Samir pulled the two behind a large shrub at the bottom of the hill motioning for them to scrunch down as they waited, for running footsteps could be heard coming their way. Nearing them three Romans were moving fast in their direction one of the guards veered left and another right with the other getting closer to their shelter. It was not yet dawn although ole Sol was about to make a full fledged move against the darkness and crown himself once more as he climbed onto his throne. The Roman loomed closer running hard, Samir smiled and Majheed and Ayoub understood. The movement of the guard brought him nearer and as he passed them Samir thrust his lance through the shrub catching the shin of the guard which careened him into the ground his speed gliding his head into a large boulder making a sound as that of a melon being dropped and breaking open this guard was out for the count. Without delay Samir bound out of the shrub motioning to the other two to follow. Samir pulled the breastplate, helmet, tunic and sandals from the body tying his hands and feet then pulled him behind the shrub where he would not be found for some time. Samir donned the breastplate, helmet, sandals and tunic of the guard then said, "Put your hands behind your back and I will bind you with the rope from the guard." Majheed started to say something then a light went on and he understood what was happening for Romans were everywhere and this would be their exit plan. Holding his lance near the back of his two prisoners Samir began his march with the two out of the forest area. "Heads down you two, do not attempt to look at my Captain, keep moving ahead." Samir shouted he also kept his head down for this impressed Captain Carmedias, "Good job soldier take them directly to the dungeon." Samir slapped his chest hard with his left hand saluting the Commander. "Yes Sir, trot you two or I shall run this lance through you!" His Captain watched smiling for he knew he had done a great job and proud of himself.

Samir and his two prisoners cut through the woods and as he did noticed a Sergeant turning his way. He saluted and shouted, "I must relieve myself my Sergeant then I will take the short cut to the dungeon." The

Sergeant waved in acknowledgement. When they were deep into the woods Samir took off the helmet, sandals, breastplate and tunic tucking them into sackcloth bags. They headed north to the farm of Aunt Ankarnina only a few mille. Upon arrival Ankarnina hugged them all welcoming them. Samir left them with distinctive instructions. "I am instructing you both to grow beards so that when you go into Jerusalem where you are known by the merchants you will create a new character I also suggest you change your names. Ankarnina smiled, "That will be easy for you should each take the name of your grandfather." She smiled nodding her head as she put together a zoowada (food package) for Samir' trek north. Now Majheed would be Toufeek and Ayoub's new name would be Shammas. They said their names over and over until they all laughed then Samir said, "I must leave now for I have a long trek ahead of me and we do not know who or if anybody made it to our leader, pray for me." They hugged showing their love for each other saying their goodbyes.

As he made his way north Samir was not sure which route to take. He was in great shape so began trotting north along the base of the mountains keeping them on the west staying near the Jordan River which stretched north into the Sea of Galilee. Some four hours later he slowed somewhat, just a little, took out some of the food Auntie had put in his pack and while trotting ate one meat pie and a pear, that would suffice until morning.

Finishing the fruit he stopped near the river. Bending down while supporting his body with his arms he sipped a deep drink from the stream of the sweet water of the Jordan. He pondered for just a moment his own image looking back at him from the stream; he thought: I drink from a stream that has been flowing since the beginning of time; a smile of wonderment shown upon his face, then quickly rose picking up his brisk trek and on his way again. Samir knew he must watch himself now and not allow strangers to come close; he would keep his head down and not permit his eyes to contact others. His mind mulled over the acquaintances in Jerusalem had he or any of the Patriots become too friendly with any within that city. The admonishment of the rule given them years before came to mind, "Keep those who would wish to become close at arm's length never giving information that might bring you or all of us down. Learn to smile when asked personal questions thus when you ignore those questions they should not be bothered; a shrug with a smile will give them all they need and if any be adamant know that would probably be intent to seek information. Once again a smile and a shrug and take leave of that person.

****

Caesaria Philippi located on the south slope of Mt Hermon loomed before Samir and a smile broke across his face for he had traveled the one hundred and twenty mille from Jerusalem in four days. He as all the Patriots were in great physical condition for as the years advanced Schmuel and Barabbas insisted they follow this regimen. He looked upwards toward the plateau where Schmuel had first come before finding the new hideaway; he paused thinking, "Wow it has been years since the establishment of this northern headquarters, good that we did for now it is coming into great need." He stopped for a second his senses taking in the aromas flowing from somewhere above. He speedily climbed the steps for there seemed to be a hole where his stomach had been and now his nostrils verified the aroma as that of lahaam mishwee (charcoaled meat) wafting across the Plateau the wind spinning it down across the heads of those climbing the stairs. Yes he would partake of a most delicious meal. He reached the plateau and his senses insisted on a direct route to that huge charcoal bed where slabs of lamb, kid and chicken hung on skewers while a young man boringly slowly turned the handle revolving the circular spit his sad eyes and the many long and loud sighs emanating from him were basically directed toward his father filling dishes with the meat and veggies and ignoring his son. Samir stopped noting what a clever device this was for by revolving over the burning coals the meat would be cooked perfectly. Smiling the proprietor asked, "Ya zalama shoo am bit hib? (Sir what would you like). Samir pointed to the lamb asking, "Do you serve this with cammash (Pita bread)? "A wah." (Of course), came the answer. He paid for his meal and stepped toward the flat rocks where he could be comfortable while enjoying this long awaited pleasure.

Half way through his meal he paused his eyes rolling across the mesa not looking at anything in particular then looked back down to his plate to wrap another piece of lamb in the pita bread a voice said, "Sir that looks like a very good meal would you recommend that lamb?" His appetite not completely satisfied he did not look up and with a mouth full of food he tried to answer, "Oh yeth thir thith ith some of tha," he paused knowing he was being rude then finished the large bite, looked up and almost choked for looking down at him was Braheem, Claudio, and Zeno. Braheem said "Sir when you are finished eating I would like a word with you, I will be yonder near the drinking pool." Claudio brushed his finger over his lips indicating Samir not say anything. The three turned and walked away toward the drinking pool. Finished, Samir returned the plate to the café owner thanking him and slowly walked over to his three friends. "Did you have a question for me Sir?" Samir asked a broad grin braking over his countenance. Speaking quietly so as not to be heard above the hum of the crowd, "Why yes Sir, may I ask where you hail from, you look like a friend of mine from Chabulon (Cabul). There was the code sentence now Samir had to recall the answer. "No Sir in fact I do not know where that town is, sorry but perhaps you can lead me to a place where I may rest tonight?" He turned looking around as their eyes followed his line of sight. There was nobody within ten feet of them and Braheem nodded saying quietly, "Come follow us." They all started down the steps toward their headquarters. They strode away from the Plateau and up a small hill toward a row of trees and dense greenery on their right. "How far are we from headquarters?" Samir asked, anxiety in his voice. Zeno answered, "Not far Samir," pausing he put both his hands on Samir' shoulders and looked into his eyes, "but what is bothering you, your face is drawn and you seem very apprehensive?" Braheem interrupted, "We are here Samir; you will be surprised now, pull on that large shrub in front of you, yes that one, yank hard on it." Samir yanked on the shrub and it pulled toward him. Surprised he said, "Wow how in the world did that happen." "Go in." Zeno said and they all stepped through then turned to watch Samir's astonishment as he watched the shrub spring into place. "Boy that is something, has any of the other southern members arrived?" They stood looking at him uncertainty in their eyes. "Are you expecting more," and turning to Zeno and Claudio Braheem asked, "are we having a meeting I know nothing about?" his face a study in wonderment. Samir, "Well I guess I must be the first one here, hurry, I must speak to Barabbas for I have bad news to report." Knowing they would hear no more from Samir they headed up the hill to the mesa. Samir was so very impressed with the northern headquarters but nursing his rightful concerns his mind was directed to relaying his message to Barabbas and the Patriots. Just then Barabbas rounded a corner toward the back of the cave and seeing Samir shouted, "Well would you look here ya zalaam (Gent's)," surprised, "Are you part of a delegation or?" Seeing Samir' downcast face he knew something was not right. "What is it Samir, your face tells me things are not right, am I correct?" They met in the center of the large cavern and after exchanging hugs and greetings Samir told them all that had taken place. When he finished the questions came fast. They were of course happy for those who made it out safely but somewhat irate to know that so many of their brothers had been taken prisoner. "There is not a lot we can do at the present time, you say Schmuel is safe, do you know what route he took to get here, and by the way what course was yours?" Samir answered, "I came directly north following the line of The Jordan, and thanks to that gentleman cooking the meat atop the Plateau, Braheem and his men found me hungrily feeding myself the first real food I have had in three days." "Are you healthy, feeling good is there anything you need?" "No, no, I'm fine but my thoughts are now of Schmuel and the rest. I am sure they took other routes to get here Barabbas, can we check the other routes they may have taken?" Barabbas gently pulled Samir to him holding him tight as a father might care for a son saying, "Do not fret my dear Samir for you and I both know our Captain is the most resourceful member of our organization and remember he purchased this farm himself and knows more of it than any." They all sat down while Jodan and Yonaton brought them cups of coffee. "I see you have designated cooks as we have," pausing his mind going back to his Aunt, "I forgot to tell you I dropped Ayoub and Majheed with Aunt Ankarnina and instructed them to use their fathers names, Toufeek and Shamus. Also they will not go into town unless in disguise, my Aunt is a very wise and creative woman and she will be quick to guide them although you and Schmuel have schooled them well." Barabbas said, "All right now let's all get some rest for we will need our strength tomorrow as we await the arrival of our brothers.

****

Toward evening of the following day they were whiling away time playing chess, rumikub and other games and making small talk when one of the Patriots jumped up from his position. "Shush." Yahcoob said and pointed to the roof exit. They could hear the straw and limbs being removed from over the trap door. Barabbas screwed his mouth up while they all kept their eyes on the escape door. Yahcoob and Vigilius grabbed their weapons standing near the ladder while the others drew away from that area. The trap door opened slowly and a head poked through and at that Barabbas laughed that happy laugh of his as he shouted, "Schmuel, Schmuel we should have known! Jump down and bring the rest with you!" Schmuel along with the twelve slumped to the floor in exhaustion and were brought food and drink immediately.

****

Next day found the Patriots outside in the warm sunshine awaiting the decision of Barabbas, Schmuel, Braheem and Samir who were at the top edge of the mesa under several large chiku (sapodilla) trees planning the strategy to be used. They were all deep in thought when Barabbas took a sip of his drink than turned to Schmuel, "We must devise a perfect plan with no errors to free our bother Patriots have you come up with anything, how about either one of you?" He pointed to Braheem and Samir then along with Schmuel shook their heads, "I think it benefits us to return to Jerusalem soon but yet not too soon for I am sure our nemesis will be expecting us." "Yes," Braheem spoke next, "and I am positive they will strengthen the rear entrance into the dungeon for the reports received here in the Tetrarach's office from Jerusalem said they were quite perturbed at our use of their weakness." Snickers came from the others as they recalled their success at that prison. From Barabbas, "All right, if we are all agreed than we will return to Jerusalem to study the situation and decide our next move. Samir please inform them all that they may ready themselves for the return. Remind them they all have their return routes and do not return to the cave but to the farm of

Ankarnina." "Just one moment please," from Schmuel, "Braheem perhaps you should remain here in Caesaria in your capacity at the Magistrates for we will need you in the event any pertinent information makes its way to Jerusalem. As he looked up he noticed all the Patriots of the northern group had their belongings and were ready to march. "Gentlemen we want to thank you for volunteering to go south to assist your brothers but we will not need you. In the event we do we will send for you so continue your normal duties meanwhile as you know Braheem is in charge and Manjour and Kallial will be aides. Again thank you all! Oh yes some of the men do not know there is a cavern behind the Anakarnina house we will be using until we find another location for we do not want to add any more pressure to Ankarninas life farewell for now and think of us.

****

The Patriots made their way back to Jerusalem and maintained their secrecy following their daily regimen, rigorous exercising including running as well as mock duels with weapons awaiting orders from Barabbas or Schmuel. After three days they received a briefing and were told, "Be ready at a moment's notice for we are preparing to free our brothers." During that time Barabbas, Schmuel, Samir and the two giants Tanoush & Haleem all dressed as beggars assuring they would not be noticed, spent two full days circling the site of the dungeons hoping to come up with a plan. Barabbas standing back of Schmuel both dressed in dirty sack cloth and cowls covering their faces said, "Do you see a way in yet Schmuel or have you come up with a plan?" "Possibly Giant I have a plan, I will signal the others to go back to the farm."

****

Anakarnina was in her element and happy for now she was cooking for a family (as she called them). She continued refusing any compensation over Barabbas' insisting just the opposite and once again she smiled and held up her hand palm facing him, saying only, "Shush." For she *would* feed all the Patriots so for the first time in years they relished a home cooked meal.

Later Schmuel presented his plan. "I am asking for two volunteers," but before he could say anything he had to raise his hand to halt their enthusiasm, "I appreciate your eagerness but please wait until I finish presenting my plan." Many minutes later when he finished his presentation the entire group stood all of them acknowledging their willingness to volunteer to aid their brothers. "On second thought," Schmuel said, "First Sami and Maloof will be needed later and will not draw, that will leave forty four of you to draw let me say if whomever is selected wants to withdraw after you hear what it entails we will accept that." He turned to the

Two Men Named Jesus

others for agreement, without hesitation they all nodded their assent. When the drawing was over the two winning the drawing was Youseff and Hunna so now Schmuel explained what was expected of them and when they heard the plan they smiled then the group laughed out loud understanding Captain Schmuels plan.

The following day Tanoush and Haleem dressed in the finery of wealthy merchants accompanied by Kodaan the seven foot Eunuch holding a rope attached to the wrists of Youseff and Hunna approached the office of the Magistrate. Hesitantly, for not knowing who these wealthy merchants might be and not wanting to err, the Captain of the guard genuflected asking politely, "Sirs how can I be of service?" Playing the part to the hilt Tanoush spoke with authority, "Take me to Governor Lysinias immediately." With the utmost speed Captain Carmedias led the way to the Tetrarchs office; sticking his head inside the door he was about to speak when Lysinias asked, "Captain what have we here," than seeing the wealthy merchants backed into the room, "please gentlemen come in what can I do for you?" Entering Tanoush, seemingly upset said, "Governor my men have captured these two thieves found in our compound stealing from our wagons. I want them jailed immediately for perhaps they are of that group you told us of last month." "Aha," shouted Lysinias, "now we have two more of that thieving group. Thank you so much my

Lord we will take care of them." Taking the leash from Kodaan the Captain bowed walking away toward the dungeon with his two prisoners. As an afterthought and not wanting to be rude, "Can I be of any other services gentlemen." Tanoush and Haleem shook their heads no and turned walking in the direction they had come. None noticed the snickers coming from the Patriots watching among a crowd that always seemed to be near the Magistrates Headquarters. Three Patriots who had placed themselves not far from the entrance into the dungeon watched as the Captain of the guard escorted Yousoff and Hunna through that steel door barking orders, "You and you take these two to the lower dungeon and place them in a cell near the other so called Patriots, ha, ha, ha." He laughed with much arrogance for, as he thought, his side had finally won a battle. Remember not more than four of those prisoners to a cell."

****

That night the work planned by Schmuel began in earnest. The eight men who had drawn the first nights work reported to Tanoush and Haleem to begin. The two leaders met their men at the edge of the clearing facing the dungeon. Tanoush took his four men skirting the left side of the wall and back into the dense forest surrounding the dungeon while Haleems group took the other side they also went into the forest at that point. The wall surrounding the dungeon had been raised to twelve foot initiated by Lysinias after the big break out of the Patriots previous incarceration. They were thankful, for this night blacked out a day which was quite warm but now a cool front had descended from the mountains in the north inviting the clouds to hover over the entire area.

Each group selected a spot ten feet into the forest and began digging following Schmuel' plan digging straight down. From time to time they would come up out of the hole then pull up baskets of soil which two others would scatter back into the trees. Being in excellent physical condition they knew to take a break from time to time. After two hours the four were relieved by four others and this went on throughout the night. Just before old Sol was to begin his morning traverse across the sky they ceased the digging. Covering up the mounds of dirt with brush and leaves; it was not likely any would be walking that way for each corner of the wall butted up against a dense growth of trees. They would rest and once again continue their digging after that day's nightfall arrived.

****

Samir and Maloof were taken below to the fifth level of the dungeon. When the other Patriots saw them they said nothing and so as not to encourage the guards of any display they watched as the two were taken to a cell and locked in. The Sergeant of the guard laughed loudly, "Look you thieves here are two more of your ilk why don't you welcome them this will be your new home." Samir and Maloof were shoved into the cell pleased to see Phillip and Herman. The guard laughed as he locked the cell and climbed the stairs. Nothing was said until the guards were out of sight and the prisoners knew their conversation could not be heard. They spoke softly through the small opening in the doors of the cells. Speaking to them Phillip asked, "How did this happen were you caught or," Samir interrupted him, "Shh quietly now and listen. Starting this night and each night until finished our men are digging a tunnel that will lead directly to our cells." He stopped while this soaked in for they could not fathom what he was saying. "Do not worry for we have tools with us to help get through the walls." Samir and Maloof raised their tunics and under shirt and there tied around their waists were chisels, not one but several. They lifted each one of the tools out of its place under the felt belt used to keep them in place laying them under the pallets. Phillip asked, "How are we to know when they have reached our level, and when are we to begin digging and," this time Maloof interrupted him, "Phillip is your head made of lead, just follow directions and everything will come out right and don't ask, we do have hammers as well." Unwrapping leggings, worn by a few people, he undid felt strips under the leggings holding a hammer to each of the inside thighs. "Phillip," began Samir, "we will begin by chiseling each chance we get night and day. Do you recall the sack cloth wall Judith put up once, he painted it to look like the wall behind it. Remember we could not tell it was not the wall. That is what we are to do here." Now pleased Phillip smiled, "I should know better our Captain Schmuel is a remarkable man. His mind works overtime, wow that's great."

****

The following day a dark haired lady approached the gate of the prison. The officer of the guard asked, "What is your business here woman why do you stand there looking through the bars?" She answered quietly, "I have brought the only thing I have for my husband and son." "Who is your husband and son are you sure they are here in this prison?" She replied emphatically yet with that same quiet voice, "Yes I was told by a friend you have them here." What are the names and what have you brought for them?" She pointed to a tightly bound roll of sack cloth atop her head, "This I have for them so they will be warm and dry we are poor people and I have no clothes to bring to them. The names are Thomas and Gabriel, may I be allowed to see and talk to them?" The guard answered rudely, "I see you do not know the rules, in order for you to see them you must go to the Magistrates office, put in your request then check back the next day and that office will give you the time to visit although do not be surprised if your request is denied. Now," and he turned to one of the guards standing near, "take this sack cloth and make sure it gets to," he paused looking at the woman, she answered, "Thomas and Gabriel," "Yes take it to them." Zaina walked away her eyes to the ground for she must pretend sadness. The young guard took the roll of sack cloth down to the fifth level telling that Chief floor guard, "Take this sack cloth to Thomas and Gabriel a woman brought it for them." The Chief guard turned and shouted toward the four cells where the Patriots were held. "Which of you are Thomas and Gabriel?" Stepping up to the door of the cell Thomas answered, "I am he."

The door was opened and the guard tossed the roll of sack cloth into the cell and left. They removed the outer roll and inside found another roll with the identical color of the dungeon wall. As they opened it up more chisels, hammers, a six foot wood slat and nails. Samir pulled the slatted wood cots together one atop the other using them as a ladder. He climbed atop them saying, "Hand me the sack cloth to be hung and you Thomas climb up by me." When Thomas stood on the cots with Samir he said, "Hold the slat over the cloth allowing it to drape down while I hammer it to the ceiling." From below Gabriel said, "Be careful they will hear the pounding!" "No if you look out the window in the door you will see the guards there in that room, see, where the light comes from they cannot hear for the cement is thick and will not reverberate." Gabriel and Maloof watched from below, Gabriel not convinced backed away to see

Samir use the hammer." They folded the sack cloth over the slat than Samir slowly hammered four nails through the slat into the ceiling. Thomas and Samir climbed down then walked around to admire their handiwork. Gabriel walked to the door of the cell turned looking hard and said, "Wow I don't believe it, and it looks just like the wall." This would give them ample room to work because from the curtain to the wall measured eight feet. "Listen men," Samir explained, "we must be aware of the habits of the guards so they will not surprise us, so we will study them for a few days then begin our work. "Gabriel, station yourself at the window and study the movements of the guards; when we are working on the wall if they move toward us throw a rock against the back wall to warn us for if they look in and do not see all of us we will be in trouble, how much time do they spend in their room, how often they make rounds and how long it takes them, and what hour they bring us food." Thomas said to his son, "My son steel yourself for we will depend on you to warn us of any problem." After a few days of watching while the others began a test hole through the wall so that they might send Barabbas information of their work, Gabriel had done an excellent job determining the guard's movements and now they were ready to begin their work in earnest.

While Gabriel maintained his position the other three began the grueling work ahead of them. The pounding was absorbed by the natural wall of the dungeon that had been carved out of the side of a hill and down into the existing chasm for this must have been a rock quarry years before. Samir would make the first blow. Picking up a chisel he put it into a small crevice and holding the tool tight hit it solid with his hammer. "Wow I hit that as hard as I could and it did not seem to give much." Trying again he drew his hammer slowly back and hit the mark again driving the chisel into the wall just $1/8^{th}$ of an inch. "Okay fellows pick your spot and get with it." He told them as he renewed his efforts. Soon they each had a hole driven into the rock and after pounding for some ten minutes they stopped to rest for a few seconds. Samir stopped and motioned Thomas to follow him. In front of the curtain he said, "Thomas you are assigned to your sons position for we need his strength behind the curtain." Thomas smiled saying, "I thought you would never ask." Gabriel was signaled to take his father's place and it was not long to notice that the young man's age improved the work load much better than the other two. The hammering continued for some and the first day revolved into the next and the next until the scratching on the wall showed the eighth day of work. Samir stopped his work stepped away stretching his body, twisting his neck and generally exercising when suddenly Maloof, having turned one of the cots against the wall to climb higher hoping he would find a softer spot, fell backwards fortunately landing on the pile of straw they used to keep themselves warm. Samir and Gabriel could not help but laugh for there was Maloof his left hand holding a chisel high in the air while his right held a hammer laying in the straw yet seemed to ready to make another blow. As Samir looked he said, "Maloof what do you have in your left hand?" "Can you not see Samir I have the chisel in my," and as he held his hand up it was empty, "what the heck happened to my tool?" he asked than looking up to the point where he had been working he pointed and there in the wall was his tool. Samir laughed, "You must have unloaded all your energy on that blow for you drove it into the wall so far I can barely see it." "Not to worry Samir I will climb up and retrieve it." Maloof slowly climbed back up his improvised ladder and extended his hand to twist the chisel out of its trap in the wall. "Samir throw up another chisel so I can work this one out of its jam." He pulled on the jammed chisel and it fell landing on the straw again. "Darn that must have been stuck in solid mud for it came out too easily." Samir said, "Catch," and he threw a chisel up for Maloof to catch, "hammer that in to see what kind of material we are up against." Maloof pushed the chisel into the hole and then twisted the handle with some force. "It seems there was a really hard crust which we have gone through but this is soft limestone we've just gotten lucky!" He jammed in his chisel again hitting the head with his hammer than stopped. Standing on the ladder he said, "Look just when I thought it would be easy going forget it for, wow, I've hit really hard rock this time in fact it feels like marble or agate." He pounded for a good ten minutes not making any headway. Samir waved him down off his perch than motioned them to sit down. "We must work as hard as possible, choose another spot and begin working on that."

They continued working day and night sleeping as needed and working between the changing of the guards and the occasional peek into the cells. Each cell was having the same problem with the walls so Samir told them to cease until he could find a solution if there was one. The work went on although they were making no progress.

During this time it seemed Samir was in another world so they spoke to him only as needed for they knew his brain was hard at work on a new project, they would wait. Finally, after two full days he told them to cease their work and listen up. "I have been searching my brain for a way out of this and now this is so simple I cannot believe I have not thought of it before and if this works we will have no problem escaping, but I must get a message to Schmuel as soon as possible." They waited for a few minutes until Samir asked, "I must get information to our spy Dean" he paused than, "in the Magistrates office but how do I do it, any of you have an idea how we can do this safely?" They all looked at him uncertain of what Samir was saying. Gabriel asked, "Who is this Dean you speak of and why do we want to get information to him?" Samir forgot for a moment that he was the only one of this group having this information. "Forget that name I am sorry I mentioned it for knowing it could put you in jeopardy." And he shook his head as if attempting to clear his mind as he held his hand in the air waving to quiet them. They watched while Samir paced back and forth across the floor of the dungeon for some ten minutes thinking when he abruptly stopped. "Listen closely to what I have to say, and get my words to the other three cells. I will need you Maloof for this next act in this little program of mine in order to get word to our headquarters. I have in my packet some of the weed that the Greeks brought us, you may recall they brought two kinds the first being an awful tasting leaf that turns the stomach making one deathly ill. The other is the one that puts one into a total sleep resembling death, do you all recall?" They nodded their head in understanding. "I am sorry but Thomas you must be the guinea pig for the first part of this plan, I hope you understand for as the eldest you are supposedly the most prone to illness." He explained his plan which they then relayed to the rest of the prisoners.

****

The following morning from Samir's cell came blood curdling screams for almost a full minute while Maloof and Gabriel shouted, "Help guards my father is dying we need help." Maloof hollered, "Hurry hurry this man is dying and we can do nothing for him." Samir knew it would take some time before help would be forthcoming for it was the Sergeants job to be extremely cautious. Thomas' screaming and regurgitating continued while the others in all three cells shouted pleading for help. Prior to all this Samir had given Thomas a few of the bitter non-toxic leaves to chew and almost immediately became ill.

Almost five minutes passed before the Sergeant and three guards arrived and opening the cell door froze as if hitting a steel wall their eyes bugging out watching the body erupt into spastic tremors shuddering and bouncing from side to side throwing his body into terrible turmoil. Samir sprang to the aide of Thomas putting a few leaves of the stupefying drug in his mouth. Chewing the leaves only a few seconds he abruptly stopped screaming as his body settled down upon the floor. The guards backed off frightened, terror in their eyes then, still bent over the body Samir reached into Thomas' mouth and pulled out the leaves closing them in his hand that they not be discovered by the guards. The Sergeant indifferently yet scared, "Hah I guess you are shy one man now," and leaning over the body put his ear near Thomas' mouth, "yes he is dead, dead, dead," turning to his men, "get him out of here right away; bring a stretcher and the rope." One of the guards ran up the stairs and soon returned with the carry cot whereupon the sergeant wrapping the rope around the body securing it to the gurney, then attached a heavier rope to the top of the gurney. They pulled the stretcher out of the cell and all the prisoners watched

Two Men Named Jesus

while it was hoisted up on a pulley the five levels. Samir said to the Sergeant, "Sir would you please send somebody to this man's wife they live near the outer edge of the south gate just ask for Thomas Fahrnia' home thank you;" with an angry look the Sergeant opened his mouth to talk but Samir leaned close to the man's ear, "If you say her son is doing well and mention his name she will tell you where to go to receive your reward." The word reward opened the Sergeants ears which made him smile as he sprang up the stairs shouting, "Guards I will take care of this poor man's body, bring the large four wheel chariot." He went into the Tetrarchs office saying to his Captain, "Sir one of the prisoners has died should I take him to his wife before he begins rotting?" "Yes by all means get rid of the body, good job Sergeant." The chariot arrived and he told the guards, "Get back to your work I will return soon and make my report." The Patriots watched as their friend was raised to the top of the dungeon. When the guards were finally back to their stations Samir and his men clapped quietly some holding hands over their mouths so not to laugh too loudly.

****

Barabbas, Schmuel and several of the Patriots were sitting away from the east gate of Jerusalem watching and waiting when the Sergeant from the dungeon approached a man sitting at the gate drinking coffee and eating sweet bread. This would be Raaph who on this day was the contact man for any messages coming to the Patriots. "You there" and he touched the man's back, "is your name Fahrnia?" "Yes," the man answered what is it you want Roman?" The Sergeant answered, "I have just returned the body of Thomas to his home and his wife told me to seek you out for a reward." Taken aback the man seemed stunned and began weeping, "Did you say Thomas is dead, how do you know this, where is his body, why you a Roman guard are bringing me this message, please explain!" Somewhat irritated the Sergeant said, "Just pay me I have no time to explain all these things, if you are curious go speak to the widow." Confused the man reached into his packet inside his tunic taking out two daric's handing them to the Sergeant attempting to ask another question but the guard hastily jerked the money from the man's hand his lip curled in indifference as he turned and walked away without a word. The man, a Patriot by the name of Raaph rose from his table running in the direction of the Fahrnia home. Barabbas and his men followed, making way to the east gate and the home on a hill nearby. Stepping into the house they did not know what to expect seeing Thomas sitting sipping hot tea showing signs of illness. Barabbas took his hand, "Thomas my friend what happened are you ill and did they let you out of jail, Raaph was told you were dead, uh, uh?" Looking up at Barabbas and smiling said, "No my General I am fine now but I thought I would die." Relating the incidents in the dungeon and more;

Thomas related Samir's plan laughing as he disclosed the plan. "For a week or longer we attempted to break through the wall of the dungeon but with little progress than about the time we thought we had hit limestone it turned out it must have been a very small layer. We tried punching holes throughout the wall but ran into what seemed to be slate or marble we could not tell. By that time we were extremely frustrated whereupon we ceased working while we all gave it much thought when finally Samir came up with this idea. Fortunately Samir had a bit of the drug the Greeks had with them upon their arrival to join us. Now slowly one by one the Patriot prisoners will become sick and die and Samir is convinced that before we all expire the Romans will become alarmed that we may have a contagious disease and instantly release us." The guffaws and hilarity almost laid the Patriots out for most of them were laughing so hard they were falling down tears in their eyes. Schmuel laughing turned to one of the Patriots saying, "Tell the men to cease the digging it seems we have a much better and easier plan." Barabbas said, "We must give Samir a bonus for such an ingenious plan, and to you Thomas you are a very brave man to have allowed your body to be put in jeopardy for your friends, both you and Samir are commended for your exceptional thinking and bravery." Thomas smiled, "No my General I did nothing for my brothers would act the same for me and I deserve no award for I am a Patriot." Cheering followed his words.

****

The following day a lady arrived at the prison claiming to be the husband of Thomas the dead prisoner asking to see those who were with him at the end. The Sergeant shrugged his shoulders looked at the Chief guard and said, "Why not; you," indicating one of his men, "accompany this lady to the fifth level and let her speak to the prisoners in cell A." The guard led her down to the fifth level and stood back for fear the area was contagious pointing to the cell of Samir. She approached the steel door putting her hand through the opening, "I do not know your name but I want to shake your hand and thank you for helping Thomas." Samir took her hand and she was holding a small bag which he took from her she than gave him her left hand giving him a second bag. "Goodbye and I hope you boys are out soon." Thinking that statement was not realistic the guards laughed one of them saying, "Come Mrs. that is all the time you have," and escorted her upstairs to the exit.

****

Back in the dungeon Samir directed them. Whispering loud enough for those in the next cell to hear, "Yanatoun, sometime tomorrow you will pretend to be ill while Narouth and the others make note of it to the guards of course they will pay little attention; the following day you will chew the weed that will make you ill and like Thomas you will officially be dead, ha, ha, ha, be alert and maintain a sober and stern expression when the guards come." The following morning the prisoners in level five, cells A, B, & C began shouting for the guards, "Come down here we have a very sick man in cell C, help, help!" Again the guards on level five awaited their Sergeant who would soon come to see what the alarm was. All the Patriots looked toward Samir for any answer and shrugging his shoulders, "They could care less if we are sick, or ill or even if we die." Soon the Sergeant accompanied by three guards arrived looking into the cell he saw a body in convulsions and shouted, "It looks like you will lose another of your brothers for that is what happened to the other one a few days ago;" turning to his men, "wait for the convulsions to stop than do as I did the other day and get him out of here." Coming to the porthole in cell a he motioned to Samir to step forward. Samir stepped up to the opening, "Is there another reward if I contact that same person?" "I am not sure perhaps you should just set his body in the courtyard letting all know his name so his family can claim him." The Sergeant nodded, "Ok sure that's what I'll do." Samir said to them, "We will let it rest for two days then another of us will become ill and die than we will see what they do." Upon the death of Narouth when the Sergeant was called he shouted down to the guards in cell block five saying, "Guards do not touch the body! I will send the stretcher and the ropes but make the prisoners attach the body and let us know when it is ready to raise and again *do not touch the body!* When the stretcher was lowered the cell block Chief shouted to the prisoners, "I will unlock your door and you will back away then come get the stretcher, tie the body upon it and we will raise it, now stand away from the door!"

****

The Sergeant had sent a message relayed him by the Captain who had spoken to the Tetrarch contemplated discussing it with the Magistrate council's in house Doctor. Lysanias asked, "Doctor do you not think it somewhat unusual that in cell block five we have had three deaths in six days, should I worry perhaps this may be an epidemic of some kind." The Doctor suggested, "Have these men separated from the rest of the inmates and I would not worry as of this moment but if there *is* another death within the next three days than my suggestion is to turn them out forcing them into the desert where their illness will not come upon us." "Thank you Doctor." and nodding to his Captain who understood what he was to do. So Samir's plan advanced as set forth and he learned from the Patriot spy Favarh of the intention of the Tetrarch to run them off, fearful this were the beginning of an epidemic. Samir, to his men, "We will let them relax for a few days and when they think safety is on their side we will subject them to two additional deaths, hah, what do you think of that?" From that fifth level of the dungeon came a roar of laughter but because of the density and depth of the dungeon it only awoke those guards on that level and from the Chief of level five shouted, "Quiet you thieves before I come in and give you another taste of my lash." The Patriots snickered at that whereupon one of them whispered, "I look forward to our next action I predict it will frighten you to your end." Once again snickering and quiet laughter, what fun!

****

By orders from Tetrarch Lysinias the prisoners were watched closely but not directly. The Captain of the guard would not descend to the fifth level and ordered cell doors to be opened and all guards be brought up. Steel gates were installed across the steps which barred the way up the steps and a wooden cage carrying food and water to the prisoners was lowered three times a day. This new isolation seemed to please Samir and his men for they had the run of the entire fifth level. After the fourth day Samir told his men, "Now they must be certain there is no cause for alarm for the Doctor informed them that they wait but three more days so let's give them that and an additional *three* days when we will make their lives miserable and full of terror." The fifth day the Chief of the fifth floor came down the steps to the steel wall that had been installed urging them, "Come out prisoners let me have a look at you!" Samir was the first to step out of his open cell and when the Chief saw him he fearfully backed away slowly his eyes narrowed seeking any sign of ailment in the prisoner. "Bring them all out; let them stand near you." Samir turned, "Come out men show your selves." When they started out Samir caught the eye of Maksoof in the back of cell B and winked. Maksoof caught on quickly and waited for the others to circumvent Samir, then slowly and feigning a definite although imaginative illness with his head hung low and his hand upon his lips attempting to hold in the foam leaking from his mouth pulled himself up near Samir. Looking up at the guard he seemingly forced a smile allowing a piece of soap he had been chewing to make it foam so when he spoke he lisped and an ugly trail of bile slithered out of his mouth and down his chin dripping off onto the floor. Terror gripped the Guard and for a split second he froze on the step screaming he turned running up the steps shouting, "They are sick; send for the Centurion; run tell the Tetrarch we must get rid of them, *"Help, help, help, help what am I to do?"* his voice trailed off as he ran out the prison. Samir said nothing but waved the Patriots back into the cell where they could laugh and enjoy the events they had acted out. Now all of you return to your cells!" He waited until he saw they had removed themselves from the common area.

They watched as two mechanics came down tearing the steel gate out of its moorings and hurried back up the stairs. The voice of the Captain boomed at them again, "We are throwing down ten huge cloaks of canvas which you will wrap yourselves in; wait until we tell you then you will climb the steps turn left at the head of the stairs which will lead you toward the desert. You will march into the desert with my men following; you will be forced deep into the desert and do not come back for you are banished from this area and if you attempt to return you will be slaughtered. Now move, GO, GO, GO he shouted."

Samir whispered to them, "Move slowly as if you are ill and follow his instructions I am sure our leaders will meet us and lead us away." They were led north up a very narrow hill sloping from north to south. Arriving to the top of the hill they could easily see the Kidron Valley to the east and to the west they could see off to the Tyropoeon valley. "Well," spoke Samir, "I finally get to see that peak above the valley." Now as they looked there was a great crowd, noisy as it moved behind an ass carrying a man coming into Jerusalem. The noise grew as they came closer and closer to the gate of the city. Nasr asked, "Can you hear what they are shouting and who is riding on the ass." They stopped to look toward the growing mass of people and finally they heard the word they were shouting. "Hosanna, Hosanna," they were shouting as the donkey moved slowly toward the gate. Following behind them but not very close the guard shouted, "Move on you thieves down the hill toward the valley." When they had descended the hill they could see the desert as the face of the sun glared down on the sands and the heat radiated into their faces like a blast oven off the sands. As they stepped onto the sands they could feel the difference in the temperature for it was a sharp contrast to the hill they had just descended. The Sergeant of the guard shouted at them from a distance, "Go now into the desert for that is your only course and we will watch to make sure you do not return. I will post guards along this edge of the desert to make sure you do not return." Samir and his men looked back searching for a familiar face in those traversing the green hills. Nasr whispered to Samir, "I believe I saw Haleem and Ayoub but they are far back, oh look standing on the hill looking this way I am not sure for the sun makes a haze that is hard to see through, can you make them out, is it them?" Samir shrugged his shoulders for he was not sure although he said, "Perhaps, it looks like Ayoub, oh yes and there is Majheed standing next to the Giant, they know we are here." Nasr said, "They have turned and are watching something below them, it must be the man on the donkey and I can still hear the crowd although I cannot tell what they say." They stopped then for they heard a great commotion coming from the direction where Barabbas was standing. They watched as the guards who had lead them here turned toward a voice from near the hill. The words were indistinct but the guards turned and sped toward the noise on the hill. Samir said, "They are going back something is taking place and they have left us, come on we may be needed." As they stepped out of the desert onto the surrounding oasis and looked up the hill they saw the Patriots were now surrounded by a large number of Roman soldiers. Nasr shouted, "Samir what can we do we have no weapons and it looks as though they have them blocked on all sides." "Yes I see but I am going to their aid but I give the rest of you leave to your own desires!" Samir ran up the hill toward the surrounded Patriots as the other ten followed. Samir neared two of the guards and dove for the feet of one of them and as he did he twisted the guard' ankle hard and one could hear the *crack* of the man's leg as he shouted in pain and dropped to the ground. Arresting the guards sword Samir cut down the guard nearest him and he heard Nasr shout, "I have taken care of one of them and now I have a lance, c'mon men!" The others charged into the fray and one of the Patriots was cut down for they heard him scream. Samir grabbed a second sword loosed into the air by another Roman Nasr had slapped across the head with his lance. Samir caught the sword as it was settling toward the ground and tossed it toward Barabbas shouting "Giant catch!" Barabbas sprang into the air catching the sword and bringing it down into the side of a Roman guard and at the same time shoving Ayoub toward Majheed shouting, "Run my brothers, run seek shelter where they cannot find you," and returned to the melee.

All the Patriots had appropriated weapons and were now fighting for their lives. Barabbas looked to make sure Majheed and Ayoub had escaped and heaved a sigh of relief when he could not find them. As he fought his way through the oncoming Roman guards his mind wrapped itself around a very pleasant idea and in his mind's eye he saw Majheed and Ayoub circled by their loving families and all of them were happy and this thought flowed over him making him a happy man for he felt strongly that the sight in his mind was true. Barabbas felt a sharp pain in his side and he speedily turned grabbing the shaft of the lance the point of which had gouged him. Now jerking the lance with all his might the Roman on the other end of the lance, although he did not look as though he enjoyed the trip came flying toward the mountain of a man. The Roman guard clinging tightly to his lance, his feet off the ground and his body in the air met Barabbas' huge fist with his head and slumped quickly to the ground. His eyes caught Samir who swiped his sword toward a soldier who ducked but yet caught the business end of the weapon on his shoulder and as Samir' body continued on an arc the hilt of his sword slapped against the rear skull of another soldier knocking him to the ground. Barabbas shouted, "Samir there are three coming at you from behind." Samir nodded, "You had better watch your own rear my friend," he shouted back, "Nasr is down," and he gasped, "and I see only four others," gasp, "it looks dire we may have lost more," gasp, "I am not sure how long I can hold out." It looked as though Lysanias had released the entire garrison for everywhere one looked there were Roman guards. One of the Roman Sergeants took three of his soldiers aside, "Watch now, watch the big man when I say so jump him all of you swinging your weapons, wait until I give you the signal. There were very many soldiers fighting and only ten Patriots charging the soldiers fighting for their very lives each clashing with three or more soldiers at one time. The Sergeant waved his hand toward Barabbas and the three guards jumped him. The first, thinking he would have a definite advantage leaped upon the back of Barabbas and at the same time another thrust his sword toward the thigh of the big man, the third stood back for just a moment hoping to gain a better advantage. Feeling the man clinging to his back Barabbas reached back with his empty left hand locking the wrist of the man in his huge hand. Barabbas dropped to the ground gripping hard on the young man's wrist than swinging the young man over his head and at the ideal time released the man's wrist allowing the guard to fly through the air and his head met the Sergeants the sound resounding in the air as that of two melons being crushed while the sword the guard grasped sliced into the chest of the third guard who had been waiting to make his play. The battle continued for almost an hour up the hill than down then back up until finally they were so exhausted and drained they slowed feeling as if they were in outer space looking down upon themselves knowing they were ready to fall to the ground in complete exhaustion. The Roman Captain seeing this whistled and circling his hand in the air and signaling a group of soldiers holding nets who sprang forward throwing the nets over the head of Barabbas while the remaining Patriots were wrestled down each by at least four guards.

Now it was all over although the Patriots had leveled, killed or maimed at least thirty for they were lying all around the area as Physicians and medical assistants tended them. The Centurion rode up to the battle area shouting! "Hold that mountain of a man, tie additional ropes around him or he will loosen himself, the carriage is coming and we will load them all on it and take them to the dungeon and hear this, I want six men on that giant at all times!"

Soon the flat bed chariots arrived and they were transported to the dungeons. When the dray carrying Barabbas pulled into the great courtyard upon the huge marble Dais were Pilate, Herod Antipas, The High Priest of the Temple and a few of the seventy one members of the Sanhedrin. The Centurion took the chain which was attached to Barabbas' wrists and ankles jerking on it attempting to pull him off the chariot toward the dais where Pilate stood. "Take the rest of them to the dungeon," said the Centurion. Pilate spoke, "Hold; take those others to the dungeon but take Barabbas below to the cell where the Nazarene is being held for they will make good company together, hah, ha, ha!" He laughed at what he thought was a joke. Barabbas could barely walk for the chains were tight and short forcing him to decrease his normal stride as they led him onto the ramp into a depression in the jail. He thought to fight again but by now he was resigned to the fact that he knew this day would come and yes that day was here and now. They then retied his hands in front of his body and extended a lance handle through his elbows holding them behind his back so the pole extended out on each side of his body. The Centurion shouted at him, "Down big man take the steps down to the next landing." As Barabbas stepped onto the landing there before him was the Man he had seen many times throughout the past years, the man who's face he could not forget for when he saw Him there had always been a tug at his heart. His mind reached back in time to Cana where he, Majheed and Ayoub had witnessed Jesus wave his hand over jars of water which when taken out was wine; yes that was He. Barabbas also recalled this soulful appearing man with the sweet face of a saint feeding five thousand or more people at the edge of the Jordan River many years ago. He watched as the guards swore at him hoping to make him angry which would give them a chance to hit him.

The soldiers took them to the center of the large grotto and telling Barabbas, "Sit back, move toward the back of the cell while we dress the King for his coronation." Then Pilate took Jesus and scourged Him. And the soldiers twisted a crown of thorns and put on His head, and they put on Him a purple robe. Then they said,

"Hail King of the Jews! And they struck Him with their hands." Pilate went out again, and said to them, "Behold, I am bringing Him out to you, that you may know that I find not fault with him."

Then the Governor left Jesus with the guards and they began scourging him again. This normally calm giant of a man Barabbas could not witness anymore and he dove at the guards his body flailing them with the chains connected to his body and the guards fell back away from Jesus as Barabbas twisted his body as to utilize the long lance handle as a weapon, diving left then right into the midst of the guards throwing them off their feet knocking them down, inflicting wounds upon them. He shouted at them, "What has this man done that you are scourging Him, did you not hear the Governor, He has done no wrong. everybody he has come in contact with will tell you he is a more than just a man!" He thought, I know this man is God, and accepting this in his mind softened his demeanor. Looking down into the grotto the Chief Centurion shouted to his detachment, "Go below and subdue this giant now!" They dove into the depths of the grotto grabbing onto the chains holding Barabbas and with great effort drug him away.

They took Jesus out before the shouting crowd. Pilate said to the Jews, "It is your custom during the feast that you release one of the prisoners. Who will it be Jesus

Christ or Jesus Barabbas?" "Then they cried out again, saying, "Not this Man, but Barabbas!" Then the Jews took Jesus Christ leading him away that they may crucify Him.

Barabbas not knowing why he sat watching them taking Christ away for he wanted to run after them and shout at them but something told him to leave it alone. Pilate nodded toward the Captain of the guard, "Release that man, for the Jews have selected the other Jesus to be crucified. The Captain faced Barabbas at a distance saying, "Barabbas you have heard the decision of the Sanhedrin, if you will sit on the top step I will send the jailers to release you and you must promise verbally you will stay calm and not cause any more problems; do I have your word?"

One word only is all Barabbas could speak for he knew something had entered his heart which held him in a calm silent embrace; and understanding although it be a poignant blush which engulfed his entire being, "Yes." He said as his eyes caught the eyes of Jesus and immediately he knew what he must do. When they had cut the chains off his legs and wrists he stood stretching his body as he reached toward the heavens than walked down the twelve steps of the marble platform. Until now he had not noticed the clamor of the masses had settled to a quiet unlike one would be aware of during a time such as this. He saw the crowd grow and as Christ rounded a corner carrying the cross and the crowd swelled behind that terrible procession. Now Barabbas, not knowing why, fell in several feet behind the others. He felt an urge to go forward that he might carry the cross for this Man and his heart was pounding with pain and love for Christ. Then he saw the Captain of the Guard point to a man in the crowd, "You, come help your King carry this cross." The guard looked around at the crowd for approval of his comment and laughed loudly, when none laughed with him his smile drained and his face became blank. Barabbas walked along slowly following the curious and falling further and further back from The Man carrying the cross. As he walked a feeling of melancholy and utter despair came over him he knew not why and his body launched forward his pace quickening and in less than ten steps he was even with The Man called Christ. As Barabbas was about to speak he heard unspoken words in his mind and he knew Jesus was communicating with him although no sounds were uttered. The voice in his mind convinced him that what was happening was a prophecy being fulfilled and neither he nor any other earthly person could halt the happenings now or within the next hours. Barabbas stood motionless for some time while the procession made their way out the city gate and into an area on a hill just outside Jerusalem city.

He knew the name of this infamous hill for others had been crucified here as well and but for the Jews selecting him to be released it might have been him carrying his own cross to Golgotha.

He felt familiar hands clasp in his own and looked down to see his two favorite people Ayoub on his left and Majheed on his right quietly sauntering along with him and now holding his hands and looking at their upturned faces it was as if he had never really seen these two lads whom he dearly loved for he had been their protector and a father figure to them for years. Mimicking the two of them his face broke into a soft smile and he squeezed the hands firmly but softly. "You two do not know how great it is to see you and to have you walk with me I thought we were lost to each other but now I know we will be together forever." Majheed said, "Giant that is The Man we saw in Cana many years ago is it not He turned water into wine?" "Yes my little one that is He and we have seen Him other times as well," answered Barabbas his melancholy falling away gradually for the presence of his two buds holding on to him as they had done years ago when they were but children warmed his heart. Ayoub said, "Let's find our way back to the farm for I feel in my heart this Jesus is who He says He is and I do not want to look upon Him hanging upon that cross again for I feel we should leave it to his Family who we see standing below the cross weeping and mourning that great loss." Barabbas smiled down at him, "Yes wise young Ayoub you speak as I would expect to hear from your own grandfather; come let us return to the farm and begin a new life and we will pray for our brothers who may not have been as fortunate as we yet who knows how many we will find at the farm." They started off on their way to a new life for these past hours had changed and in their minds they had come to realize they had seen the Son of God and witnessed a scene very few would ever experience yet in their hearts knew His word would spread over the World and change those lives who would realize this would be the Man to follow making it a more understanding World as one makes ones way through this same World knowing His love will dwell in the hearts of those who invite Him in.

THE END

About the Author

Sunny Eugene Cohlmia was born in 1928 and spent my early years in Waynoka a small town in northwest Oklahoma there attending grade and high school. I did not excel in anything other than the arts, and only after being encouraged by my dearest Mother and a Teacher of whom I will never forget, I began writing at fourteen but laid it aside when I learned of and became interested in girls. I moved to Tulsa Ok where I began my Career meeting the girl who would become my wife. Subsequently I quit an exceptionally high paying position with a huge retail store so to move to Wichita Ks where I courted and married the finest lady in the world.

We are married fifty six (June 2011) years and are blessed with four fine sons. I have spent some 60 years in several business endeavors of which I thoroughly enjoyed. Upon my retirement I returned to my love of writing. I continue writing and at the time of my retirement I picked up at the fourth chapter of the first story I had begun when fourteen years old writing by hand in my father's retail store. Since the time of my retirement I have written seven children books, four fictional manuscripts, hundreds of poems, short stories etc. As of July '09 my first publication hit the streets and to the date of April 1, 2011 sold near 1200 copies, "The Chains of St. Peter" ISBN 9781606966976.

*The Orthodox Study Bible (O. S. B.) * John 18:38, * John 19:1, * John 18:40.

S. EUGENE COHLMIA PERSONAL FAMILY COAT OF ARMS

KNIGHT HOLY ORDER ST. MICHAEL THE ARCHANGEL

DUKE OF AFQA - MINISTER INTERNAL AFFAIRS COUNTRY OF HASSAN IN EXILE

(Explanation of the Duke S. Eugene Cohlmia's Personal Family Shield)

Squared Shield::
1st quarter - The Scimitars and the Cedar of Lebanon, the refuge of our family after the fall of the Kingdom of Ghassan (this is from our Royal Crest and its present to all of the noble COA of Ghassan.)
2nd quarter - The Christian Cross
3rd quarter - The crescent (Arab Symbol) - although we are not Arab we utilize this symbol for the years spent in Yemen as Governing Body of the Arabs in the Syrian Peninsula.
4th quarter - The falcon (Royal Arab Sport)

The supporters:
The lion (we came from the Azd tribes (known as The Sons of the Lion.)
The Arab stallion

The helmet and crown of the Royal Duke.

Motto: "To the greatest & Only God"